Colonial Angels

Colonial Angels

Narratives of Gender and

Spirituality in Mexico, 1580–1750

ELISA SAMPSON VERA TUDELA

 University of Texas Press, Austin

Cover illustration credit: Reproducción autorizada por el Instituto Nacional de Antropología e Historia. CONACULTA.-INAH.-MEX Reproduction authorized by the National Institute for Anthropology and History. CONACULTA.-INAH.-MEX.

Portions of this book in revised form first appeared as: "Voyages in the New World Cloister" in *History and Anthropology,* Vol. 9 Nos. 2–3 (1996), reprinted with permission of Harwood Academic Publishers; and "Fashioning a Cacique Nun: From Saints' Lives to Indian Lives in the Spanish Americas" in *Gender and History,* Vol. 9 No. 2 (August 1997), reprinted with permission of Blackwell Publishers.

First edition, 2000

Requests for permission to reproduce material from this work should be sent to Permissions, University of Texas Press, Box 7819, Austin, TX 78713-7819

♾The paper used in this book meets the minimum requirements of ANSI/NISO Z39.48-1992 (R1997) (Permanence of Paper).

LIBRARY OF CONGRESS
CATALOGING-IN-PUBLICATION DATA

Sampson Vera Tudela, Elisa.
Colonial angels : narratives of gender and spirituality in Mexico, 1580–1750 / Elisa Sampson Vera Tudela.
    p.   cm.
Includes bibliographical references and index.
ISBN 0-292-77747-7 (alk. paper). — ISBN 0-292-77748-5 (pbk.: alk. paper)
    1. Mexican prose literature—Women authors—History and criticism.   2. Nuns' writings, Mexican—History and criticism.   3. Mexican prose literature—To 1800—History and criticism.   4. Literature and society—Mexico.   5. Sex role—Political aspects—Mexico.   6. Mexico—Church history.   I. Title.
PQ7133.T83   2000
868'.08—dc21   99-20697

For my parents

For Hamid

Contents

Preface   *ix*

Acknowledgments   *xvii*

Chapter 1.   Moving Stories: *New Spanish Hagiographies and Their Relation to Travel Narrative*   *1*

Chapter 2.   Chronicles of a Colonial Cloister: *The Convent of San José and the Mexican Carmelites*   *14*

Chapter 3.   From the Confessional to the Altar: *Epistolary and Hagiographic Forms*   *35*

Chapter 4.   The Exemplary Cloister on Trial: *San José in the Inquisition*   *55*

Chapter 5.   *Cacique* Nuns: *From Saints' Lives to Indian Lives*   *76*

Afterword   *98*   Notes   *163*

Appendix 1   *101*   Bibliography   *188*

Appendix 2   *118*   Index   *199*

Appendix 3   *148*

Preface

. . . los que son naturales españoles, si no tienen mucho aviso, a pocos años andados de su llegada a esta tierra se hacen otros . . .

BERNARDINO DE SAHAGÚN, *Historia general de las cosas de Nueva España,* bk. 10, chap. 27[1]

Bernardino de Sahagún's concern about the power of the New World to transmogrify the Spaniards who traveled to it is one that was shared by any number of writers, readers, and, above all perhaps, inhabitants of the Indies. Nuns immured within their convent walls were not exempt from worries about what the New World environment might do to their search for personal and communal spiritual perfection. By the eighteenth century, the powerful ecclesiastical reform movement that grew in New Spain to curb the "abuses" and "relaxation" of convents seemed to confirm that the nuns had succumbed to America, abandoning the purity of their Peninsular origin and becoming *otras,* just as Sahagún had warned happened to all things and persons Spanish.[2]

There were, of course, exemptions: nuns and convents that tried to remain faithful to the Old World models of piety that had been exported to the New World and who resisted both the real and the imaginary differences of the Americas. To this day, for example, the Carmelite nuns of Puebla, Mexico, keep in a well-protected box a Carmelite habit sent to them by a convent in Spain in the seventeenth century. By way of explanation, the nuns tell how their predecessors were uncertain whether they were wearing the correct habit and keeping to the exact rules on clothing. Sta. Teresa of Avila appeared in a vision to the mother superior, assuring the convent of her help. Soon afterward, they received a complete Carmelite habit from their sister convent in Spain. The contents of the box were intended to instruct the New World nuns in the path of orthodoxy and to confirm their kinship ties to the Old World Carmelites.[3] The vast distances of the discoveries cohabit here with the intimate and familial space of the cloister and its customs that unite two communities in sisterhood across the oceans. The story of this box and what it encloses is fundamentally also the story of this book.

In applying to their Peninsular sisters to provide guidance on matters of correctness and decorum in religious practice, these Mexican nuns make vivid the uncertainties attached to the validity and legitimacy of colonial practices. There are, of course, competing versions or stories of what exactly these practices were and how they constituted New Spanish culture in the period. One characterizes Mexico as perennially in opposition to the Peninsula: black to Spain's white; while the other sees the colony as eternally subservient to Madrid, copying its every move slavishly. These interpretations go from political appraisals of viceregal government, seeing it either as an instance of independent municipal traditions inspired in the medieval *fueros* of Castile, or as a typical example of the encroachment of royal absolutism, to economic analyses that propose radically divergent opinions of the extent to which the colonies were implicated in the "decline" of Spain. More broadly cultural judgments also display this tendency to polarize the constitution of the colony. In these cultural evaluations, academic culture, artistic production, and civil society in general in New Spain are alternately praised for their perfect execution of European models or condemned for their provincialism.[4] This book argues that both these extreme explanations are inadequate. The material examined in *Colonial Angels* suggests some very complex ways of thinking about and overturning, more than once, the simple oppositions between colony and capital, center and periphery, New and Old, as well as the distinctions, hardly ever discussed in this context, between male and female, and enclosed and free.

The New World in this period is less El Dorado or Utopia than the land of Cockaigne—a land, that is, of change and exchange. Take, for instance, the two most often quoted examples of the exchange involved in colonization: the building of Mexico City's cathedral on the site of the most important Aztec temple in the city, and the adoption by the Spaniards of the Indian maize tortilla as a replacement for the wheaten bread of the Peninsula. The stark disparity between the two examples means they could easily be thought of not so much as evidence of exchange but of brutal imposition, on the one hand, and pragmatic appropriation, on the other. Without in any sense negating the trauma of the Conquest, it is possible to see that even the adoption of the tortilla carried with it considerable cultural weight. Bread of either kind was a staple food, quotidian and yet symbolically resonant, especially in the Roman Catholic tradition. Maize grows more quickly than wheat and requires less care. Tortillas were prepared exclusively by women at specific times of the day. All these factors would have meant that the switch from the one to the other inevitably entailed cultural shifts, in this case particularly in the distribution of time in agricultural work and in the sexual division of labor.

Colonial Angels is in part an attempt to understand the histories and stories of such negotiations as these. It stresses the reciprocity of the exchanges while not ignoring their often unequal nature. There are hundreds of examples of the kind of "down-up" transmission of culture embodied in the tortilla example, where the dominant Spanish group in some measure acknowledged the existence and value of the conquered and marginalized indigenous group. The investigation of these kinds of exchange is a difficult one to document because it concentrates on spheres that leave less obvious "traces" than the reproduction of institutions or the ideological import of the evangelical work of missionaries. The writings connected to convents and their inhabitants provide such a source. While certainly a record of the transplantation of an Old World institution to the New World, they also reveal aspects of this transplantation that have less to do with the machinery of imperial domination than with the personal experience of cultural exchange and negotiation.

Colonial Angels studies this kind of transmission of culture with an emphasis on the issue of gender and its place in the imposition of the Spanish empire. This takes us back to the Mexican Carmelites and their precious box. Any Old World inheritance had to make a hazardous journey in order to reach the New World, but the dangers and difficulties encountered on this journey by women and by a "feminine" tradition, if we may call it that, were especially perilous. The founding mother of the Carmelites occupies an important role in this respect. As a writer and spiritual model, she is the figure that dominates the Mexican Carmelites and that influences nuns of every religious order in the New World.[5] Sta. Teresa of Avila's spiritual and textual legacy, however, is not easily assumed—how, for example, does one inherit a "tradition of reform" without falling into paradox?

Access to women's texts of this period is itself complicated and often tangential. It frequently involves the examination of works by male authors who use primary material written by women. Thus, an important part of *Colonial Angels* involves an attempt to understand the cultural context, the imperatives and sanctions, in which the re-elaboration and use by men of texts written by women took place. The writings by women that I examine were absolutely necessary to the being of their authors as nuns. Writing defines these women; it is their "work." The very existence of the nuns is justified by their representation, their writing of themselves as virtuous individuals, even as potential saints. Their ability to represent themselves is both a source of vulnerability (because it was always monitored by the authorities) and of strength (because it was impossible to control completely). Although this literature is in many senses similar to propaganda, its techniques are never straightforward or univocal. *Colonial Angels* may not reveal the literary sisters of sor Juana Inés de la Cruz, but in this context it is of little significance that the nuns in this book appear at first sight to be less artistically talented than sor Juana; their importance lies rather in the fact that they write in another ambiance where exemplarity is more important than aesthetic virtuosity.[6] This does not mean that they are conformist. Their exemplarity is, in fact, better thought of as a negotiated originality: negotiated with priests, with literary traditions, with cultural values. What it reveals are novel literary forms that, though not necessarily outstanding according to aesthetic norms, are nonetheless dynamically creative.[7]

Colonial Angels examines various examples of the range of this creativity and the literary acculturation it illustrates and argues that the New World context necessitated the creation of a new kind of writing. The first chapter concentrates on the shock of the new, on the transformations undergone by women and their convents when they were transplanted to the New World, and on how these were represented. Its principal focus is to see how the hagiography succumbed to the influence of that other genre so intimately connected with the discovery of America: the travel narrative. It is intended to be read as an extended introduction to the book, laying out the principal concern of the other chapters in a very precise form; what is the relationship between generic change and historical change, and what is the gendered dimension of both?

In the next three chapters, which form the center of the book, the convent and its collective and individual histories are the focus. In the first, the founding of the Carmelite convent of San José in Mexico City and the narratives of disunion, rebellion, and reform that it gives rise to are discussed in relation to how they borrow from and change both the Teresian narrative tradition and the more general inheritance of hagiography as a guiding genre. In the second chapter, the focus is more refined and concentrates on the individual, examining the letters written by a nun to her confessor and his reworking of them into her hagiography. In the third, we return to the Mexican Carmelites, only this time to find them in the Inquisition, accused of heresy. The testimonies and letters connected to this trial provide an opportunity of seeing how the cloister and its nuns represent themselves and their community in this extreme situation, what the literary models they recur to are, which they privilege and which they ignore. In the Inquisition, the hagiographic topoi of reforming nun and recalcitrant community are rehearsed to suit the requirements of the Holy Office's forensic rhetoric, and their terms become very political—a politics connected to institutional struggles in the New World and to the power of different ecclesiastical factions. Once again, questions of the exchange and negotiation of cultural values in the colonial context are raised. The central quarrel between these Mexican Carmelite nuns and their archbishop is the same as that which brought Sta. Teresa of Avila into conflict with the clergy in Spain and eventually led to the splitting of the order into opposing factions. In both the Peninsular and the Mexican cases, the Carmelite nuns argued about whether their spiritual purity and the integrity of the Carmelite reform was better safeguarded under the jurisdiction of the regular or of the secular clergy. The Carmelite tradition was transplanted whole to the New World; that is, with its heritage of fractures and fissures intact. Significantly, however, as the chapter shows, the New Spanish version of the tradition splinters in specifically New Spanish ways.

The book closes with a chapter on the foundation of a convent for noble Indian women, a piece which, like the first chapter, confronts the differences of the Americas directly and tries to evaluate the new kind of narrative system through which they are represented. To ascertain the feasibility of the foundation, the authorities demand reports from priests who have had varied and long experience of ministering to the spiritual needs of Indians. Their testimonies certainly form part of the classic debate as to whether the Indies were truly Christian (and civilized) or still pagan (and barbaric). However, through the transformation of the intimate material exchanged between priest and Indian woman in the confessional into information of a more general nature, these accounts also contribute to a newer kind writing on the Indies—one which shares the comparative and epistemological stakes of ethnography and which, in this extraordinary case, also considers issues of gender. Once more, the strict association of feminine piety with the hagiographic model is broken in these narratives.

The shape of *Colonial Angels* then moves from direct contact with the difference of the New World, to the more complex, if attenuated, differences of established colonial society, and then back again. Hagiography is the genre at the heart of the book, serving as the medium through which to narrate every stage of contact with the New World. As a genre, hagiography has a very distinct form that relies on well-established conventions, and it is the modification and transformation of these that is so revealing about the transmission of culture in the colonial situation. For example, a recurrent pattern in the genre is for the virtuous individual to find herself in conflict with the sinful society around her. In the convent chronicle, this pits the saintly nun against her monastic community. In many of the Mexican writings, this conflict is expressed in terms of birthplace, the sinful nuns being insulted variously for being criollas (of Spanish blood but born in America), *gachupinas* (Spaniards in America), or *Indias* (indigenous women), and for exhibiting the supposed characteristics of these peoples. Thus, the *gachupinas* are condemned as *modernas* or lovers of novelty, the criollas are *regalonas* or spoilt and indulgent, while the *Indias* are *chocolateras* or eaters of chocolate in a period when it was considered an aphrodisiac.

Throughout the New Spanish *vidas*, the sins of the less virtuous find exempla rooted in experience, in the politics of the moment. Greedy nuns add chili to their food, revealing their decadence and their inability to eat simply, in an opposition where "decadence" is connected to the new spice discovered in the Indies, and "simple" qualifies the food of the pure Peninsula. Vain nuns wear numerous jewels, a complaint usually directed at criollas, who were considered to be utterly superficial and ostentatious, while lazy nuns are described as *Indias,* ruined by the climate whose pernicious effects were well established. The specificity of these insults reveals how the issues of birth were social and cultural before they became racial. They also reveal the extent to which the chronicle hagiographies were a literature of everyday life in the cloister. In this respect, they are an extraordinarily valuable source because descriptions of this kind do not exist in more official literature. In the manuscript chronicle of the Carmelite convent, for example, the conflict between the reforming nun who is a *gachupina* and the criolla monastic community is represented exclusively in the cultural terms described above. However, when *Parayso occidental,* a version of the same chronicle, comes to be published, the conflict is represented as pertaining only to spiritual virtue and religious orthodoxy. Nevertheless, it is the other versions that remain vivid, versions telling the stories of wicked nuns, lazy and indulgent, lulled by the climate and rendered lascivious by the food, who smoke, who watch plays and listen to concerts in their cloisters, and whose convents are like small cities where Indians, blacks, and children also live and work in a misceginated social chaos far removed from the more official pictures of the stately order of baroque Mexico City.

The convent, which seemed initially the perfect institution to transplant to the New World (because of its implied rejection of *any* world), became instead an important arena where political influence was negotiated strategically by the New Spanish elite and the Peninsular authorities. Similarly, though the subject matter of the texts associated with convents was supposedly transcendental, these writings became instead histories of the cultural values in the colony. The New World cloister—in its theoretical distance from the world and in its real submersion in it; in the silence vowed by its members and in their lived communication, writing, and sociability—provided the space for the representation of what more usually remained silent: women and their creative role in colonial society.[8] The tremendous force of the writings about New World nuns, and especially the writings by them, lies in their revelation of other prodigies, new conundrums, and situations notably *unlike* those presented by the America written about and marveled over by missionaries, colonizers, adventurers, and philosophers and with which we have by now become so familiar.

Acknowledgments

As befits a study of the relationship between the Old World and the New, this book owes its existence to both worlds. In particular, to Italy, where at the European University Institute I did much of the initial writing, and to Mexico, where I carried out the research for it. Among the many people in both worlds to whom I owe substantial debts of gratitude, I will mention only a few: in Europe, Fernando Cervantes, Olwen Hufton, Richard Kagan, Jonathan Murphy, Anthony Pagden, Gianna Pomata, and Ulinka Rublack—all read and commented on different parts of the text at different moments of its writing. Special thanks to my mother, Ana María V. T. Sampson, who checked all my translations. In the Americas, Asunción Lavrin read the vaguest of first outlines and encouraged and advised, and Lourdes Villa Fuerte García and José Antonio Robles Cahero introduced me to the Mexican group Historia de las Mentalidades and, more important, welcomed me into their circle of friends. Thanks to his knowledge and love of the library, Roberto Beristain of the Biblioteca Nacional in Mexico City provided me with sources untraceable in catalogs. My thanks also to my family in Peru, among whom I finished the manuscript. Later in its progress, the book was fortunate to have two very attentive and generous readers, Catherine Jaffe and Stacey Schlau. I am grateful to David Brading for help in locating the cover picture and to Alberto Islas, Alejandra González, and Carmen Flores Vallejo for their generosity and kindness in securing permissions. I would also like to thank Sheri Englund of the University of Texas Press, who guided me through the process of preparing the manuscript for publication.

Colonial Angels

Moving Stories:

New Spanish Hagiographies and Their

Relation to Travel Narrative

Basta decir que impelida de su ardiente fervor del bien de las almas y zelo de propaga-
ción de la Fe y derramar su sangre, andubo por mar y tierra seis mil leguas, que en una
mujer y monja es muy ponderable.

BARTOLOMÉ DE LETONA, *Vida de Gerónima de la Asunción,* 1662[1]

. . . de romera a ramera hay poquísima distancia.

ALONSO DE ANDRADE, *Tratado de la Virgen,* 1642[2]

The foundation of the first convents of the Spanish empire in the Indies
required a number of women to undertake the extraordinary journey to the
New World. This voyage, with all its dangers and insecurities, constituted a
challenge for even the hardiest of men at the time, and the participation of
women in such adventures elicited the reverential shock and allusion to martyrdom that the quotation from Letona exhibits. Nevertheless, women were
not just in physical danger when traveling, and their movement was not only
a sign of physical strength. Their journeying was both moral vulnerability
and sexual deviance as Alonso de Andrade's comment in his treatise makes
apparent. In his opinion, there is but the slightest distance separating the
movement of the pilgrim woman from that of the prostitute, a slip in virtue
being mimicked by a corresponding slip in language.[3]

In this context, the travel narratives contained in the convent chronicles and hagiographies of New Spanish cloisters provide an extraordinary source, retelling not only the progress on the path to salvation of pious nuns and their cosmic spiritual journeys but also the real transatlantic voyages of women whose virtue was unimpeachable. These narratives marry a spiritual representation of travel with accounts of the personal experience of journeys most often associated with the "discovery" of the Americas. The narrative reconciliation of hagiography with the testimonial genre that these texts achieve is an important moment in the context of Spain's evangelical empire-building mission. Moreover, the presence of female protagonists in these stories provides a unique opportunity to assess the role of women in the colonial project.

The protagonists of the chronicles and *vidas* are predestined to be good travelers. The saint has always been a classic mediating figure in Western Christendom, providing a bridge between heaven and earth, between the known world and the unknown. The *Vida de María de Jesús* (1676) by Francisco Pardo provides an extended and rhetorically developed version of this notion. In a dream that bears clear parallels with such classical forebears as Scipio, María de Jesús is transported by two guardian angels through the cosmos. The summary that prefaces the chapter gives a good idea of the kind of voyage she undertakes. She is an alert sentry, a look-out tower for all the planets, who rises to explore all the hemispheres, discovering the delights of Glory. She passes over the diaphanous regions of clouds and sees the horrors of the center, outwitting the cries and desires of the abyss, penetrating the immensities of the sea. Her journey takes her to the lakes and other out-lying parts of purgatory, until by the end of it, she has traversed all the "provincias y naciones del universo, y rodea en palmas de angeles todo el mundo . . ." [the provinces and nations of the universe and encircles the world with triumphing angels].[4]

This kind of journey is clearly reserved for the chosen few, but the virtuous nuns who aspire to sainthood also share a more generally diffused spiritual notion of travel: that of the continual movement of the soul on its voyage to heaven and salvation. When Isabel de la Encarnación experiences her religious calling in a vision, its nature is that of a metaphorical journey. She is shown a very long path, full of brambles and sharp thorns and at the end of which there is such a small light it is almost impossible to see. At this moment in the journey, sor Isabel hears a voice that tells her, "This is the path you have to walk, and to reach the joy of the light and of rest, you will have to travel on it and be torn to shreds, leaving your insides on those thorns."[5]

The contradiction between the imperative that women remain cloistered from the world within the walls of their homes or convents, and the spiritual movement and drive for progress that they are also urged to undertake is enormous. In some cases, as a response to this double imperative, the language used to describe the effects of prayer, which is the chief tool the saintly "mediators" use to travel between heaven and earth, is so ambiguous it leaves an image that embodies the contradiction perfectly: a completely breachable cloister. It is in her small cell that the wings of sor Catarina's heart spread, and she flies up to the breast of her Husband. From this place she is shown the deepest secrets, seeing many of her confessors flying up to heaven at the moment of death, rising up to where the Divine King promised that none of those who had guided her soul would lose theirs. From here God shows her many souls that live in mortal sin so that she can chastise and correct them and intercede for them so that they reform their lives. From here also she is transported for many leagues, traveling in spirit to the provinces where the Jesuit fathers had their missions. This part of her journey is especially vivid, and she is able to describe the land and the new conversions as well as how the houses and huts are constructed, what dress the Indians use, and what the missionaries looked like. Apparently, all of this was later proved to be true [. . . viéndose después todo cumplido].[6]

In the didactic literature of the day, there is a clear attempt to resolve and contain the contradiction between the nun's enclosure and her role as holy voyager, mediating between heaven and earth, through a dichotomy that separates the body from the spirit. The New Spanish hagiographies, however, show the impossibility of such a project, most obviously because of the *real* nature of the voyages recounted. It is significant that the breaching of the cloister described above should primarily concern the action of the nun in purgatory and in evangelization. The conception of purgatory, as argued by Jaques le Goff, significantly modified categories of space and time in the Christian imagination.[7] The idea of purgatory as a "place," though theologically contested, was in practice widely accepted and is very much linked to the pastoral and evangelical role of the Church. Most notably, it was used in the diffusion of the faith because it provided instances of instructive exempla. Purgatory could be traveled to and its inhabitants described, the accounts of their torments serving as valuable information for the preparation of the spiritual journey the listener's or reader's own soul would inevitably have to undertake. Le Goff argues that the introduction of purgatory in the form of exempla into the narrative mode common to the hagiography and the sermon (which addresses a concept of time that is transcendental, that of salvation and conversion) implies an introduction of historic time that cuts across and interrupts this eschatological time.[8] The voyage of prayer that carries Catarina de San Juan in the above quotation from her cell to purgatory and then on to specific Jesuit missions where she is able to report accurately on the customs of the land she sees and on the dress and character of those who inhabit it, makes vivid how versions of the spiritual narrative of the cosmic tour often succumb to the allure of a kind of description most often associated with the account of "real" journeys. This type of narrative has perhaps as its distinguishing characteristic the "historic" treatment of time as opposed to the transcendental, and it is plausible to suppose that the New World provided particularly attractive exempla of this kind. Even the stylishly polished hagiography of María de Jesús can be seen to indulge in this other narrative mode. The references to the paradise she sees on her journey are in consonance with the most conventional requirements of learned hagiographic form, being a reproduction of the classical *locus amoenus*. There are green forests, crystalline rivers, colorful birds, all in a luminous and pleasant space.[9]

This description of a place that is effectively "no place" breaks down when the journey reaches purgatory however, and it is notable that the regions she sees here could be interpreted as representing the recent past of the land she travels from (New Spain), when it was still the place of idolaters. It is as though the New World, like purgatory, once acknowledged as a real geographical destination, different from the terrestrial paradise it was at first thought to be (and which is, in effect, "nowhere") can only be narrated in the historic rather than eschatological mode. So, the angels take sor María to other "remote and different" climes—those of infidels—where she makes out "muchas riquezas, profanas pompas, sobrados placeres, amenas arboledas y agradables frutas . . . [great wealth, profane pomp, excessive pleasures, pleasant trees, and delicious fruits . . .] in a description that owes much to the tradition of representing the Americas as an extraordinary cornucopia.[10]

Without a doubt, the New World presented enormous difficulties for the imposition of European cultural and spiritual norms. The kinds of distortion that travel and the New World could bring to the hagiographic model of feminine sanctity is evident in the hagiographies examined, which exhibit the strain of adapting a narrative form that was becoming more and more rigid at the time to stories telling of different lands and different experiences.[11] The frequent reference to martyrdom and the "desert" the New World presents for the traveling nun is an indication of how a predominantly masculine hagiographic model had to be invoked to explain the presence of female saints whose lives were more traditionally ones of immobile and virtuous enclosure.

The far-reaching implications of this kind of modification for conceptions of the feminine itself can be identified in the *vida* of Ana de San José, a Spanish nun who lived her entire life in a convent in Salamanca but whose hagiography was reprinted in Mexico in 1641. In a spiritual voyage, sor Ana not only journeys to a land of evangelical enterprise, but she becomes a preacher herself, usurping that most sacred of male privileges, direct access to the Word of God:

Otras vezes me sentía llevar sin saber de quién y estando yo en arrobamiento veía mi cuerpo así vestido con el hábito, y de la misma manera que ando; y estando yo elevada, como si fuera otra, veía que me llevaban. Esto me ha sucedido muchas vezes ir andando por el aire como volando; y algunas vezes me hallo entre multitud de Indios de diversas naciones, con la doctrina Christiana en la mano, y ellos estan de rodillas oyéndola.[12]

The absolutely unorthodox, not to say heretical, behavior that Ana de San José describes herself as indulging in can only be imagined because of the distance separating her real cloister in Salamanca from her dream destination in the New World. Arrival in the Indies clearly placed the travelers and their cultural and religious "baggage" in an extreme situation where such certainties as sexual difference can already be seen as challenged by this if not "world-turned-upside-down," certainly "otherworldly" situation. New Spain, however, did not confuse only the categories of sexual difference but also those that divided civilization from barbarism. In the Western tradition, the journey of a saint was generally understood to imply an entry into a different world, and more specifically it often meant abandoning civilization for barbarism, the city for the desert. Paradoxically, the presence of convents and their inhabitants in the Indies was supposed to signify precisely the imposition of civilization, of the Spanish state, and of all its cultural, religious, and political adjuncts. The strict entry procedures that legislated the race and social class of the nuns, the political intrigues and competition surrounding the foundation and patronage of convents, and the important part they played in processions and celebrations in the city makes apparent their central role in the creation of a civic politics, a politics that was necessarily also a racial, religious, and cultural one. The city as conceived of in classical thought was the model upon which many of the discussions about the good government of the Spanish empire in America turned, and the establishment in such an empire of a community of women (the convent), within the *civitas* (as reconceived by Christianity) would serve as symbolically resounding proof of its civility.[13]

The New Spanish hagiography has thus to narrate the "exportation" of Spanish civility to an idolatrous land in narratives that range from the histories of heroic conquest by Spanish soldiers to stories of the equally heroic martyrdom of missionary priests. These narratives, however, also have to affirm that the idolatrous nation in which such adventures unfold is ultimately, or will become, Christian and orthodox—the fitting place for such pious heroes. It is in the representation of travel that the complexity of such a project is made evident. On the one hand, there is a desire to assert the specificity of the New World setting—its status as land of idolatry for example, and, on the other, a wish to deny the pernicious effects of its "difference"—the fact that it might prove impossible to eradicate such beliefs completely.

One narrative strategy that can be traced in many of the writings involves an attempt to register movement without representing change. In a curious version of the relationship of time and speed to distance, the spiritual mathematics of nuns' journeys allows the representation of their voyages to consider these variables while bracketing the question of place. Nuns in the chronicles certainly travel on real as well as spiritual journeys, but they effectively go nowhere, for it is precisely by acknowledging no change in the matter of place that the New World's difference is neutralized and its religious (and political, racial, and social) orthodoxy asserted in terms of its asymmetry to the Old World.[14]

An enlightening explanation of the importance of place in such a kind of journey is given in the remarks attributed to the abbess of the convent of Sta. Catalina, a Capuchin foundation, on her being offered decorations for the cloister:

¿Quién a visto que los pasajeros que caminan ligeros al termino donde van, busquen comodidades en los oficios y ventas? Pues nuestra casa es una venta donde estamos de camino para el fin que deseamos, que es lo eterno.[15]

Place, in this case the cloister itself, which is figured as an inn on the route to heaven, is clearly of no importance on the journey to salvation. Nevertheless, it is crucial to represent movement in this Christian eschatology because of its inexorably teleological nature, and so the convent chronicles provide very detailed topographical information of the founding mothers' movements. The itinerary on arrival in New Spain is an established one: Veracruz, Puebla, the Shrine of Guadalupe, and then Mexico City. The journey certainly takes on the value of pilgrimage with the visiting of holy sites and relics in convents along the way. The geographical detail provided, however exact, remains, as Michel de Certeau puts it, a "backdrop" against which the comedy of the nuns' immutably constant desire for salvation is played out.[16]

In a philosophically rigorous working out of this "geography of the sacred," one would expect from these narratives a representation of traveling that involves no experience of such movement and change on the part of its subjects. The nun, as ultimately innocent woman, would always be the dupe of the experience of travel that she would never experience *as* experience, her innocence turning it into events, places, things that happen to her but do not affect her. The chronicles certainly gesture at this in the emphasis on the enclosed nature of the journeys the nuns undertake. They move from covered coaches to ships' holds, staying overnight in convents and keeping to their liturgical hours in a representation of continual enclosure, emphasized by the insistence that their veils prevent them from both seeing and being seen. In the sermon that Juan Ignacio de la Peña uses as a source for his chronicle of the foundation of the first Capuchin convent in Mexico City, during the journey, as the group crosses the Sierra Morena, the confessor accompanying the nuns encourages them to look out at the view because of its beauty. They refuse to lift their veils, saying they will see everything in heaven. As compensation for their sacrifice, the nuns are rewarded with a much more significant sight, which refers them to a place in the geography of the sacred rather than that of Spain: a vision of the Virgin.[17] In a similar rhetorical strategy, the nuns are represented as exempt from the usual "female" constraints on travel; they have no special demands and do not endanger the efficient progress of the expedition. In fact, they are not women but that most hardy traveler of all, a male apostle: "unas mujeres varoniles, verdaderas apostólicas."[18] The function of this kind of description is to make clear that the huge distances covered in the journeys elapse outside historical time, the nuns never entering the world, Old or New, but transporting their cloister and its special "time" to a different place.[19]

Despite the considerable strength of this hagiographic narrative imperative to present movement without change, travels without places, the chronicles also exhibit the influence of a radically different mode of writing about journeys that is resolutely "historical" to use le Goff's terms. The manuscript chronicle of the convent of Sta. Brígida is an excellent example of a narrative open to influences of this sort. In the chapter devoted to description of the journeys undertaken by the founding mothers, a considerable amount of attention is paid to circumstantial detail, the personality of the accompanying men, the kind of places chosen to sleep in overnight, and the weather. Perhaps the most blatant modification of the hagiographic genre is the explanation of the foundation's enforced postponement due to war breaking out between England and Spain. The nuns are forced to remain in Cádiz for four years and are only eventually able to embark because of the danger of an invasion of the city. This situation is clearly translatable into hagiographic terms: the nuns as potential martyrs, the prey of evil heretics. Although this is gestured at in the chronicle, what seems to interest the nuns writing is more a historical explanation, along the lines of cause and effect (giving an abbreviated account of European politics at the time) and an interpretation of individual reactions in very "naturalistic" terms (particularly of the bravery and determination of the captain of their ship).

It is arguable that the principal contribution of the narratives of discovery written about the New World concerns the status of the writing subject and the issue of authority in the text. One can thus see that the representation of travel in conventual chronicles allows an exploration of the issue of gender and authority in the texts. Traditionally, it was clear that a woman writer's authority in her writing came through divine sanction, not a simple concept to assert as the increasingly "juridical" character of Curia inquiries into *vidas* shows.[20] The accounts of voyages to the New World reveal other strategies for asserting authority in writing. The main problem for writers of histories of voyages to the New World was the textual void they were also venturing into.[21] It is apparent that one solution was to invoke the personal experience of the writing subject. The influence of forensic rhetoric in constructing the "I" as witness in hagiography cannot be underestimated. The increasingly legal nature of the hagiography also meant that often narrative events took the form of a legal deposition, or at least gestured toward this type of "truth." In the chronicle of Sta. Clara, Antonio de la Rosa Figueroa in his introduction to the extant second book, which is devoted to the description of the fire that destroyed the convent, comments on the greater historical value of an experiential account than one based on hearsay:

> Siempre es templado en la verdad lo que vemos y siempre es sublime en la grandeza lo que [viera] de nuestras noticias la antiguedad o la distancia; alocución que el juicioso Horacio advirtió en su *Arte Poética,* diciendo que se concedía más la admiración cuando son testigos los ojos que cuando [resuena] solamente al examen de los oídos.[22]

The writing of Bartolomé de las Casas is classically taken to present the contradictory narrative pulls between the desire to invoke the authority of tradition in the form of an authenticating text and a wish to assert the value of his own experience by constantly invoking his "presence" in the Indies. Although examples of the recurrence to "experience" in the chronicles may be found, and forensic rhetoric is certainly used extensively, it would be inappropriate to identify such marked contradictions in the conventual *vidas.* Hagiography certainly provided a very authoritative form and canon of texts, yet it was flexible to change, especially when its instrumental use as history, as in the New Spanish examples, called on it to represent categories such as travel and difference, usually outside its epistemological scope. Moreover, the didactic function of hagiography meant that issues such as the status of the writing subject and its relation to authority in the text were focused on in a very different manner, much more concerned with the text as "tool" and as "practice"—in fact, with its reception and consumption rather than its production.

Once this focus on reception is acknowledged, the significant differences between how printed and manuscript works represent travel and its contradictions begin to make sense.[23] The accounts of voyages in the manuscript chronicles were meant for "domestic" consumption in the cloister itself. Their reading at moments of recreation in the convent would have served to create a notion of a community with a shared history expressed very much in terms of the "experience" of the founding mothers. The conventional use of the same pronoun to designate the protagonists of the history and its voyages (*nosotras*) and those who read about their exploits (*nosotras*) emphasizes this. The audience's degree of estrangement from the experiences constituted by the wondrous real voyages recounted in the chronicles could be seen as complicating the construction of any sense of community around such extraordinary experiences. Nevertheless, this supposition must be mitigated by acknowledging the ease with which spiritual voyages of a kind the modern reader finds incredibly bizarre were narrated. This sort of travel was particularly good at illustrating the mediatory power of saintly individuals in the community, and there are innumerable instances of pious nuns traveling to purgatory, being shown their convent, and learning about the very private vices and virtues of its members. This knowledge of *interiores,* as it is called, is of transparent didactic use but also functions to create a sense that the cloister and its particular nuns were carried toward salvation and redemption precisely through this continual traveling of its more pious members. When the plague strikes Mexico City in 1633, Agustina de San Juan's privileged knowledge is demonstrated in a vision she has of the nuns to be saved. Her mediatory role is emphasized by her post as gatekeeper of the convent, and it is while walking toward the gate that she retells her premonitory vision. The Holy Trinity appeared on its throne to sor Agustina, summoning nuns from one side and young girls from the other, making her incredibly happy.[24]

The power these journeys to purgatory and other celestial spheres have to create a sense of community rests on their appeal to a shared experience, achieved in great part by the introduction of exempla. These examples furnish the narration with an element of historic specificity, mentioning events and people who are "real" protagonists in the community's past. In this way, the spiritual journeying of pious nuns can be argued to carry them closer to the community they travel from. The mise-en-scène of their voyaging is certainly often staged in startlingly naturalistic terms, the trance being fixed precisely in time and its accompanying gestures being minutely recorded:

> El día de los Santos Niños Innocentes del año de 1630, estando la Madre Isabel de la Encarnación muy fatigada de sus trabajos y dolores, y en especial en el costado, a las diez de la noche entró la enfermera a verla . . . en esta ocasión llegó la Prelada . . . Estuvo pues la Prelada en compañía de otras dos religiosas en la celda acompañando a la enferma. La cual como

si estuviera buena se sentó sobre la cama, arrimándose a la almohada, y quedó arrobada, con el rostro y los ojos tan hermosos y encendidos, que parecía un serafín. . . .[25]

In contrast, the printed versions of nuns' journeys, both spiritual and real, address a much wider audience and their authors often have a transparent political agenda. In some cases, their concern is the promotion of a specific religious order or what might be called a precocious patriotic desire to defend New Spain from all charges of inferiority by intervening in the issue of the New World's difference and the modes of infusing its representation with authority. Nevertheless, the valorization of "experience" in creating a sense of a community and of its history that is evident in the manuscripts can also be found in the printed versions where the nature of the community created is necessarily much more diffuse. Significantly, the work of pooling experience achieved in the manuscripts through the consummate simplicity of the pronoun *nosotras* devolves in the printed sources to the narration of travel. Here, the private perusal of the text through its reading takes on the character of a journey and appeals to the readers by constructing a homology between any real journey they may have made or can imagine and the metaphorical voyage of reading. For example, the readers of *Trono Mexicano* are invited to become as itinerant as the subject matter and to consider their own travels when reading about that of the nuns:

¡Ponderen los que han navegado, y experimentado los riesgos del mar! Y los que no los han pasado, por lo que han oído admiren lo que padecerían unas pobres religiosas; que si las molestias y trabajos de una navegación son grandes, tanto tuvieron de mayores en las madres, cuanto su instituto de más rígido, con el prolijo recato de su retiro.[26]

The postscript to Isabel de la Encarnación's life is even more explicit about the shared "experience" the hagiography alludes to. It addresses its "dear Christian readers," telling them that God did not create us for this world but for the next, and that to reach this other life only two paths exist. One, though narrow, difficult, and unattractive (that of virtue), has a sure and guaranteed end, there being no danger of getting lost. The other, though it may seem more easy and delightful, is deceptive because its pleasures are false. "Halt!" the book orders its readers, pleading with them not to be stupid and blind but to walk on the sure and true path of the sufferings of the Cross, so that by imitating the venerable nun who is the subject of the book, they may gain their inheritance of Eternal Happiness. The author ends his exhortation claiming that this is the happy end "a que he dedicado el trabajo de esta Historia" [to which he has dedicated the plot of his History].[27]

In this injunction, the reader's personal spiritual voyage and the example set by sor Isabel's own journey are joined in the notion of the traveling constituted by the reading experience itself. As the reader reads sor Isabel's *vida,* he or she learns from the examples given. The consumption of this kind of text was clearly meant to have a direct bearing on the actions of such a reader. How successful this didactic intent was remains a question for another study. Here, what is important to note is the mode in which such a transference from text to action was conceived as taking place. To return to the categories used earlier, the deployment of didactic examples introduces a "historic" time to what would otherwise be an eschatological narrative of a saintly life. In the New Spanish case, the introduction of such examples necessarily meant confronting and negotiating the "difference" the New World presented. Although the New Spanish conventual chronicles and *vidas* may have wanted to affirm in their exempla that only the "place" was new, not the institution or the orthodoxy of its inhabitants, the very recognition of place meant a compromise of hagiographic form. At points, the parallels to be drawn between exemplary women (*ave raris* by the period's own definition) and strange monsters of the New World are baroque temptations too attractive for the male writers to resist. They use such a happy conjunction to display their learning by comparing the nuns to the monsters in the works of Pliny and other classical writers. In Rodrigo García Flores' sermon on Teresa de Guzmán, she is compared to the monsters in Aulus Gellius, who live only off the scent of flowers, as well as to the anthropophagi in Pliny, who can only survive and breathe in a specific country, hers being that of prayer and peace.[28]

The affinities between the New World, the evangelical mission it suggested, and the narrative modes associated with both point to the demise of "pure" hagiography in this context and, paradoxically, to its resurrection and success as a heterogeneous narrative form. The narration of the extraordinary real journeys made by these nuns from Spain to the New World is clearly the most obvious example of how the colonial hagiographies were called upon to be as flexible and permeable as the cloisters they represented in order to answer to the needs of the historic and cultural context they were written in. The narrative adaptations required by the New World context were not confined only to the chronicling of "real" journeys however. These texts invite their readers to embark on emulative journeys to reach the virtues they advocate, and in this didactic project, the travel narratives they contain are shown to represent not only the voyages of Spanish nuns and institutions to the New World but also those of a range of Spanish cultural, sexual, and spiritual orthodoxies. It is precisely in the narration of both metaphorical and real voyages, which require a degree of detail and historical specificity that militates against any desire to neutralize the New World's extraordinary difference, that the stories of virtue in the colonies are never quite able to escape the exoticism of the real adventure that brought them to such a far-away place.

Chronicles of a Colonial Cloister:

The Convent of San José and the Mexican

Carmelites

[México, ciudad] . . . dignamente merecedora de que en los ecos de la fama haya llegado su nombre a los más retirados términos del universo, aún no tanto por la amenidad deleitosísima de su sitio; por la incomparable hermosura de sus espaciosas calles; por la opulencia, y valor de sus antiguos reyes; por la copia y circunspección de sus tribunales; por las prendas que benignamente les reparte el cielo a sus ilustres hijos; conseguido ser la cabeza y metrópoli de la América; cuanto porque a beneficio de éste, y de otros innumerables templos, con que se hermosea su dilatado ámbito se puede equivocar con el cielo empíreo, cuando desde ellos, sin intermisión, se le envía a Dios Nuestro Señor el sacrificio y holocausto de sus debidos elogios, y a donde viven los que los habitan con pureza celestial.[1]

CARLOS DE SIGÜENZA Y GÓNGORA, *Parayso occidental,* 1683

Llegadas a la casa, entramos en un patio. Las paredes harto caídas me parecieron, mas no tanto como cuando fue día se pareció. . . . Yo no sabía qué hacer, porque vi no convenía poner allí altar. . . . Comenzáronse a buscar [clavos] de las paredes; en fin, con trabajo, se halló recaudo. Unos a entapizar, nosotras a limpiar el suelo, nos dimos tan buena prisa, que, cuando amanecía, estaba puesto el altar, y la campanilla en un corredor, y luego se dijo la misa.[2]

TERESA DE JESÚS, *Libro de las fundaciones,* 1610

Sigüenza y Góngora's extravagant idealization of civic space celebrates convents as some of the most important buildings in the ultracivilized and pious metropolis of Mexico City. His description forms part of the introduction to a chronicle that contains an account of the foundation of San José, the first Carmelite convent in the viceregal city. Another Carmelite convent, also called San José but located in Medina del Campo, Spain, is the subject of the second quotation, but in this case idealism is abandoned in favor of an account of the prosaic realities of founding such institutions. Sta. Teresa of Avila recounts how hard physical labor was required to convert buildings that were in dilapidated conditions. Her description of this foundation, and indeed of all the religious houses included in the *Libro de las fundaciones,* gives the impression of Carmelite convents as essentially improvised institutions, springing up in the interstices of metropolises that were unaware of their existence and often indeed openly hostile to them.

What change did the perception of the Carmelite Order undergo for the first of its convents in Mexico City, founded scarcely one hundred years after the rather ad hoc and precarious establishment of the Peninsular convents, to figure as the centerpiece of an official account of the glories of the colonial capital? What happened for this most radically ascetic of monastic reforms in the sixteenth century, whose essence was embodied in Sta. Teresa's comment that God was to be found *también en los pucheros* [even among the pots and pans] to become the subject of such pompous and triumphalist rhetoric? This surprising change in the Teresian tradition, and the journey and place of destination that played a part in occasioning it, is the focus of this chapter.

We are used to thinking of the New World as a place in which European culture re-created itself. In terms of religious communities, the two most salient examples of European traditions interacting dynamically with the New World context are the millenarian dreams of the Franciscans and the utopian projects of the Jesuits. My intention here is to study an instance of precisely this kind of exportation—of a spiritual tradition that was also an intellectual and a writing tradition, but which in this particular case had a woman at its center. In some senses, to claim that there existed a female "tradition" in this period is to be purposefully anachronistic, for women were generally excluded from the ability to create powerful genealogies of any kind. Nevertheless, the long history of misogynist writings in Europe is itself a "tribute" to the existence of this illegitimate female line. What is so interesting about examining the Teresian tradition, and particularly in the New World context, is precisely that it constitutes an instance of a female tradition being deemed acceptable and indeed co-opted by the ecclesiastical and political hierarchies that usually worked to marginalize such phenomena. And this situation is even more intriguing because, as we will see, the Teresian tradition in the Indies is being championed within the context of a crucial argument about the orthodoxy of the New World, the success of conquest, and indeed of the evangelizing enterprise itself.[3]

The number and variety of the chronicle histories of San José give us an extraordinary insight into what the exportation of the Teresian tradition meant for very different authors and their equally diverse intended audiences. There are manuscript writings by the nuns themselves, telling the history of the foundation in biographical and autobiographical form.[4] There are also three accounts of the foundation by men: one, a secular academic (Sigüenza y Góngora); one, a Dominican preparing a general history of the Carmelite Order (Avendaño); and the other, a chaplain of the convent writing a history of its foundation (Méndez). All of these stories of how San José came to be established have as a literary model the writings of Sta. Teresa, and their relation to this body of founding texts is an important indicator of how the tradition fared in the New World.

All the authors agree that the foundation of San José is an event of momentous importance in the colony. Avendaño and Méndez go so far as to claim the foundation to have been divinely ordained. Indeed, both historians declare that Sta. Teresa herself had often expressed her desire for such an event. In his history, Avendaño documents the devotion to Sta. Teresa shown by eminent people before the foundation and argues that this is a pious portent of San José's success. Among these devotees is the hermit Gregorio López, an acclaimed "holy man" of the Indies who was revered as a saint at the time and whose support would have been both spiritually and politically very valuable.[5]

The fortunes of the Carmelite Order in general in the Americas are distinguished by the drama and speed with which they unfolded. The years 1600–1606 were some of the most active of the Counter-Reformation. They were also a period in which Sta. Teresa's fame in the New World grew. By 1604 Lima had its Carmelite convent and in New Spain potential patrons and founding mothers were numerous. Inés de la Cruz and Mariana de la Encarnación, the nuns who went on to found San José, mention various other attempts that disrupted their own during these years. These involved nuns from other New Spanish convents, *beatas* from Spain, and female members of elite Mexican families.[6] Sor Inés and sor Mariana eventually succeed, but in order to establish San José they and their companions have to leave the Conceptionist convent of Jesús María in which they were professed nuns. Their abandonment of the Franciscan Order and their breaking of the rule and of the cloister are the painful episodes that give birth to San José.

The reaction of the nuns left behind in Jesús María is to accuse the departing women of being nothing but *noveleras* [modish] and to allege that their wish to leave the Conceptionist rule has no more substance than a fashionable whim. The perception of the Carmelite Order as a "reforming" force was widely held, and the vehemence of these nuns' condemnation of reform is a response to the fact that it necessarily implied criticism of existing norms. In this case, criticism of an established religious institution to which they belonged. The situation was a delicate one and serves to remind us of the status of the Carmelites as relative newcomers in a hierarchy of religious orders that stretched back many centuries. Indeed, Trent's promotion of the Carmelites (however patchy and inconsistent this sometimes was) would have lent the order an ultramodern aura. The founding mother, Mariana de la Encarnación, clearly wants to avoid the ecclesiastical scandal that such accusations of superficiality could lead to, and in her account of the foundation she emphasizes the fact that the Carmelite confessors first concentrated on making the nuns who were intent on reform keep to their Conceptionist rule perfectly before moving on to ideas of taking on a new or different one.[7]

The arrival of Archbishop Pérez de la Serna to Mexico City in 1612 provided the ecclesiastical backing that made this kind of diplomacy irrelevant. The archbishop had spent the transatlantic crossing reading Sta. Teresa's writings and believed that he had been saved from shipwreck by her intervention. Opposition to the foundation of San José was at an end—the convent was to be the archbishop's magnificent *ex voto*.[8] Pérez de la Serna was certainly very energetic in ensuring that his chosen object of devotion accrued as much "saintliness" as possible and as quickly as possible. In 1618, the year of Sta. Teresa's canonization, he also named her patron saint of Mexico City, a title that would have conferred great honor on the saint's representatives in the city—the nuns of San José. The archbishop had already made sure the convent had as its chaplain Francisco Lossa, possibly the most celebrated holy man in the Indies at the time because of his past friendship with the dead Gregorio López, who was himself considered a saint. Moreover, Pérez de la Serna also ensured that López' bones were held in the convent, thus making it the possessor of very powerful relics.[9] The weight of these associations charged San José and its inhabitants with a considerable spiritual aura. It also confirmed that the Carmelite convent and its nuns had come to be the exemplary signs of an orthodoxy that the Church aspired to communicate to the entire colony.

The ceremonies connected to the foundation of San José confirm the political importance of the event as well as baroque commonplaces about how public display could be used in ratifying institutional power and world order. The written account of these ceremonies, of the magnificent altars erected along the route, of the illuminated streets, fireworks, and public squares covered in rich carpets and flowers, certainly serves to record and acknowledge these instances of benevolence on the part of a devout patron or group of patrons. It also serves the more broadly political and ideological projects that San José had come to embody. This second function is transparent in two descriptions of particularly significant images: St. James and Sta. Teresa herself. Both images are life-size and richly decorated. The image of St. James, the saint of the Crusades against the Moors and who had been adopted by the conquistadores as their patron, is described as breaking through crowds, forcing them to give way in a dramatization of the triumphant victory of the most orthodox of Spanish *reconquista* values—values that were, of course, to be guarded in the new convent.[10] The altar devoted to Sta. Teresa also stage-manages a transparent political meaning. Accompanying the image is a "spectacle" consisting of a forest populated with animals and *Indios* who prostrate themselves as the procession goes by. Once again, San José is associated in these shows with a notion of the spiritual conquest of the New World as accomplished, triumphant, and celebratory.

Of course, the most important objects and displays that San José possessed were its nuns and their pious lives, and the written accounts of the nuns themselves provide the material required for confirming their own as well as their convent's saintliness. The most elaborate accounts are the two versions of the foundation of the convent by the founding mothers, Inés de la Cruz and Mariana de la Encarnación. There are also autobiographical *vidas* as well as other biographies of virtuous nuns. Most of these have Inés de la Cruz or her protégé Bernarda de San Juan as subjects and are written by different nuns, although Margarita de San Bernardo emerges as the chief author. The writings of these women are used as a source by all of the male chroniclers.

Parayso occidental by Carlos de Sigüenza y Góngora is the only published chronicle; Avendaño's and Méndez's works and that of the nuns exist only in manuscript. Both these last male authors often refer the reader to the nuns' accounts through marginal notes, allowing the reader to conjecture that their work was meant for a convent audience who would have had access to the women's manuscripts. In contrast, the panoply of dedications, approvals, and prologues that accompany *Parayso occidental* make apparent its very public status as a piece of writing. It is also the history of San José that most abandons the texts by the women as a writing base. In Sigüenza's version, the main story concerns the convent of Jesús María, and the inclusion of the story of the foundation of San José by nuns who leave this first convent is subsidiary to the main narrative.

All the versions of the foundation, whether by men or women, whether more or less elaborate, are greatly influenced by Sta. Teresa's own writings and in particular the *Libro de las fundaciones* and *Camino de la perfección*.[11] From some of the nuns' accounts, it is clear that these writings were available in manuscript in the convent. Inés de la Cruz' account of her own life develops the Teresian parallels most systematically. She describes herself as avidly reading the *vidas* of hermits as a child as well as "mirror" books, just as Sta. Teresa claimed to have done. Later, when sor Inés' father decides to go with his family to the Indies, sor Inés sees in this her opportunity for martyrdom, in a manner reminiscent of Sta. Teresa's wish to die at the hands of the Moors. It is, however, Sta. Teresa's admission of her love of secular literature, and in particular of novels of chivalry, that is most often echoed by the New Spanish Carmelites. Often the seductive texts are poems or plays rather than novels, but the guilty enthusiasm is the same.[12] Moreover, the tone and style in all these Mexican writings is intimate and personal, something that has often been remarked on in relation to Sta. Teresa's own work.[13] In the accounts of the New Spanish nuns, this is particularly notable in the way personages representing enormous political power are written about. Both founding nuns, for example, are careful to reproduce Archbishop Pérez de la Serna's speech, usually the jokes he makes at their expense. The relation to Juan de Rivera, the patron, is described in terms of the flirtatious techniques of persuasion the nuns have to use on him. In a similarly light and mischievous vein, their dealings with the oidor Quezada are characterized as "complicated" due to the fact that the men in Quezada's family have a history of falling inappropriately in love with nuns, a weakness that predictably makes Quezada's wife unsympathetic to his patronage of the Carmelites.

An instance of the chronicles making direct allusion to Sta. Teresa's writing in their narrative structure occurs in accounts of the taking of legal possession of houses in which to found the convent. Each of these versions is inspired by passages in Sta. Teresa's *Libro de las fundaciones,* which have been described as "picaresque histories" because of their irreverent and comic tone.[14] The ironic fact that in order to do God's work Sta. Teresa must dupe and out-maneuver landlords and officials from the town council is reproduced in the New Spanish versions when it becomes clear that the houses that the patron Rivera had bequeathed in his will to the Carmelite foundation are inhabited and so must be vacated before the nuns can move in. The archbishop decides to do this by taking legal possession secretly at night—again, an action with numerous Teresian precedents.[15] He arranges for someone in the house to set up an altar, and he arrives in the early hours of the morning to say mass and so consecrate the building and force its inhabitants to leave. Méndez' account is a transcription of Mariana de la Encarnación's, adding only the explanation that the archbishop used a bell to wake up the neighbors because this reminded him of Sta. Teresa's way of taking legal possession of a building. Mariana claims her account comes straight from the archbishop's oral version and is very effective at describing the speed and confusion of events as well as the archbishop's obvious delight in the adventure. We are told Pérez de la Serna breaks out into laughter at the sight of the startled tenants emerging "unos medio desnudos, otros cubiertos sólo con frazadas y algunos en camisa, dando voces que no los podían sosegar" [some of them half undressed, others covered only in blankets, some in their shirts, and all screaming so loudly that nothing could calm them].[16]

The New Spanish versions share Sta. Teresa's own pleasure in narrating the absurd details of such nocturnal adventures. For Sigüenza y Góngora, the episode presents an irresistible opportunity to describe a moment of enormous dramatic potential that he takes on with enthusiasm, producing an account of comic confusion that finds resolution with the coming of daylight.[17] Moreover, his framing of this episode within the device of a dream and an (entirely geographically specific) earthquake constitute the kinds of rhetorical effects that have encouraged critics to claim the hagiography as a precursor of the novel.[18]

Other examples of how the New World versions of the foundation story take the Teresian tradition of adaptation and transformation of literary form to heart abound in the chronicles. In this respect, the Teresian inheritance can be seen as an extremely liberating and creative one. A marginal note by Mariana de la Encarnación to Méndez' chronicle supplies a particularly telling instance of this. In her note, sor Mariana tells the story of a miracle that the male chronicler did not include in his version; she elaborates on the man's text, appending her own version of events. The roots of the story she tells lie most probably in the fables that would have been the staple both of oral storytelling and of many of the sermons that she would have heard, but the comic pace and irreverent tone are absolutely sor Mariana's own:

> Siendo novicia tenía a su cargo el corral de las gallinas y estando un día haciéndoles salvado, llamaron la campana para comulgar (y como había de ser la que [oraba] en el acto de comunidad) dióse más prisa para acabar con la ocupación, dió el gallo en meterse el lebrillo de salvado estorbándola a que lo acabase incorporar [*sic*] y afligida, dióle con el cucharón en la cabeza y quedó muerto; la pobre novicia le metió la cabeza en el salvado y se fué a comulgar pidiendo a Dios la vida del gallo, con gran fe de que lo había de alcanzar; así que salió del coro fué a ver su difunto y hallólo muy brioso paseando todo el corral.[19]

Sor Mariana's talent and creativity point to how both the nuns and the men writing about San José enjoyed a considerable amount of formal freedom and innovation in their compositions. They adapt the Teresian model, which was so evident a reference point, but they also adapt the generic model behind all these accounts, and behind Sta. Teresa's writing itself— namely, the hagiography. This genre had come to be the privileged form through which to write the history of religious orders by way of catalogs of their illustrious members. In one sense, this use of hagiography to record history seems contradictory, given that the epiphanic and didactic uses of the genre allow very little room for narrative, instead producing works that are an "exposition" of the saint's life and of the universe itself as the Divine Book. In this kind of narrative, plots are always already written by God

Himself, who orchestrates all events, acting through the saint. Despite these very strong formal characteristics of immanence and repetition that hagiography's continual reference to exemplary events brings about, the representation of virtue in hagiography can in contrast be seen to "fix" the genre very firmly in worldly concerns, situating it on the side of the status quo. Michel de Certeau has argued that the representation of virtue rather than that of the extreme states of martyrdom or of a hermit's existence can be seen as an attribute of the established Church's hagiography.[20] In de Certeau's analysis, martyrs and hermits predominate in hagiography when the Church represented is under siege, attacked and vulnerable. In contrast, the established Church gives rise to hagiographies of nuns and monks, both essentially products of its fixed institutions and whose lives conflate religious virtue with social conformity.[21]

It is significant in this context to recall that the concept of "heroic virtue" was itself first used in the canonization process of Sta. Teresa in 1602 and was introduced specifically as a measure meant to lessen the importance usually attached in such procedures to the miracles performed by the saint. "Heroic virtue" was designed to separate bona fide saints from practitioners of magic and the black arts. Candidates had to exhibit the three theological virtues of Faith, Hope, and Charity as well as the four cardinal ones of Prudence, Temperance, Justice, and Fortitude, all to a "heroic" degree that ensured no demonic interference was possible.[22] From these very precise elaborations of the concept, we can see how the figure of Sta. Teresa was adopted by the Counter-Reformation Church in its evangelical mission to staunch any manifestations of spirituality except those it itself promoted and sanctioned.

The unmistakably political projects that hagiography was associated with make it apparent that the genre could then also be fairly easily assimilated into an apologetic project for the Catholic Church's evangelical mission in the Indies and, more generally, for the colonial enterprise itself. Problems remained, however, with the representation of exemplary spirituality and particularly with a specifically feminine spirituality.[23] The difficulty of expressing spiritual truths in narrative had, of course, been raised by St. Augustine himself, whose *vida* constituted the model for all hagiography. His rejection of a career as professor of rhetoric may be read as a symptomatic distrust of form, of the figurative power of language. Thus his praise of Cicero's *Hortensius* focuses on the force of the text's content: ". . . not to sharpen my tongue did I employ that book, nor did it infuse into me its style, but its matter."[24] Notwithstanding this caution, it is precisely the rhetorical figure of metaphor that achieves Augustine's conversion: ". . . especially after I had heard one or two places of the Old Testament resolved, and oft-times 'in a figure,' which when I understood literally, I was 'slain' spiritually."[25]

Capable of slaying and resurrecting simultaneously, "spiritual language" was a contentious issue and, by the sixteenth and seventeenth centuries, much policed by the Inquisition. Given the Pauline injunctions on women's silence, their exclusion from theological knowledge, and the recuperation of misogynist patristic and scholastic texts by Renaissance moralists, women's access to such language was much disputed.[26] Hence Sta. Teresa's cautious introduction to her use of the metaphor of a garden for the soul in her own writing:

> Habré de aprovecharme de alguna comparación, que yo las quisiera excusar por ser mujer, y escribir simplemente lo que me mandan, mas este lenguaje de espíritu es tan malo de declarar a los que no saben letras como yo, que habré de buscar algún modo, y podrá ser las menos veces acierte a que venga bien la comparación; servirá de dar recreación a Vuestra Merced de ver tanta torpeza.[27]

Sta. Teresa's claim to simplicity and her association of this with her sex is a strategy also adopted by the nuns of New Spain and is in marked contrast to the learned approach of Sigüenza y Góngora or other male compilers of convent chronicles. The description of incredible spiritual events and mundane domestic ones in the same tone, which is so characteristic of Sta. Teresa's writing, was strongly disapproved of however by Luis de Granada (1504–1588), who attempted to limit the use of examples to strictly biblical ones.[28] Although the Curia was never able to implement such strict control over the form of the *vida*, it is clear that during this period the text of the potential saint's life was as much an object of scrutiny as the life itself.[29]

In the writings produced by nuns in San José, the women are careful to avoid the worst consequences of being caught in theological or doctrinal error by expressing their access to spiritual knowledge through the trope of *docta ignorantia,* a well-established figure for affirming female religious and literary inadequacy. The deployment of this trope in the *vidas* reproduces the dichotomy that may be understood to inhabit the body of the female mystic. In this body, the radical disjunction between the divine male voice and the female body it speaks from is dramatized through a spectacle that serves to illustrate the anomalous position of women in relation to language.[30] The woman may speak powerfully, but the voice is not her own; it is God's. Nevertheless, the fact that in the chronicles of San José the theater for this knowledge is the page and not the body makes a crucial difference. In writing, the nun is not only transmitting spiritual knowledge but reproducing it; she is creating, as we have seen from the instances of departure from tradition and generic form discussed earlier.[31]

As a consequence, though these nuns certainly claim "entendimiento rudo y torpe lengua," their simple wits and clumsy tongues are liberated in their writing, where access to spirituality is often figured and celebrated as access to articulate and fluent language itself:

> Elevábase el entendimiento en estas ocasiones tan altamente que, admirándose ella misma de lo que razonaba (que solía ser en versos suavisísimos y elegantísimos), exclamaba diciendo: "¡Qué es aquesto! ¿Quién a mí me ha hecho poeta? ¿Quién es quien me ilustra mi entendimiento rudo y le sugiere semejantes palabras a mi torpe lengua?"[32]

This type of articulacy and inspiration is readily mentioned in the chronicle *vidas* but certainly not reproduced in quotation. Similarly, Méndez' description of Inés de la Cruz' theological knowledge concentrates on her delicate deployment of the correct vocabulary to describe the nature of the Holy Trinity. Her actual words are not transcribed for the reader, however.[33] The fact that sor Inés' record of her mystical experiences is written for her confessor goes some way to explaining this reticence. The kind of subjective experience of the spiritual that is alluded to, and figured as perfect speech, is meant for a very select public: the nun's confessor. Nevertheless, it clearly remains what Asunción Lavrin describes as an "opportunity" for the subjectivity that was erased through the novice's vows at profession to be in some measure restored to her in the writing of her *vida*.[34] And it is through the politic deployment of reticence when describing spiritual matters that the writer secures the orthodoxy of her *vida* by differentiating it from the disreputable mystical model of feminine spirituality. This reticence is also indicative of a more general evasiveness in the chronicles connected to the representation of spiritual knowledge. The convent history certainly wishes to lay claims to the sanctity of its nuns, but it does not narrate the content of this access to knowledge, though it often narrates the effects of such sanctity: miracles, prophecies, and so on. These miracles and prophecies have their representation justified by appeals to their demonstrable "truth," clearly something much more difficult to claim for an interpretation of a vision or a theological explanation given by an ecstatic nun.[35]

The image of the convent community that emerges from a reading of works by both women and men is by no means a consistent one; at points unity is emphasized, at others, dispersion. This variation is most easily explained by the plot of the chronicle narratives, which set out to record the life and history of a community and which come into conflict with the hagiographic plot that had as its subject the individual. The principal plot "device" in the histories of San José could be described as rebellion followed by reform. This narrative dynamic requires, on the one hand, the exaltation of a virtuous reforming individual (and achieves its effect by contrasting this individual with a recalcitrant community), and, on the other, it requires that this virtuous individual be seen to be the exemplar of a community whose own perfection makes it heavenly. Clearly, this double narrative imperative implies quite serious formal problems in terms of keeping generic decorum.[36]

The problems of representing reform were not confined only to the elegant execution of the recommendations of rhetorical handbooks—it had a direct impact on and relation to the institutions and persons represented.[37] It was also intimately connected to an important contemporary debate on the virtue of religious institutions in New Spain. A new and adapted Conceptionist rule published by Archbishop Francisco Manso y Zúñiga in 1635 addressed this debate. The convent of Jesús María would have been subject to this new rule, and Jesús María is also, of course, the convent abandoned by the reforming would-be Carmelites on the grounds that its enclosure was not "strict" enough and that it infringed many of its own laws. Manso y Zúñiga's pamphlet begins by hinting that the archbishop's political and spiritual power is not all that he would wish it to be, the nuns being unruly and reluctant to accept his authority.[38] It goes on to specify necessary reforms in sections covering dress, the method of electing an abbess, the distribution of the community's economic possessions and income, the regulation of entries and exits from the cloister, the keeping of the vow of silence, and the preservation of a "peaceful" atmosphere within the community.

These areas designated as a problem are strikingly similar to the features of convent life in Jesús María, which the would-be Carmelites choose to complain about in their justifications for breaking away.[39]

The fact that the breakaway nuns focus their case for reform and spiritual purity on this contrast between their contemplative and ascetic desires and the mundanity of the community they found themselves in has curious narrative consequences. In most cases, it leads to a reproduction of misogynist topoi on female sociability by the author, regardless of the latter's sex. Thus in the *vidas*, without exception, the convent figures as a space from which to escape the veniality the aspiring nuns are understood to be condemned to by virtue of their female sex if they remain in the world. Consequently, spiritual weakness in the convent is signaled precisely by a reversion to these worldly values. Hence, the outcry against ornamented habits, servants, and the presence of lay persons in the cloister.[40]

The communal "paradise" of rational flowers envisaged by Sigüenza y Góngora in his prologue to *Parayso occidental* will simply not function as an image of the convent if reform of the community and the virtue of a particular individual has to be represented. For reform to be justified, both in spiritual and narrative terms, it is necessary for the cloister to replicate the sins of the world within its walls, producing a convent community fractured in many ways, the most important clearly being the division between the saved and the damned. The reforming nun's *portentos* [premonitions] often work to confirm this kind of division in the community. A striking example is Inés de la Cruz' vision of the nuns who sang hours in the choir gently ascending to heaven. She recounts the vision to the community, reciting the names of those she had seen rising up, and her reaction to the anxiety her account causes those nuns absent from the pious roll call is to laugh, exhorting them to keep the rules of the order in future.[41] The heavy-handedness of this crude blackmail tends to obscure the sophisticated claim it makes, and the fact that such a claim was perfectly "orthodox," however much the ecclesiastical authorities might complain about divisions within convents. Reform was divinely sanctioned.

The groups and "bands" that convents were accused of breaking into were often determined by friendship and by kinship; that is, by the kinds of strong emotional force that Inés de la Cruz appeals to in her manipulative vision. The story of Marina de la Cruz and her daughter (with whom she professes after becoming widowed for a second time) is revealing about the kinds of ties and affection that are licit in the convent. Sor Marina loves her daughter dearly and spends most of her time dressing and ornamenting her. God intervenes and kills the daughter in a particularly bloody and spectacular way, leaving Sigüenza y Góngora to comment that worldly affection will bring only eternal death to its devotees.[42] His later approbation of sor Marina's adoption of Inés de la Cruz as a "spiritual" daughter makes clear that affections in the cloister were precisely differentiated and that the convent represented a space where the affective ties of the worldly family were invalid and, on occasions, sinful. Thus, Inés de la Cruz' vocation is confirmed early in her life when she abandons her mother in the cathedral in order to pray alone.[43] What makes the representation of this very traditional topos of *contemptus mundi* so interesting in the chronicles is how often the ties the nuns are represented as having to throw off are connected to the family.

The overtly didactic purpose of the official convent chronicles alerts us to the fact that such an emphasis is carefully calculated in texts. That this should be so is not so surprising given what we know of the powerful systems of patronage and influence that depended on ties of kinship and how they linked ecclesiastic and political institutions in the colony. These "networks" are clearly visible in convents where sisters, nieces, cousins, and so forth, would profess in the same institution.[44] Though all convents, European and New World, absolutely depended on such systems, in strict doctrinal terms they were all too worldly—and often caused competition and conflict between the different groups. Inés de la Cruz' refusal to accede to Archbishop Pérez de la Serna's request that the founding nuns for San José be chosen from each convent in Mexico City could then be interpreted as an attempt to ensure not only spiritual coherence (she argues that taking nuns from different religious orders will make it difficult to impose a new order) but also political stability, by ensuring that a completely new system of solidarity and community identity, designed by sor Inés herself, can be set in place.[45] In fact, sor Inés' request echoes various comments of Sta. Teresa's in *Libro de las fundaciones,* where she describes the harm that powerful groups within the convent can bring. Sta. Teresa's drive to abandon the use of titles, which was the custom in the convent she left in order to found the reformed branch, also has a dual significance. On the one hand, it is an assertion of pious humility (all nuns, whatever their station in the world, are equal before God in the cloister) and a politic implementation of reform meant to break up social and kinship groups in the convent. For example, all the histories of San José condemn "particular friendships" or the ties of worldly affection in trenchant terms inherited from Sta. Teresa.[46] This type of affection, especially among women, is considered to threaten the downfall of convents. Without having to look for psychosexual explanations of this anxiety, it is obvious that such friendships and alliances challenged ecclesiastical authority and the union of the convent community.

Inevitably, the family becomes the focus of the "reform" plot just described. It provides a simple way of describing allegiances in the convent and of assigning nuns to "groups." Mariana de la Encarnación herself becomes a victim of these divisions when she contemplates the idea of reform, a wish that is immediately identified as a threat to the community. The convent is full of her sisters and other relatives, as well as friends who were educated there with her as small girls before professing. None of these people can understand her desire for change and try to dissuade her by appealing to her sense of solidarity with this group.[47] These women speak of their shared experiences in San José, of the difficulties overcome and the happiness secured. They also tell sor Mariana that by siding with the reforming *gachupinas* she will be reneging on all this. Almost obscured by the emotional force of her friends' complaint is the fact that these nuns describe the women responsible for taking sor Mariana from them in terms of their birthplace. The nuns in New Spanish convents like Jesús María were all of Spanish race, as was stipulated by their entry requirements, but there was a distinction between those born in Spain and those born in the Indies, between criollas and *gachupinas,* and it is this distinction that sor Mariana's friends invoke. This difference begins to be expressed in increasingly biological terms in contemporary sources such as sor Mariana's account, and I will reproduce this terminology, but it should be kept in mind that the difference between *gachupinas* and criollas in the convents should be thought of as primarily cultural or ethnic rather than strictly racial.

The detail of birthplace reveals the plot of reform regarding the foundation of San José to be organized around divisions that are as much rooted in culture as they are in family or kinship structures. That kinship and family structures should also be marked by culture is a fairly obvious revelation, but given the context of the New World, what happens in the chronicle stories of reform is that the plot of religious orthodoxy is transformed into one of cultural (and racial) orthodoxy. This interesting and significant development means that the enclosed nun comes to symbolize the honor of contesting power groups in the Indies and that her story becomes the reflection of their histories and the projection of their imagined futures.[48]

The nun as heroine of the New World narrative is not altogether unexpected if we remember the important role played by hagiography in supporting established values—both those of generic form and those of ecclesiastical hierarchy. If it becomes possible to write hagiographies of the New World in which women shine for their piety and orthodoxy, the piety and orthodoxy of this erstwhile pagan land is confirmed and, along with it, the success of the Spanish evangelic mission. The difficulties of convincing anyone of the truth of this story, and the virtue of its heroine, are palpable in the attempt by Juan Ignacio de la Peña to describe the success of the Capuchin Order in Mexico. Peña has to insist on the "legitimacy" of the nuns for their vocation—they may be born in the Indies and subject to the malign influence of the food, climate, and air of the place, but they are, nonetheless, "true" Capuchin nuns:

> . . . Señoras vírgenes Capuchinas, criollas, hijas legítimas del espíritu y aliento de sus primeras madres Capuchinas, para que vea la Europa, que hay alientos de su tamaño en la América, porque aunque los influjos, los alimentos y los aires pueden debilitar las fuerzas, hasta hacer en los cuerpos más delicadas las complexiones, es poderosa la gracia para formar espíritus gigantes. . . .[49]

This extended assertion of equality in spiritual matters pivots, however, on the very difference between the Old World Capuchins and the New, a difference that Peña acknowledges as physical and material and spiritual. It is these differences that only the extreme virtue of the criollo Capuchin vocation can overcome.

We know that New Spanish convents at this time were populated with women of very heterogeneous racial and cultural backgrounds. The nuns may all have in theory been of Spanish "origin," but the children in their care, the women taking refuge, and the servants working there could have been blacks or Indians or members of one of the *castas*—the name given to the groups of misceginated peoples that makes apparent the beginnings of a project to categorize them. It would be a mistake, however, to assume that this kind of problem was exclusive to the New World. In some ways, such a concern for purity of birth and of blood is a resolutely Peninsular one and, given that we know Sta. Teresa came from a "New Christian" family, it is particularly resonant in the Carmelite context. The saint's Jewish ancestry and the blind prejudice and suspicion that such people were subject to in the period lends her appeals for the annulment of worldly ties in the cloister a more urgent and precise tone. So the transplantation of the Carmelites to the New World involved both the transplantation of the idea of "purity of blood" *and* the critique of that same notion. Moreover, it was as if this notion and its opposing idea had been placed in a context so exaggeratedly designed to test them that it seemed almost parodic: a land of indigenous pagans and of other peoples of recently created and suspicious lineages, as well home to any number of migrant Jews and heretics.[50]

It is no wonder then that the reformatory stance taken by many of the virtuous nuns in the chronicles should be interpreted not merely in terms of religious ambition but also of social and "racial" advancement.[51] The nuns of Jesús María see Inés de la Cruz' desires for reform as being intimately connected to her status as a *gachupina* in a convent overwhelmingly made up of criollas. They warn Mariana de la Encarnación that she is being deceived by what are described as *gachupina* proclivities: the love of novelty and the desire for celebrity.[52] Ana de San Miguel, who is abbess at the time of the breakaway, goes further and presents a global interpretation of the privileges enjoyed by *gachupines* in New Spain. Clearly, what is at stake may nominally be religious orthodoxy, figured as greater austerity, but there are a host of political interests, represented as cultural and racial purity, also involved. Sor Ana's comments are made during the period when Archbishop Pérez de la Serna became the patron of the would-be Carmelites and link the patronage he proffers explicitly to the fact that the leading reformer, Inés de la Cruz, is also *gachupina*.[53] The abbess' identification of the political rather than spiritual reasons for Pérez de la Serna's behavior is quoted by Mariana de la Encarnación, who, in the same account, provides information that would seem to confirm this as being the principal motivation the archbishop had. Sor Mariana describes how he berates the founding mothers when they try to refuse the grand entrance ceremony he has planned for the inauguration of the convent buildings. Pérez de la Serna classifies their complaint that such ceremony is unnecessary as disingenuous hypocrisy. He at once consoles and reprimands them, saying that they will have time enough in which to display their orthodoxy as Carmelites and all the austerity this implies.

On this particular occasion, however, the politics of the moment is the pre-eminent concern, not spiritual etiquette.[54]

The enormously complex political and racial situation these comments point to is further revealed as being of central importance, both in the cloister and outside it, by Méndez' extended aside on racial politics, meant as an explanation of Ana de San Miguel's remarks mentioned above. Méndez' opinions are an elaboration of a profoundly "democratic" Christian argument: that all people, no matter where born, are equals spiritually. Crucially, he does not argue for their equality outside the cloister. The existence of *buena o mala tierra* is not questioned, difference in these matters clearly being admitted, but the convent thus becomes the utopic homeland — *nuestra verdadera patria* — where this difference is dissolved in the same way as other worldly attachments:

> Y contención de Indias o España, de esta o la otra tierra es cumplirse al pie de la letra lo que la mística Doctora de la Iglesia, Nuestra Madre Sta. Teresa de Jesús dice: que es pelear sobre si esta o aquella tierra son buenas para adobes o para tapias. Dejemos tierras, con todo religioso y religiosa hablo, los que hemos profesado el hollar y poner debajo de nuestros pies al mundo y sus vanidades. . . .[55]

His reference to Sta. Teresa is to her dry words in *Camino de la perfección*, where she declares that discussions about which is the best *tierra* [homeland] are but a debate over which soil is better for making walls of sun-dried mud or of simple mud.[56]

Although Méndez quotes Sta. Teresa in an attempt to close off argument once and for all, his words in fact make it clear that the belief in the differences existing between *gachupines* and criollos held great currency. It was used throughout the arguments about laxness and reformation in convents to support opinions about the spiritual inferiority of criolla nuns. The stories of the other contenders for the foundation of San José only serve to confirm this. Inés de la Cruz describes how the patron Rivera sends to Spain for nuns, as he does not want to found the convent with Mexican women. She writes to him explaining that she herself was born in Spain, in order to secure his support. Although sor Inés does not explicitly mention the racial values at issue in the foundation attempt, Mariana de la Encarnación's account of Archbishop Pérez de la Serna's words make transparent how important these were. Pérez de la Serna believes criolla women to be incapable of keeping the strict Carmelite rule and associates them with features characteristic of "relaxed" convents:

> Que mientras que él fuese prelado no consentiría fundasen convento de religión que profesa tanta perfección criollas regalonas y chocolateras. Que traeríamos tres o cuatro criadas cada una que nos sirviesen. . . .[57]

At this point it is useful to consider the two charges of which the prelate accuses criollas: *regalonas* and *chocolateras*. The first is connected to the nefarious effect the climate of the Indies was believed to have on its inhabitants, making them lazy and morally lax. The second charge is a refined version of the first, chocolate at this point being considered a drink of indulgence and luxury, consumed primarily by women of the New Spanish elite.[58] The misogynist assumptions underlying both charges are obvious: the criolla in this reasoning is simply an excessive woman. This excess of sexuality is precisely what the perfect Carmelite does not signify, and as a result of the cultural specificity of the arguments put forward, the criolla is thus not a Carmelite because of what is classed as her "racial" difference. In other chronicles of the same period, nuns often take distance from their New Spanish heritage, using exactly the same logic that extends the concept of inheritance and purity to quotidian matters such as food, the consumption of which necessarily had implications for the purity of the body. Thus, María Josefa de Gracia, though born in the Americas, is also "born" a Capuchin, her vocation signaled by her rejection of the staple New Spanish food of chocolate.[59]

Gerónima de la Asunción, the founding mother of the Carmelite convent of Manila, whose spiritual opinions are recorded by Bartolomé de Letona in his *La perfecta religiosa* (1622), acknowledges the differences between Peninsular women and those born in the Indies but points out that where such a difference has led to a change in practices, the criolla nuns cannot be accused of laxness. Apart from making clear that many of the procedures that are considered as being relaxed are in fact permitted by learned prelates, sor Gerónima also points to the different financial status of the convents in Spain and in the Indies as an explanation. She describes Spanish convents as being assured of an income from which to provide food for their "robust" inhabitants. American convents, in contrast, "no tienen tanta providencia ni tanta salud." That is, they have no fixed incomes and are populated by less healthy individuals. Her mention of these factors means that the polarities of what was considered a monolithic "natural" difference are opened up and made relative by acknowledging its cultural valence.[60] This relativizing movement is confirmed by her comments on fasting, where she makes apparent that the Carmelite rule is adaptable to regional and cultural differences and that these cannot then be regarded as indicators of religious orthodoxy:

> Del ayuno: En las Indias hay costumbre legítima de comer todos en las cuaresmas y demás días de ayuno huevos y cosas de leche. Con que la prohibición que de estas cosas pone aquí la regla no obligará en este reino ni en los demás donde hubiere semejante costumbre. Y más diciendo la regla que las monjas guarden la costumbre de la región.[61]

Sor Gerónima's words argue that quotidian practices are in a different realm to the kinds of practice that determine correct religious belief. However, from the evidence of the chronicles, it is clear that, though these quotidian elements may indeed be in a different realm, they remain laden with significance; they are in fact as much markers of identity and orthodoxy as declarations of faith or spiritually correct renditions of visions. In relation to fasting, it is not surprising to find that a New World substance, chocolate, is the one that causes sor Gerónima difficulties in terms of justification. Several of the nuns are described as drinking chocolate only in order to fast, and sor Gerónima takes up the point that this practice has been criticized by people who allege that chocolate is in fact a solid food and that one cannot therefore fast on it. She attempts to defend the substance saying that *chocolate natural y ordinario* is a liquid, and therefore it is licit to consume it while fasting.[62] Several of the references in the chronicles to the use of chocolate also make this caveat, claiming the chocolate they refer to is not the luxurious and spiced drink usually consumed, but a more primitive and simple version made with water rather than milk and containing no condiments. The ultimate impossibility of rescuing chocolate for ascetic signifying purposes, however, is signaled by the new rule added to the Carmelite's vows: the nuns promise not to drink the substance. This extra, and American, vow serves at once to affirm the purity of their spiritual archetype and their difference from it—their New Worldliness.

It seems then that the details of the New World Carmelite chronicles are irredeemably condemned to "giving away" the fact that these stories of virtue happen in a place that makes them difficult to believe with complete confidence. If this is true for the details of the stories retold, it is also true for more structural elements as well—from the echoing of Teresian plot designs, to the organization of the story of reform around specifically New World themes, to instances of individual writing talent and creativity.

Part of this vitality that the hagiographic form shows in its New World manifestation is due to the fact that however conservative the genre may ostensibly be in theoretical terms, in practice, the didactic impulse behind it makes its writing an incredibly "modern" enterprise, in that it is always directed at the future.[63] No wonder hagiography seemed the perfect vehicle with which to trumpet the victories of the conquering and evangelizing Church in the New World. And the attraction and significance of placing women at the center of this celebration is apparent in the way the Carmelite tradition is transported to the Indies. Sta. Teresa no doubt would have imagined herself in the New World as a martyr—along the lines of her desired Moorish martyrdom in childhood—embodying an extreme form of piety whose manifestation depended on the complete removal from civilization and from worldly concerns. Instead, her legatees, her New Spanish Carmelite daughters, are utterly compromised with the politics of the colony and with arguments about social and cultural hierarchy and orthodoxy—just as Sta. Teresa herself had been in the Old World.

From the Confessional to the Altar:

Epistolary and Hagiographic Forms

Hasta aquí la Venerable Madre, a cuyas ponderosas, eficaces palabras no tenemos que añadir en la narrativa de este punto; pues añadir, o poner algo, sería derogar mucho de las expresiones y viveza con que lo refiere todo.[1]

José Eugenio Valdés, *Vida admirable y penitente de la venerable madre sor Sebastiana Josefa de la Santísima Trinidad* (1765)

José Eugenio Valdés takes his task as hagiographer of Sebastiana Josefa de la Santísima Trinidad, a professed nun in the convent of San Juan de la Penitencia for Poor Clares in Mexico City, with evident gravity. He shows a lively concern for authenticity and accuracy, claiming to want to preserve the moving and expressive character of the nun's writing by transcribing it without annotation or addition. His actual practice in the hagiography he writes of her is quite different. But this is in itself an old story, and a great deal of recent research has been dedicated to telling such tales differently, to righting the balance by unearthing the works of women and allowing them to speak for themselves.[2]

This tracing of women's texts across geographical and cultural boundaries offers a significant and valuable critical option, allowing women's writing to be located within a female textual lineage. In relation to convent writing and the *vida*, we must be wary however of thinking of writing nuns as an isolated community. Previous chapters have already demonstrated how the symbolism of an unbreachable cloister obscures a reality in which social, political, and economic factors played a crucial part in establishing convents, maintaining nuns, and, in the New World, sustaining an imperial mission. The *vida*, in particular when written by women, is distinguished as a literary genre by its mediated nature. The figure of the confessor or spiritual father is always present. This is certainly the case in sor Sebastiana's letters, which are the subject of this chapter. My principal concern here is to read and interpret the story of the confessor Valdés' relation to sor Sebastiana and her writing, and more generally her relation to the various confessors who solicited writing from her. The focus then is on the interplay *between* writing practices and on the intentions—historical, spiritual, and political—that guided them in the New Spanish context. As a consequence of this emphasis, exploring sor Sebastiana's relation to a tradition of feminine autobiography and hagiography is not central to my argument, while elucidating her relation to broader colonial writing practices (including the work of men, and in particular of her confessor) is.[3]

This does not mean abandoning an examination of gender and its relation to writing practices in the colony. Indeed, in this instance, my more general concern about surveying the transformations undergone by generic forms in the New World has the issue of sexual difference placed at its center. Do men and women write differently about the same thing? The contrasts between the two accounts we have of the "same" subject—sor Sebastiana's life—would indicate so. Valdés' is a heuristic relation of sor Sebastiana's life, designed to unveil the nun's virtues in a plot where experience is dissected into types and reorganized so as best to serve the essentially didactic purpose of the work. This is very different to sor Sebastiana's own narrative, which is teleological and forms an experiential story structured around events and their repercussions, either for sor Sebastiana personally or for the convent as a whole.[4] These contrasts invite speculation both as to how gender is related to genre and as to how sexual difference dictates writing practices. By this, I do not intend to imply that men and women write differently because of their sex, rather that different writing practices and strategies are available to male and female authors, and that, in the narration of hagiography, these different authorial possibilities and proscriptions are especially marked.

The sixty extant letters by sor Sebastiana make up three hundred folios of closely written text. On the cover page of the sewn booklet, a note tells that the collection of letters was given to Ana de San Bernardo, the abbess of sor Sebastiana Josefa's convent, in November 1760, three years after sor Sebastiana's death.[5] They were donated by sor Sebastiana's brother, Miguel de

Maya, a Franciscan friar. Sor Sebastiana's writing is part of a tradition of works carried out by women to fulfill a vow of obedience and is intimately related to the sacrament of penance and the practice of confession. General confession as an annual requirement had been mandated by the Fourth Lateran Council in 1215. Later the deliberations of the Council of Trent (1545–1563), which defended the sacramental system and encouraged frequent communion by the laity meant that confession, which was a necessary prerequisite for communion, became the privileged method of religious acculturation.[6] Confession involved the priest in a dialogue with an individual whose boundaries were redefined precisely by this process of constructing and narrating the passing of time and the actions that occurred in this temporal space. New Spanish nuns would have been used to giving a written account of their conscience to their confessor, and many *vidas* written by men use this kind of material as a primary source for the biographies of their pious spiritual daughters.[7]

There may be several reasons why confessors obliged women to write rather than simply to leave the recounting of sins to the usual auricular form. The most obvious was that it allowed a more precise evaluation of the authenticity and orthodoxy of the narratives recounted. The confessor caught up in the production of saints and venerable persons was able to sanction or to claim credit for the spiritual adventures of his confessants much more authoritatively if there was a text upon which to base his judgment. Given that the normal condition of being a woman in this period prohibited access to writing in all but the most extraordinary of situations, it is important to note that the condition of the nun seems to have *enforced* writing upon certain women. The audience for this kind of writing was very particular, however, and most nuns certainly never saw their manuscripts go into print.[8] Their audience could, nevertheless, be fairly large, consisting of the various confessors who were the addressees of many nuns' writings, the entire body of ecclesiastic authorities entitled in theory to keep track of such spiritual narratives, and the convent community itself, which would often circulate manuscripts among its members for didactic purposes. Although sor Sebastiana ostensibly addressed her letters to a particular confessor, the privacy of this form would have been well understood by all to include a considerable number of people as potential readers.

"Enforced" is certainly the correct word in relation to many nuns' writings if we are to attribute more than purely rhetorical compliance to the many protestations of unwillingness proffered by women in this situation, from Catherine of Siena to Sta. Teresa to sor Sebastiana herself. The trope of writing as suffering belongs to a Christian tradition that associated martyrdom with spiritual enlightenment, and in this context, it was clearly intended to secure belief in the writer's words.[9] Sor Sebastiana's pain is the guarantee of her truth, and such truthfulness is important to prove because the process of writing exposes the nun not only to the censure of her confessors but to that of the Holy Office. Although references are indirect, fear of the Inquisition certainly plays a part in sor Sebastiana's reluctance to write. That this fear was well founded is apparent from the very real persecution of *beatas falsas y embaucadoras* [feigning holy-women impostors] in which this institution was involved in this period.[10] So the emotive and moving voice that Valdés is so keen to preserve was considerably less unconstrained and spontaneous than his description might lead us to believe.[11]

Although the censorious eye of the Inquisition watched vigilantly over sor Sebastiana's expression of her voice in writing, her narrative can also be seen to be influenced by more oblique and less dramatic, but equally strong forces—those of generic form. At one point in the letters, sor Sebastiana suggests that her confessor actually provides her with models on which to base her writing.[12] The extant letters are indeed very coherent in structure and fairly repetitive. Although sor Sebastiana's use of a thematic template provided by her confessor is not out of the question, what can only be described as the individuality of the language and tone of the epistles rules out any mechanical copying. Sor Sebastiana's verse, which is transcribed in various sections of the letters, can also be considered as marking her as an independent writer. The poems are all devotional and fall into very traditional lyric types. They show a powerful command of rhythm that recurs in various prose passages in the letters. Moreover, both the verse and the letters are indeed full of lively expressions, as Valdés has advertised, and it is these expressions, "¡Oh, cómo quisiera ser una santa!"[13] which leave us with the strong sense of sor Sebastiana's individual presence as an author. Often, they are exclamations of despair or inadequacy, and in one case an autoaccusation of heresy. Sor Sebastiana could not have been unaware of the resonance of such vocabulary in this context, and her use of it reveals a confidence in her own ability to manage the codes governing the representation of spiritual experience. The extreme terms she employs and the emphasis on emotion to secure belief, however, underline the vulnerability of this entire enterprise of saintly self-representation. Reason, not emotion, was, of course, the better guarantee of truth, but the fact that women's access to full rationality was held in doubt in the period means that sor Sebastiana's claim to truth could indeed only legitimately be made through this risky strategy of deploying emotion. In the universe of spiritual experience, emotion enjoyed a privileged position, but sor Sebastiana's expression of it remained problematic. Holy women were frequently in danger of seeming to be feigning or simulating, and the invocation of strong emotion as the touchstone of feminine truth constituted something of a paradox. The wide dissemination of the figure of a woman dressed in a nun's habit, which badly conceals her vulpine feet, doing an act of charity, as an icon of hypocrisy in the period shows how popular the conflation of religious dissembling and femininity had become.[14]

In contrast to the modest pamphlet containing sor Sebastiana's letters is José Eugenio Valdés' hagiography of the nun that was clearly intended for a large audience. The book runs to nearly four hundred printed pages and as a frontispiece has a grand engraving of sor Sebastiana gazing devotedly at a Christ child in a cradle. Behind the nun, high on a shelf, are the books that make up her spiritual library, and the Holy Spirit in the form of a dove hovers over her inclined head, illuminating her thoughts. In his prologue, Valdés says sor Sebastiana's brother Maya commissioned the book from him, and it would seem reasonable to suppose that Maya identified an interest in promoting his sister's spiritual fame. Maya's collection of Sebastiana's letters and his commissioning of a hagiography, the printing costs of which were financed by devotees of the nun, certainly fits very much into the pattern of investments made by elite family and religious groups in the colony to promote the cult of individuals who would bring them prestige in the present and divine grace for the hereafter. The nuns of Mexico City in the eighteenth century professed a style of spirituality consonant with the dynastic concerns of their benefactors and of the aristocracy—the class from which they themselves overwhelmingly came. This kind of religious practice gave prominence to anniversary masses and to intercessionary and commemorative prayers and served to strengthen the bonds between spiritual and earthly patronage and prestige. It is therefore no surprise to find that sor Sebastiana's brother was himself employed as a confessor in his sister's convent, but the networks of kinship and solidarity that crystallized around the publishing of a hagiography of sor Sebastiana encompass a far wider community than her immediate family. Sor Sebastiana was in fact promoted as a particularly virtuous criolla nun; an exemplar of piety with which to vindicate the orthodoxy—spiritual, cultural, and political—of this sector of colonial society.[15]

Mexico City, the viceregal capital of New Spain, was saturated with convents, monasteries, and other religious institutions in this period. It was a place where the presence of the Counter-Reformation Church in every sphere of life was hard to ignore. The many church buildings would have been a very concrete manifestation of the imposition of civilization—that is, of Spanish culture, religion, and politics on the erstwhile pagan México capital. Numerous encomiastic and apologetic books of this period sing the praises of the city, extolling its perfect urban design (its streets laid out in grid plan, its fountains evenly distributed, its vistas pleasantly interspersed), and the magnificent convent buildings are often at the center of these perorations.[16] This kind of extended praise, of course, betokens more than a lively interest in architecture, and as so many critical studies of baroque culture have shown, space is power.[17]

If we consider the convent from this symbolic perspective of urban planning as the embodiment of social, political, and religious ideologies, then the tradition of female asceticism that led to the establishment of the first Christian convents can be seen to be in direct opposition to the male tradition. Female asceticism grew not from the notion of removal from the city to the desert, as in the case of the monks, but was based precisely on an idea of retirement within one of the most significant of the city's institutions: the household. By immuring themselves in the home, women were meant to bring down grace upon a community, and the withdrawal and immobility of virgin women was metaphorically associated with the integrity of their bodies, which came to have an exceptionally charged significance. There was always, of course, a demographic political dimension to this, with convents becoming repositories for women who could not marry "honorably"—that is, in accordance with their status. This became particularly important in the Indies, where not only class was an issue but also race. Hence, the American convent literally was a fortress for racial and cultural values.

Once enclosed, these women and their institution were moving proof of the resounding civility of a society that could regulate its own reproduction so successfully that many of its women could be reserved in marriage for the Deity. And most prodigiously, these extraordinary women showed piety bordering on the holy, making convents the producers of saints. The importance of a native production of saints in the Spanish Americas as a way of confirming their spiritual conquest is self-evident, and the speed of Sta. Rosa of Lima's canonization is testament to the enthusiasm of the Church itself in this project. So José Eugenio Valdés' overblown rhetoric could almost be anticipated when he describes sor Sebastiana's birth as the most magnificent of the splendors with which God, in His mercy, had seen fit to grace the city of Mexico. In Valdés' account of sor Sebastiana's life, the saintliness of this criolla nun is portrayed as being of enormous symbolic worth, the jewel that sets off the value of the viceregal capital, the seal confirming its civility. Although having "otherworldly" referents, these kinds of concerns are, of course, ultimately very mundane, directed as they are to notions of cultural and religious hegemony and to the consolidation of imperial power and of colonial identity. Sor Sebastiana, predictably, does not share these concerns, or at least not in her writing. On profession she would in fact have declared herself, as every nun did, to be removed from the world *tamquam vera morta,* and her writing is valuable for such worldly enterprises precisely in the measure that it is the writing of someone dead to the world, someone who because of their distance from it, could mediate between it and the Almighty.

The dilated American empire, so rich in mineral wealth, may well have found its spiritual touchstone in the criolla sor Sebastiana according to Valdés, but his own mining of the textual treasure left to him reveals a rather more anxious relationship than that suggested by his optimistic rhetoric. In fact, caution rather than triumph defines the tone of most of the relationships between confessors and spiritually inclined female confessants for which we have any evidence in this period. The suspicion surrounding false mystics and spiritual women in general was strong, and the Church's desire to regulate the production of writing about such subjects is evident from Urban viii's Bulls of 1625 and 1631 that no hagiographies be published of pious persons who had not been officially recognized as such. Nevertheless, the publishing of strictly-speaking unauthorized *vidas* was prodigious at this time, and their reliance on the kind of source Valdés uses was very frequent.[18]

Valdés' task as the writer of a hagiography based on these sources is different from that of the scribe or that of an objective historian. It involves the manipulation of these sources as well as of others, and such an elaboration of the narrative denotes how his relationship to the truth of sor Sebastiana's writing has less in common with historical notions of the integrity of source material and more with an interpretative approach that is in itself creative.[19] Valdés' description of sor Sebastiana's childhood, for example, with details of her breast-feeding habits and miraculous escapes from accidents is completely absent from her own writings and is almost certainly more of a rhetorical gesture signaling sor Sebastiana's saintliness than a real account of her early years. A similar hagiographic commonplace, which is reproduced by Valdés and not mentioned by sor Sebastiana and which is more probably a piece of propaganda for Tridentine reforms and access to devotion, is her conversion during a sermon. The sermon inspires sor Sebastiana to request confession, and she spends two hours recounting her sins, deciding to profess at the end of it. In this anecdote, Valdés' concern is for the verisimilar, not so much for the historically accurate; but this should not be interpreted as leaving his writing in a disembodied realm. Paradoxically, the constraints involved in preparing a narrative of sor Sebastiana's life for general public consumption actually lead Valdés to be more factually informative than sor Sebastiana herself on occasions. Thus, it is he who supplies the information that sor Sebastiana's parents were candle makers in order that the reader may make sense of an early miracle where she escapes death by drowning in a pot of molten wax. This information is absent from sor Sebastiana's account of the miracle, it being assumed the reader of the letter, her confessor, would know her family background.

The description Valdés gives of the spectacular effects of sor Sebastiana's trances where holy fire rises up from her chest is a good example of the different relationship to truth displayed in the book and in the letters. Valdés' account conforms perfectly to hagiographic tradition and is in fact rather tame, but no such description is to be found in sor Sebastiana's writings, where it would constitute an impious assertion of her own sainthood.[20] Valdés' writing was, of course, also constrained by theological rules and regulations lending legitimacy to some spiritual experiences and not to others. The long list of all the saintly qualities exhibited by sor Sebastiana's visions that he appends to their description makes this apparent. The list is modeled on the parameters set up in Gerson's *De probatione spiritum* for distinguishing false from true spiritual visions, and Valdés' citation of Gerson makes vivid his need to insert what he writes into a tradition of acceptable and holy works.[21] Adherence to the genre's form is thus taken as signifying the orthodoxy of the events described, and hagiography certainly provided Valdés with a canon of authoritative texts. It is to these texts' repetitive structure and formal characteristics that he often appeals to legitimate the content of his own writing.[22]

The correct composition of a hagiography is thus clearly a matter of utmost importance. The possibility of the salvation and redemption of the reader depends upon it. In writing a hagiography, Valdés entered a series of complex theological debates where each point or interpretation had to be upheld by a learned gloss. This notion of illustrating and explaining a text is analogous to the confessor's role as interpreter of a nun's confession and, indeed, to Valdés' own relation to sor Sebastiana's writing. His annotations and addenda serve to place her in a tradition of both writing and saintly predecessors. Valdés is precise about what spiritual methods sor Sebastiana follows, reproducing the sections of Loyola's *Spiritual Exercises* that she found most useful. Sor Sebastiana's devotion to this kind of *oración metódica,* as it is called by Andrés Martín, is counterpointed by her reading of Pedro de Alcántara, one of the main exponents of a more contemplative style of prayer whose works were censored in the Index of 1558.[23] In fact, Valdés links sor Sebastiana not only to Alcántara but to Catherine of Bologna and to Sta. Teresa, each of whom had come under censure from sections of the ecclesiastical hierarchy that wanted to eradicate any traces of *iluminismo* or *recogimiento* in the saints carried to the altars.[24] The fact that all of sor Sebastiana's letters also describe her devotion to Loyola's more reputable spiritual methods saves both her and Valdés from the charge of exhibiting a contemplative style "para mujeres de carpinteros" [for the wives of carpenters] as Fernando de Valdés, the composer of the 1558 Index, characterized contemplative spirituality.[25]

The efforts in Valdés' hagiography to escape the scandalous and exhibitionistic traits associated with pious women and the popular cults they elicited are to be identified throughout his book. Instead of catalogs of *miracula,* Valdés gives us learned disquisitions about the theory of penitence, the power of diabolic visions, and, most bizarre of all, the possible volume of the angelic voices sor Sebastiana hears.[26] As is usual in the lives of saintly women, eucharistic miracles and visions are the most theologically delicate to recount because of the implicit threat they constitute to the priest's privileged relation with God, and Valdés is cautious about attributing literal truth to these events, preferring to see them as metaphorical confirmations of sor Sebastiana's piety.[27] The desire to shed the superstitious elements associated with popular versions of the genre meant that Tridentine hagiographies placed much value both on historical accuracy and on intellectual tradition, multiplying learned biblical and classical references in order to place their narratives within a recognized canon of legitimate works. This drive for historical precision and formal decorum in hagiography, however, can be seen as being in conflict with the equally important imperative to inspire devotion. Juan Luis Vives' disapproval of the *Legenda aurea* by Jacobus de Voragine is instructive in this respect. Punning on its title, Vives calls the work *ferrei oris, plumbei cordis* [iron-mouthed and leaden-hearted], criticisms directed not only at the "folkloric" quality of the historically inaccurate narrative but at its inability to engage or move the reader.[28] For Vives, it was the great classical works of biography—of patricians and generals—which should have served as models for Counter-Reformation hagiography, the resulting *vida* being both elegant and true. Though Vives envisages the recuperation of rhetoric in his ideal hagiography, he also recognizes that the power of rhetoric to persuade and move to devotion and virtue (what Voragine's clumsy text does not do) is inextricably linked to its power to lie and to be inaccurate (what Voragine's text does so well).[29]

The didactic purpose of hagiography then can be understood to place its author in this awkward position, caught between the role of conscientious historian and that of effective preacher. In the prologue to sor Sebastiana's *vida*, Valdés emphasizes the historical truth of his account by stressing the trouble he has gone to to find accurate sources as well as how methodical his approach has been.[30] To a great extent, of course, Valdés' claims to historical accuracy and truth are substantiated by his use of sor Sebastiana's writings as primary sources for his own. In this primordial sense at least, his book does not efface sor Sebastiana's letters, but rather presents itself as a kind of commentary on the truth they enclose. Valdés' reliance on sor Sebastiana's written testimony as truth comes across dramatically when he rests his case for her abject humility on the entire corpus of her letters, written to fulfill the vow of obedience. Their very existence annuls his need to convince the reader any further:

> Los sesenta argumentos que ofrezco son otras tantas cartas que escribió a sus confesores. Porque cada una de ellas es prueba de su humildad. No puedo dar testimonio más cierto que ellas mismas. Leerlas y admirarse de su abatimiento, todo es uno; porque no puede ser menos que admirarse el leerlas.[31]

This exaltation of a woman's writing as source of truth relies, however, on the writing's simplicity and innocence. Valdés' comment on sor Sebastiana's verse is indicative of an attitude to female spiritual writing that valorized it only insofar as it remained the inscription and confirmation of the woman's *docta ignorantia.* He cites from her poetry, making clear that he includes it not for its artistic merit but for its sincerity and emotiveness.[32] Valdés' approbation of sor Sebastiana's writing must thus be understood as in some sense depending on sor Sebastiana's own declared aversion to it. Hence the relish with which he describes her apprehension and the analogy he draws between her writing and the extraordinary penitential practices she also undertook. Writing in this context signals absolute submission to Divine Will, and the pain and suffering it causes are a guarantee of the (female) writing subject's authenticity.[33] It is interesting to note that both nun and confessor express the same emotions about women's writing in this context. Indeed, it is only by expressing such orthodox opinions that either of them can sanction such writing.[34]

But the orthodoxy of the writing nun was impossible to guarantee unconditionally, and it is interesting that Valdés should take refuge in his role as faithful historian in order to distance himself from any theoretical errors sor Sebastiana's experience or her writing might contain:

Lo que aconteció a la Madre Sebastiana no sé si fué milagro, o prodigio, refiérolo como consta de los instrumentos que tengo en mi poder.[35]

Valdés' most emphatic defense of his own authorial integrity relies on a very fluid interpretation of his role as "historian." Sometimes this means "interpreter," sometimes simply "scribe," but this solution is very much an interim one that works within the confines of the *vida* as a book. Valdés' role as confessor and preacher, however, means that the notion of truth in the writing of hagiography will always also refer to the text's effect, to its reception and to its extratextual life, where it is expected directly to influence other lives. The didactic function of Valdés' writing means the problems of rhetoric and figuration must always be considered from the point of view of reception as well as production, and it is here that the persuasive character of rhetoric and representation in general become most ambiguous, just as Vives' consternation with the *Legenda aurea* made apparent.[36]

Valdés' art can both save through persuasion and damn through lying, but it is impossible to have one effect without the other. This doubleness in words cuts against the humanist optimism that Ciceronian civility might indeed repair the ravages of the Fall. It is clear that the power to "make-believe," displayed by writings on spirituality like Valdés' or sor Sebastiana's, could slip dangerously into a power of "make belief." Valdés resists this degradation of his own didactic enterprise by using the metaphor of other mimetic practices. He expresses disdain for painting and instead praises sculpture—a distinction that attempts to distance the effects of his didactic project from those of "pure" representation in painting by associating them instead with the more tangible (and violent) mimetic work of sculpture, which actually transforms matter. Thus, his account of the construction of sainthood remains tied to the world. Even its destruction of the body, by its very fury, leaves the representation of saintliness as inescapably somatic:

> Porque no quería ser santa de lienzo que salen formadas con los suaves tientos del pincel, y con la delicadeza de los coloridos, sino santa de escultura, hecha a golpes de la fierra y de la azuela, a heridas del escoplo, a surcos del sormón, a tiranías de la gurbia; y por fin, hacerse pedazos y dividirse toda, para ser santa a rigores.[37]

The violence of Valdés' metaphor for the "fashioning" of sainthood with its distrust of any representational system that would try to communicate the process, takes us to the very heart of the instability that reigned in the confessional relationship and in the writings that emerged from it. The virtuous woman's contacts with her spiritual fathers clearly constituted a site where various kinds of influence and power were negotiated and where the male clergy's desire to control female spirituality reveals something of its own vulnerability. Raymond of Capua's relation to Catherine of Siena is a keystone for understanding how the dynamic of such relationships worked. It is significant that Raymond's *life* of Catherine, the *Vita e dialogo* published in Venice in 1517, was one of the more popular items of hagiographic literature among the nuns of New Spain, many chronicles citing it explicitly. Raymond's respect for Catherine's piety can be taken as an expression of the kind of privileged access to the Divine attributed to women by these learned clergymen. The spiritual women were considered by their confessors to be "empty vessels." That is, they were considered to have no active role or volition in their communication with God, they were simply the instruments, the mediating agents through whom the Divinity spoke and who, when their status became saintly enough, could be transformed into objects of devotion. To be responsible for a saintly woman in the role of her confessor became a matter of considerable prestige. But the public applause attached to being the promoter of a holy nun did not always reflect the priest's confessional relation to his penitent. Indeed, as Raymond's prostration at Catherine's feet and his calling her "mother" make apparent, the balance of power in the more private relationship could easily be reversed. Given the extraordinary holiness attributed to these women, this reversal was very ambiguous, being both very hard to accept fully but impossible to condemn outright.

Perhaps to demarcate boundaries in the relationship more clearly than they appear in the example of Raymond and Catherine, the role of the confessor had gradually confined itself in the Tridentine period to one of proportioning the theoretical knowledge of a correct spirituality. Meanwhile, the female confessant had become the privileged locus of a correct practice of this regulated devotion. This sexual division of spiritual labor is eloquently set out in Valdés' description of the perfect confessor not as a participant but as a guide.[38] More than information was being exchanged by confessor and confessant, and Valdés' extravagant metaphors make this clear. The confessor as deep-sea diver looking for the pearls of virtue, as the walking stick leading the blind person, played a symbolic social role that resonated in spheres much wider than the private one of the confessional. What though if the confessor were to find the perfect pearl? If the blind person being led turned out to be endowed with divine sight through revelation?

The problem of the confessional relation was in essence this: that it was mobile. Of course, the great majority of confessional relations were very stable, and the hierarchical organization was never challenged. Nevertheless, the relation did harbor the potential for upsetting this stability, and it appeared in fact able to overturn the most sacrosanct of sexually determined roles that located the priest above the nun. Although men's more direct access to divinity was in theory assured by their exclusive privilege of consecrating the host and administering the sacrament of communion, the subjection of certain priests to certain so-called saintly women seemed to place even this in doubt. Predictably, it was the sexual and emotional charge of the confessional relation that was held responsible for this mutability.[39] Luis de Granada, who had himself fallen victim to the spiritual charms of a nun, identifies the danger of the confessional relation lying precisely in this negotiation of roles and identities that were usually givens, stable categories in the ecclesiastical hierarchy of things. Thus, he declares in *De las caídas públicas,* a sermon composed in response to the Inquisition's condemnation of the nun he had admired and written a hagiography of, that the very obedience a devout woman gives to her confessor may become a threat.[40]

Valdés is opaque on this delicate matter, but sor Sebastiana's letters are much more eloquent about the ties that bind her to various of her spiritual fathers. For example, she expresses concern that a certain confessor will behave in an unexpected manner in the confessional and writes that she is upset if she perceives any difference between the attitude she anticipated and the one he displays.[41] This emotional dependence on the confessor is itself subject to all the doubts that accompany sor Sebastiana's own spiritual progress. Her comments reveal a very complex way of managing the balance of power in the relationship. Like the majority of her contemporaries, sor Sebastiana acknowledges the confessor's superiority, indulging him with phrases of formulaic modesty and humility. She simultaneously declares however (leaving no room for contestation) that in this particularly small and insignificant matter—the progress of her own soul to salvation—she is the only one privy to the truth of the matter.[42] Unsurprisingly, the most clear mark of sor Sebastiana's autonomy in her writing is expressed in relation to these men who oblige her to write and who must then deal with the real consequences of her individuality and freedom in spiritual matters:

> . . . con un enojo con Vuestra Paternidad, como si tuviera la culpa de todo mi mal, estando inocente de lo que me pasaba . . . y así tenía vergüenza, como también el que a Vuestra Paternidad le parecían muy mal mis cosas; y que si yo volviera, ya no había de tener consuelo y que sólo lo preciso diría, que lo demás era peligroso. De repente me daba un aborrecimiento a mi Padre de mi alma, que lo quería despreciar con malas palabras. Estaba como un gentil.[43]

In this instance, there is almost a sense of the "world-turned-upside-down" in sor Sebastiana's writing, a world where a woman gives her opinion of learned men and feels disgust for their opinions. Here the confessors are pawns in sor Sebastiana's emotional tumult, or as she describes it, foils that the Devil uses in his personal battle with the nun. These moments reveal the very real distress that often characterized the confessor-penitent relationship. This psychological turmoil is, however, resolutely inscribed in its so-ciohistorical context, and we have seen previously how even strong emotion was regulated and codified in this kind of writing in the period. Moreover, the links that united nuns and their confessors in the colonial city were not exclusively personal but took place within a social and religious system that was also affected by any disturbances in the relationship between priest and penitent.[44] We have seen the symbolic weight that Valdés attaches to promoting sor Sebastiana as holy criolla. The priest metaphorically extends this criolla nun's holiness to the land that gave her birth, his rhetoric claiming for it the fruits of a true evangelization that purges New Spain of its pagan antecedents. Consequently, any anomaly in the confessional relationship that "produces" such holiness, puts at risk not only the relationship itself but this ambitious apologetic project that Valdés has constructed upon it. The New World was already too much the world-turned-upside-down, and anything less than absolute orthodoxy and consonance with the authoritative model (social, religious, or rhetorical) was in danger of being unacceptably deviant.

Valdés and sor Sebastiana provide plenty of evidence of how ambiguous and complicated the project of representing sanctity was in the New World context. It is significant, moreover, that the ambiguity settles in the same kinds of textual "space" in both their writings: that of the illustration or description of the exemplary. In Valdés' writing, the passages where the apologetic argument is made and combined with the spiritual one are characterized by the use of analogy and metaphor that serve to align the nun's virtue, piety, and so forth, with the New World. Thus, the perception of the New World as different from the Old is rallied precisely to *confirm* the orthodoxy of practices and persons described. Analogously, the saintliness of women—so different from men, so removed from the masculine ideal—is taken as astounding, as exceptionally convincing.

The role the exemplary plays in the hagiographic narrative and in the apologetic narrative is then the same. In both cases, the paradox of exemplarity (the model that is unique and yet held up as the desired standard) mediates phenomena (the saint, the New World) that are not usually registered by the accepted codes of representation or understanding. In the religious texts produced in the colonies in the period, the Indies often figure as the metaphysical example to end all examples. America is thus paradoxically a hyperfertile ground for evangelization and the end of all such projects. The

New World is both Eden and the place of the Apocalypse, an attitude most obviously perceptible in the Franciscan Order's millenarian enthusiasm to convert the Indians.

The plot of sor Sebastiana's profession in Mexico City is then an illustration of the fundamental differences between entering a convent in the Old World and in the New, as well as a standard hagiographic piece designed to show her fortitude and patience. When at one point in her career, sor Sebastiana is placed in the only convent for Indian women in Mexico City, that of Corpus Christi, the Indian nuns petition for her to be removed. Valdés explains the reaction of the *cacique* nuns who want her to leave not in terms of the Devil setting obstacles in the way of our pious heroine but instead as a perfectly understandable action, given the social context he has described, in that each "racial" group of nuns in the city had to fight for its own territory.[45] The Peninsular concern with *pureza de sangre* is clearly at issue here, but in the American context it is articulated by a variety of blood groups, each of whom is anxious to vindicate its "purity." Every convent in New Spain had indeed in some sense to demarcate its territory: racial, financial, and spiritual.[46] This worldliness of the cloister and its links to other New Spanish institutions has been mentioned previously and is dramatized by sor Sebastiana's difficulties in finding a convent that will accept her and a patron who will provide a dowry. While awaiting a patron, sor Sebastiana is taken in by the viceregal household and is clearly something of a success with the noble women of the court. Her virtue and piety make her a celebrity but do not guarantee hard cash. When an offer is finally made, it is to place her in the convent of the Brigidines, a very recent foundation at the time, and as a lay nun rather than one of the choir nuns. The strings attached to the dowry are not explained by sor Sebastiana or Valdés, but they allow one to speculate that not even a recognized holy woman could easily find financial support in a society where the interests of the monastic and social elite were so intertwined they permitted very little negotiation.[47]

Sor Sebastiana finally professes in the convent of San Juan de la Penitencia, and it is from here that most of the letters are written. It is her spiritual home, and she belongs to it much like its other miraculous images and relics that also serve to mediate between heaven and earth.[48] Sor Sebastiana's holiness thus has a very practical use and is represented by Valdés as being something of a miracle in this erstwhile land of idolatry. He reproduces the topoi of wonder and admiration at the Spanish expansionist mission that has brought such goods to America and exclaims over the particularity of this virtuous nun, saying she is a "curiosity" and "marvel" that could only be found in such a New World.[49]

Valdés' account of the images and relics in sor Sebastiana's convent, however, make it apparent that things New Spanish, even saintly nuns, their convents, and their miraculous statues, were always in danger of going native, of sliding back into pagan prehistory. For example, a figure of the Christ child that the nuns turn to worshiping after it intervenes miraculously during an earthquake is described by Valdés as having "bewitched" the good women. This type of emotional attachment, especially if described in terms more usually associated with the demonic, is certainly not suitable for a community of nuns in a city so relatively recently purged of idolatrous and devilish practices.[50] Valdés is, of course, more than aware of the dangers of such words; and in his account of another image, the *Niño de la madre Sebastiana,* which actually belonged to sor Sebastiana, he attempts to narrate the potentially superstitious while resituating it within the field of the orthodox. The image grows miraculously, and Valdés excuses himself from not being able to prove this as he had not measured it before or after the event. Despite his awareness of the empirical evidence that could be marshaled to substantiate such a miracle, he insists that the image would be worthy of devotion under any circumstances.[51]

Valdés' writing is designed to construct Mexico City as a spiritual and political utopian space, and it is, of course, sor Sebastiana's life, her experiences as the exemplar of holy New Spanish womanhood, and the community in which she lives that serve to confirm the existence of such a space. Using the symbol of the city and the holy women it enclosed as proof of civility and orthodoxy is, however, not achieved smoothly by Valdés, as has been noted. Sor Sebastiana's employment of this symbolism in her writing proves to be equally compromised and complicated. For example, her description of the choir—which could be considered the heart of the convent's enclosure, as it was where the nuns would pray in community—reveals this sacrosanct space to be inhabited by strange noises and bizarre plays of alternating light. The explanation is, of course, predictable: this is the Devil tormenting sor Sebastiana. Yet the rhetorical effect such descriptions have is to make strange and uncanny what should be the most familiar and intimate part of the cloister.[52] In sor Sebastiana's nights, the wild beasts of the desert and scavengers of the urban world (both places symbolically most in opposition to the enclosure of the cloister) actually break into it and settle at its center.[53]

Similarly, her descriptions of houses that were spaces designated for a more generalized and lay female enclosure in this period are charged with an uncanniness that is in excess of the dramatization of the rejection of worldly vanities such passages usually serve.[54] This is even more apparent in sor Sebastiana's descriptions of Mexico City, which appears to be a very different place from that written of by Valdés. In sor Sebastiana's account, the public areas that are described as dark, immense, and yet oppressive are strangely devoid of people in what are very powerful figurations of both limitless space and claustrophobia.[55] There are also various references to mud and swamps that may be descriptions of how sor Sebastiana remembered the city to look after the prolonged floods that devastated it in the late seventeenth century. The disconsolate tone in which the impassable streets covered in detritus and the black and high walls that close in around her are described is so charged with emotion, however, that it seems to betoken more than the narration of an unpleasant memory.[56] Other accounts of the city by the nun confirm this:

> . . . me vi en un lugar espantosísimo, cómo él era no sabré decir, pero para darme algo a entender, sería como el más triste barrio de los más retirados; era muy grande, y había muy pocas casitas que de verlas se arrancaba la Alma [*sic*] de tristeza: andaban unos que parecían hombres, muy zancudos, hablando en lengua que no se entendía: vi una cosa muy alta que parecía torre que no sé decir cómo era; allá en lo último había como tabladito en donde estaban bailando y saltando. . . .[57]

In this version of Mexico City, there are very few houses, and the only landmark is an enormous tower with a stage where people dance and jump. The thin dreamlike men who walk across these empty squares and streets speak a language sor Sebastiana does not understand. This civic space has simply nothing in common with the city celebrated by Valdés, and it is certainly not recuperable for his civilizing and aggrandizing project. Sor Sebastiana's rhetoric cannot serve the purpose of creating the notion of a civil and orthodox society by describing the ideal metropolitan environment in which it would unfold, as her hagiographer's text seeks to do. Instead, her writing introduces doubt and instability into any representation of such ideals, and particularly into the imperial project of celebrating the successful evangelization and civilization of the New World through such encomia.[58]

Both sor Sebastiana's writing and that of Valdés are caught in this impossible trap of asserting difference (as extraordinary virtue) while guaranteeing conformity. Moreover, their writing activity takes place in a milieu predominantly hostile to female spirituality and the excesses and superstitions it conjured up. The manifestation of such spirituality in the New World represents the replaying of a resolutely Old World set of concerns—the theological and political associations surrounding female piety—in the New World, where they all take on a distinctively different incarnation. The writings of the nun and the hagiographer, because of their Mexican context, allow an identification of the specifically American cultural and political stakes involved in the association of femininity with dissimulation that the controversy over women's spirituality focused on.

In most European accounts of America throughout the early modern period, manifestations of femininity in the New World were usually characterized as excessive and hyperbolic and had come increasingly to receive the "scientific" blessing of theoreticians of climate. What then would be the place of the phenomena of feigning holy women in the Americas? A condemnatory aside from the New Spanish Inquisition, judging an instance of dissimulated sanctity in 1537, gives a good indication of how the ideas of excess and hyperbole could characterize as much the subject—the accused *ilusa*—as those pronouncing the verdict. The Inquisition's rhetoric is extreme:

> . . . en esta tragicomedia no hay otra cosa que tramoya y aparato de virtud, y el asco y fetidad [*sic*] de la lujuria de esta mujer . . . tiene más amor propio que una beata.[59]

This constellation of accusations is completely damning—sexuality, semblance, and self-love—and makes vivid the tragicomedy in which women often ended up playing the lead if they essayed a spiritual persona in the New World.

In sor Sebastiana's writing practice, the problem of representing her spiritual persona and its exemplarity is most particularly felt in relation to the exercise of authorship itself. The act of narrating herself, her life, is unbearably painful for sor Sebastiana, and many of her letters are, in fact, about the impossibility of such a project. Among the consequences of this discomfort with the act of representation are the strange rhetorical movements by which sor Sebastiana manages to write fear and instability not only into the heart of such a symbolic space as the cloister but also into that of the colonial city itself. This much would seem to indicate that the nun's narrative of her own spiritual history and of her colonial context can never be combined with the triumphalist rhetoric so common to the majority of texts telling the story of the progress of religion in the New World. Inevitably, Valdés' history, elaborated on the text of sor Sebastiana's own version of her life, is not any the more immune to narrative hitches and difficulties. The epistolary legacy left by sor Sebastiana to her hagiographer is an unquiet one, and its unruliness is especially evident when Valdés attempts to place sor Sebastiana's virtue in its cultural and geographic context. In an aside on the devotion the citizens of Mexico City display for masquerades, Valdés' heavy insistence on associating femininity with childishness, and both with bewitchment and gallantry, seem forced attempts to persuade us that these feasts are nothing but pleasing frivolities. These entertainments were, of course, no more or less superstitious than many Peninsular ones at the time, but Valdés' preciosity immediately makes us aware of the enormous cultural "work" needed to establish Spain in New Spain:

> . . . son desempeños, al fin, de la galantería Mexicana, brujerías y juguetes con que divierten a la Señora México, que aunque señora y grande, le gustan mucho estas diversiones.[60]

The figure of sor Sebastiana as holy criolla, the New World woman resplendent in virtue and piety, clearly had many colonial hopes pinned to it, for surely it was only this woman who could resist the labyrinth of significations, and their peculiarly feminine charms, that her land suggested. Writings with this figure at their center, however, immediately entered their own masquerade and wrought the transformations in terms of content, of structure, and of rhetorical figure, which representations of the saintly lives of sor Sebastiana by herself and by her hagiographer make apparent.

The Exemplary Cloister on Trial:

San José in the Inquisition

... las descalzas nos preciamos tanto de obedientes y rendidas a nuestros prelados que no admitiéramos en ésto malas doctrinas, que tuviera quien las tuviese . . .[1]

In 1661 the archbishop of Mexico City, Mateo de Burqueiro, wrote a letter to the Holy Office concerning the Carmelites in which he "let it be understood that the nuns held various erroneous and heretical ideas."[2] This explosive letter, of which there is no copy in the Mexican Inquisition archives, initiated the trial of the convent. The only documents from the archbishop actually extant in the file are two letters concerning the appointment of confessors in San José, one written in 1657 and one in 1659. In the letter of 1657, the archbishop discusses the virtue of non-Carmelite confessors, while in the later one he justifies the appointment of confessors who are not Carmelites to positions in San José.

The Inquisition trial soon makes it clear that these matters—the charge of heresy and the religious affiliation of confessors in the convent—are intimately linked. The trial is certainly about Church authority and hierarchy and extremely revelatory about how the familiar conflict between secular and regular clergy was replayed in the New World. However, the requests from the Carmelite nuns for Carmelite confessors also reveal an extraordinarily strong emotional bond between the male and the female branches of the order. This transforms the interest of the trial from being only another insight—however valuable—into the church politics of the New World, into an instance illuminating a much less familiar issue: the gendered emotional dimension of religious allegiance. In some senses, of course, the question of emotion and allegiance is also an "Old World" inheritance, and indeed the experiences of Sta. Teresa, and the rule and confessional practices of Carmelite convents in the Peninsula, are continually invoked during the San José debacle. An important source of information on this matter, one that is simultaneously cited and censored by the New Spanish nuns, is Sta. Teresa's own book on the foundation of her convents, *Libro de las fundaciones,* written at the behest of her confessors.[3]

It remains extraordinary and shocking, however, to find the Carmelite convent of San José in the Mexican Inquisition, accused of heresy. Trials for heresy against an institution rather than an individual were rare, and the idea that doctrinal error was to be found in one of the showpieces of the colonial state must have been deeply distressing.[4] Indeed, the situation inside San José and the convent's relation with the archbishop seem to have come to a head extremely quickly. On 23 January 1661, one of the nuns in San José, Andrea de San Francisco, wrote a letter denouncing the nuns who favored having male Carmelites exclusively in the convent as confessors. She gave this to her own confessor, a criollo from Tasco called Luis Becerra, who came before the Inquisition formally on the twenty-seventh. He brought not only her letter, but two supporting letters by the nuns Teresa de Jesús and María de los Angeles. Meanwhile, on the twenty-fourth, Margarita de San Bernardo, one of the leading nuns of the pro-Carmelite group, had again antagonized the archbishop by requesting a Carmelite confessor. On the day following Luis Becerra's formal denunciation of them, sor Margarita and the other members of this pro-Carmelite faction wrote to the king asking for his support. In less than a month, the affair had escalated from an internal ecclesiastical wrangle to a fully fledged political conflict involving Church and Crown authorities in both the Old World and the New.

Throughout February, the interrogation of witnesses took place, and Luis Becerra was questioned during March and April. The truncated file ends with a request from Becerra to be released from the Inquisition's prison. No further documents relating to this episode of San José's history are to be found in the catalog of the Inquisition files. The matter remained unresolved in terms of an Inquisitorial verdict, but as in so many of the administrative and bureaucratic stalemates of colonial government, this implied an effective victory for one party: in this case the archbishop who had accused the nuns and who clearly retained his authority over them and their convent.[5]

The fact that the heresy the nuns stand accused of is tied to questions of authority that are not only religious but concerned with issues of gender, involving as they do the women's obedience to male clerics, is the principal interest of the trial. Transgressions of authority in this period were particularly execrable in women in general, and in nuns in particular. Sta. Teresa herself emphasizes the hierarchical relation between prelate and nuns in trenchantly conservative terms.[6] Nevertheless, she is sophisticated in her appraisal of the politics governing such relations, and her sometimes abstract characterization of authority is often nuanced by her recognition of the responsibilities the prelate owes the community of nuns in his role as "true father" to them.[7]

Sta. Teresa's *Libro de las fundaciones* is marked by caution and by a desire not to implicate itself in direct criticism of the ecclesiastical authorities. Thus, it does not mention names, except to praise, and attempts to avoid comment on the political events in the midst of which the religious order found itself embroiled. It is clear, however, that the first Carmelite foundation was supported by the bishop of Avila, Alvaro de Mendoza, and by the general of the Carmelites, Juan Bautista Rubeo de Ravena, and that this support was crucial for its success. It is also apparent that opinion was divided in the Carmelite Order about the Discalced branch, which made matters very awkward for Sta. Teresa. The fact that there were no male Discalced Carmelites was something of a worry for the saint and, at least in this text, her efforts to appoint men of her liking and so extend her influence over the male Carmelites is evident. She thus writes very openly about the convenience of a male foundation:

> . . . porque tenía más deseo de que se hiciese el monasterio de los frailes que el de las monjas, por entender lo mucho que importaba, como después se ha visto.[8]

Unfortunately, it was clear that the institutional dependency of the male Discalced Carmelites on the rest of the Carmelite Order brought it close to ruin. With no constitutions of their own, each monastery governed itself as it saw fit, and Sta. Teresa wrote eloquently on how such heterogeneity of practices led to disagreements and divisions that came close to extinguishing the reform before it had properly begun.[9] Eventually, constitutions were written specifically for the male Discalced branch, but the political climate did not favor reform. Sta. Teresa herself was effectively imprisoned by the Carmelite general chapter that, basing itself on the dictates of the Piacenza chapter of 1575, virtually declared war on the Discalced branch.

In Spain the division within the Carmelite Order was the reflection of a division within the Church itself between clergy who obeyed the king in his efforts to reform the Church, and those clergy who gave their allegiance to Rome and defended the universality of Trent. The conflict of interests is exemplified by the coincidence in 1567 of the departure from Rome of Juan Bautista Rubeo, the Carmelite general, to reform the order "internally," with the granting to the Spanish monarchy of the Bull *In prioribus*, which gave power to the regular clergy to visit and reform Carmelite monasteries. This division between what was effectively a state Church and the representatives of the Universal Church from the papal Curia, led to absurd situations in which friars expelled by Rubeo were rehabilitated by the Consejo Real and given important posts within the Carmelite hierarchy.[10]

Immediately after Sta. Teresa's death, the situation became even more extreme. It is difficult to give a precise account of events within the Discalced Carmelite Order, as much of the documentation surrounding what came to be known as the "Incidente de la Consulta" (the Consulta being a body created to centralize the government of the order) was destroyed.[11] What is clear is that the chief Discalced nuns, Ana de Jesús and Ana de San Bartolomé, took up adversarial positions on many issues. By far the most difficult and controversial of these was the question of the government of the female convents of the order. Ana de San Bartolomé was in favor of government by the male branch, considering it to be the best way of achieving spiritual correctness, while Ana de Jesús feared it would mean the loss of the traditional freedom enjoyed by the female branch. The quarrel split the Discalced nuns into two groups: Ana de Jesús; Jerónimo Gracián, who had pushed the Carmelite general chapter to accept the primitive constitutions for the reformed order; and San Juan de la Cruz on one side; and Ana de San Bartolomé and Nicolás Doria, Gracián's very conservative successor, on the other. Each faction claimed to be the legitimate spiritual heir of Sta. Teresa. Despite gaining papal approval for their mission, the Ana de Jesús faction suffered persecution at the hands of the order itself. In 1592 Gracián was expelled; San Juan de la Cruz was temporarily sent to a faraway hermitage as a penance; and Ana de Jesús herself was subjected to a rigorous *Visita* of her convent and eventually confined to her cell for three years. It is not improbable that in appointing her to organize the foundations in France and the Low Countries, the order was trying to put as much distance as possible between itself and this unruly nun.

The conflict over the control of the female Carmelite convents, in all its complexity, was thus in a very real sense a direct legacy of Sta. Teresa herself.[12] In the New World, however, the power struggle between the Crown and the Church and between the secular and the regular clergy did not remain at an institutional level, coming instead increasingly to be expressed in terms of the influence exercised in the colony respectively by Peninsular Spaniards and Creoles.[13] In previous chapters, the importance of these divisions in New Spanish society has been made patent, as has the fact that the convent communities were not exempt from such worldly discord. In this chapter, the criollos and *gachupines* are set at each other's throats once more in the struggle of binary opposites we have encountered before, but in this case the division seems to have more depth to it, seems in fact to reveal more of what social and demographic histories of the period have taught us was a radically heterogeneous society.

In this context, it must be emphasized that already by the mid-seventeenth century the criollos of New Spain clearly felt they belonged to a country and culture that was in many respects completely different to the mother country, but in as many others again, a reconstitution of it. This pull of the Old World in the New results in what appears to be the replaying of the "querelle des anciens et modernes" in the Indies, where the modernity of the *gachupines* lies in their not being connected directly to the land but instead involved in commerce.[14] The re-creation of archaic social structures in the New World society would clearly have influenced all sorts of social and political relations. The fortunes of the concept of *pureza de sangre* in the Indies is a case in point. The Inquisition sources examined encourage a much broader interpretation of the notion as one that embraced the idea of honor almost on feudal terms and most certainly tied it into a complex system of social class.[15] Purity and nobility of blood had definitely become mixed and necessarily very resonant concepts at the time in the hybrid society of the Indies. The New World saint, moreover, was certainly not exempt from these contradictions that encourage us to read beyond the descriptions *gachupín* and criollo to the more complex systems of social organization that existed.

The great value of Inquisition sources comes, of course, precisely from this documenting of the "underside" of the cultural project in the Americas: the deviation from the model, the failure of transmission—in this particular case, the representation of the heretical convent and the heterodox nun. Nevertheless, it is crucial to keep in mind how circumscribed the Inquisition's activities in the cultural field of the colonies were. In 1571 in Mexico, a decree was passed removing Indians from the jurisdiction of the Inquisition. The most important fact about the Inquisition in the New World is thus that its social reach and influence were predominantly restricted to policing the faith of a limited, if heterogeneous, ethnic and cultural group: the non-Indians in the colony.

This meant that the types of cases that came to trial in the New World Inquisition were substantially different from the Old World ones.[16] Interestingly, even heresy seems to be different in America. Basically, there were no great heretics in the New World; the vast majority of Inquisition cases concerned the occasional Protestant, usually a northern European sailor or pirate blown off course.[17] Only when the heretic seems to be about to enter a community or become a social force does the Inquisition take any real interest in him or her. The implications of this for events in San José are evident. On this occasion, it seemed that an entire community of women of the New Spanish elite was about to be engulfed in a breach of ecclesiastical and "natural" authority. Moreover, such a breach was taking the form of that particularly transgressive phenomenon we have encountered previously: a heterodox feminine spirituality.

The persons chiefly intended to regulate the spirituality of women were, of course, their male confessors, and clearly the ideal confessor, his ideal confessant, and the ideal relation between the two were at the center of the Inquisition's scrutiny. The questions asked of nuns and of the only confessor examined, Luis Becerra, confirm the strategic role of the confessor as contributing to the ideal convent government, a government that was understood to be both political and spiritual. How could any of this, however, be taken to mean that a nun's personal preference for confessing with certain individuals was heretical?

There are three documents that appear in the Inquisition file concerning requests from nuns in San José for Carmelite confessors. Two are letters addressed to the archbishop by, respectively, the founding mother, Mariana de la Encarnación, and by Margarita de San Bernardo. The third document is a declaration to the Tribunal by María de San Leocadia. All of these nuns were on their deathbeds when they wrote, and the dramatic nature of this sort of petition should be kept in mind. The dying nuns, preparing to make a general confession that would review their whole lives, assert their need for a specific kind of spiritual comfort. Their souls are about to enter purgatory, and the unstated, but clearly present, implication is that their salvation depends on their request being granted.[18]

By anchoring their requests in a rhetoric of personal need and the fulfillment of a rigorous religious practice, these nuns clearly hoped to be able to foil any accusations of heterodoxy. This does not mean Mariana de la Encarnación's letter is not also strongly positive in its assertion of her need for a Carmelite confessor. The founding mother does not rest her defense on the notion that it "would do no harm" for the nuns of San José to confess with Carmelites. She argues instead that it is their right, a right founded in history and supported by tradition. The Carmelites, she states, have always desired to be ruled by the male branch of the order, and, she claims, God himself intervened to tell Sta. Teresa that she should submit the convents in Avila to the rule of the male Carmelites as soon as was possible.[19] Sor Mariana claims that she has heard that nominating a confessor is a free choice. At this point in a person's life, the founding mother argues, the selection of a confessor should be left to individual conscience, rather than be dictated by religious hierarchy.[20] She is, however, quick to defend herself against any charges of theological error that the claim might suggest by saying that there is no doubt in her mind that any priest, of any order, is able to absolve her sins; it is merely that a fellow Carmelite would be more suitable.[21] Intelligently, this woman is eager to represent her personal preference as obedience—alternately to tradition, to a founding figure, and, in the last instance, to God himself.

To consolidate their position, these nuns also appeal to the other principal figure of authority in the period—the king. The Inquisition file contains two letters to the king: one of 1657, which predates the scandal with the archbishop by four years, and another written during the Inquisition process itself in 1661. The letters concentrate on the issue of the confessor's experience and particular expertise. In the letters, the nuns bring to the king's attention the fact that they are in the New World—a place generally held to be hostile to religious perfection. They reproduce derogatory notions of the nature of the Mexican population in order to bemoan that, at this crucial juncture, no New Spanish Sta. Teresa is to be found.[22] There are, however, very virtuous and perfect Carmelite fathers, and logically, the letters argue that it is only through the guidance provided by these men that the New World Sta. Teresas will be formed.[23] In these nuns' opinion, only the education and care of the Carmelite fathers can amend such an irregular and precarious situation as that of a cloistered female community in the Americas. This is a very polished and elegant argument, immediately striking the tone of impartiality, careful not to accuse the secular clergy of faults, and to ascribe the convent's problems to the context in which it finds itself. The geographical location of the convent in the New World serves to confirm the need to enforce the rule of the priests of the order: the unorthodox setting calls for ultraorthodox behavior.

It is the testimony of Luis Becerra, confessor to the faction of nuns supporting episcopal rule rather than Carmelite rule in the convent, that provides an explanation of why such a seemingly innocent preference for certain confessors could be construed as a doctrinal error. In the letter in which he denounces the pro-Carmelite nuns, Becerra stresses that their stubbornness in persisting with their request is no proof of fortitude or strong emotional need but instead reveals that the dislike they have for the secular clergy is in fact theologically founded. Becerra asserts that the behavior of the nuns could be born out of a rejection of the purity and integrity of the Catholic faith.[24] This rather guarded suggestion (he is careful not to make a direct accusation) soon turns into untrammeled fantasy, with Becerra imagining the terrible consequences of these nuns being allowed to continue in their disobedient ways. If they only consider themselves to be under the authority of Carmelite fathers, what would happen if there were no Carmelite bishop to guide them? They would, of course, Becerra reasons, usurp the privilege of ordination.[25] But this is not the end, for the attitude of these nuns would have consequences for women in other religious orders. Becerra suggests that any nuns who had professed under a secular cleric rather than one from their own order, if they were to follow the teachings of the rebellious Carmelites, could consider their vows null and void and go off and marry the first man they met.[26] In a final and grandiosely anxious rhetorical flourish, Becerra claims that the pro-Carmelite nuns will come to challenge even the power of any pope who was not a Carmelite if their requests for exclusivity in confession are indulged any further.

Luis Becerra's interrogation begins the day after he presents his written denunciation and continues for at least three months and probably more.

He is the only person imprisoned by the Inquisition, and the documents show how antagonistic the judges are toward him. Becerra's letter of denunciation is taken to pieces: he is made to retract, rephrase, and modify almost all of it. His behavior as a confessor is investigated minutely. The main thrust of the questioning implies that he himself has created the divisions in the convent, that he is responsible for the anarchic situation inside it, and most seriously, that he has corrupted his confessants in order to further his aims. It is significant that the Holy Office should devote so much time and attention to Becerra, and we may speculate that its concern is related to broader considerations in the Church at the time regarding the quality and "professionalism" of clergy.[27]

Becerra's chief confessant is the nun Andrea de San Francisco, and he presents her letter along with his own when he first officially denounces the goings-on in San José to the Holy Office. The Inquisitors are certainly suspicious of Becerra's actions as a confessor, but this does not mean that they exonerate his confessant from responsibility in any error that might have been committed. Sor Andrea's evidence before the Tribunal consists of both written testimony and oral examination in various audiences. Her position is not a strong one. The Inquisition took note of the charges she brought, but her being in disagreement with her own convent superiors clearly cast doubt on the authority of any of her statements. A good nun is an obedient one, and Andrea de San Francisco is disobedient. Her behavior and her declaration, however much they may be justified, distance her from the figure of the exemplary nun to be found in the didactic texts and hagiographies of the period.[28] Perhaps the entire point is, however, that the exemplary nun could never be represented in the context of the Inquisition.

Not surprisingly, Andrea de San Francisco begins by trying to explain why she is in such an anomalous position in her convent. She tells how she was at first in agreement with the nuns who wanted to place the convent under the authority of the Carmelite fathers, believing that this would bring it greater spiritual perfection; therefore, she even worked to persuade others. When she realized that the nuns were not behaving honestly, however, she decided to oppose them.[29] Andrea de San Francisco's moment of realization comes when she asks to read a letter the community has been given to sign by these nuns in order to further their cause. The letter, which employs some very wild rhetoric, is full of insults addressed to the secular clergy and contains scurrilous rumors about the archbishop, alleging that someone who leads such a dissipated life could not hope to teach discipline, that someone who does not pray could not hope to teach meditation, that someone who drinks so heavily could not hope to teach abstinence.[30] These parts of the letter had been kept hidden from its signatories, and only by insisting on seeing the complete text does sor Andrea discover the ruse. In her testimony, this will become Andrea de San Francisco's preferred mode of self-representation: a willing and obedient nun who discovers, little by little, the machinations of a group of unscrupulous women in the convent. This narrative structure enables her to fit into the role of the hagiographic heroine or *reformadora*, who sees the evil in a convent and tries to remedy it. Sor Andrea presents herself as the innocent who is disabused of her devout and pious conception of convent life by the behavior of the nuns she has come to call the Hijas de la Orden because of their support for the Carmelite confessors. She is the naive novice who thought she was about to enter a paradise when she professed, only to discover that the convent's internal constitution owed much more to the world than to Eden.[31]

Paradoxically, the absolute loss of paradise, at least in hagiographic terms, resonates as much in sor Andrea's simple description of the evil nuns as *gachupinas* as in the behavior she ascribes to these women. In sor Andrea's introduction of such brute "naturalism" as the question of birthplace (in this colonial context indivisible from its concomitant cultural and political associations), the abandonment of the universal narrative of virtue characteristic of classic hagiography is confirmed.[32] In Andrea de San Francisco's narrative, San José is depicted as riven into a network of alliances based on country of birth, family, and affection. The interdependence of these bonds is exhibited continually in her testimony. Although she restricts herself to two categories: *gachupín* and criollo, it is possible to see that these broad categories contain nuanced perceptions of social class, of "honor," and of status more generally. A perfect instance of this is given during sor Andrea's criticism of Bernarda de San Juan, who becomes the bête noire of her testimony. For Andrea de San Francisco, the *gachupina* nun is a "mujer de poca obligación y de menos religión" [a woman of little honor and less religion].[33] At this point, the Inquisitors must have asked sor Andrea to elaborate on what she meant by honor. Her explanation is surprising, for the cloister is completely forgotten here. The measure of virtue and honor remains purely secular and totally marked by social status. Moreover, it is substantiated by personal experience and family ties. Bernarda de San Juan is of little honor and less religion because her father is an employee of a butcher, and her grandmother, though admittedly born in Spain, sold candles from her home. Sor Andrea is sure this information is correct because her own father knew someone whose slaves bought candles and meat from sor Bernarda's grandmother and father.[34]

The baseness of the *gachupina* nuns and their supporters is also evident from their rewriting of the chronicle of San José and the history of the Carmelite Order in New Spain. In the revisionist version, the path is prepared for what is represented as the pro-Carmelites' saintly cause. Thus, before her profession, Bernarda de San Juan is told that San José is not subject to the obedience of the order but that of the secular prelate. This is described as disappointing her, and she, in the manner of reforming heroines, promises to remedy the situation once she is in a position of authority. Andrea de San Francisco, in her account, is acutely aware of the power of this kind of historical revision and rewriting and points out that this revisionist version is used in the convent as spiritual reading at recreation.[35] Not only do the Hijas de la Orden invent apocryphal stories to suit their purpose, they also misinterpret the writings of Sta. Teresa. Andrea de San Francisco, sure about her own "reading" of the Holy Mother, declares that an early version of Sta. Teresa's *Visitas* has been removed from San José because it was clear from this version of the text that the saint subjected herself and her first convents willingly to the authority of the secular clergy.

Sor Andrea's description of how the Hijas de la Orden work to impose a kind of history in which only their point of view is represented, forms part of her accusation that they continually pervert the Truth. Apart from rewriting the foundation chronicles, they also manipulate the pious devotions in the convent. This involves changing the affections the nuns feel for a particular saint as well as physically transforming images of saints in the convent. Thus, San Nicolás de Tolentino is replaced in the affections of the servant nuns by San Anastasio, a Carmelite servant friar for whom the *gachupina* nuns lay on a feast and celebration.[36] Similarly, pictures that featured friars in Franciscan habits are painted over with the habit of St. Elias. Other pictures of Holy Fathers, dressed as Carmelites, are also commissioned.[37]

Significantly, it is in relation to this rewriting of history that sor Andrea finally makes something approaching a doctrinal accusation against the Hijas de la Orden. She describes how these nuns tell the story of a Carmelite convent in Spain that manages to survive not taking communion except from the male Carmelites, though this means they only take the Host, and make the confession it requires, once every six months. Apparently, the Mexican Carmelite friars explain that it is possible to remain so long without full confession because a mental confession is enough to pardon the sins and failings of a year. This claim is a direct challenge to the authority of the Church, and, not surprisingly, sor Andrea says she told her confessor Jacinto de la Serna immediately about this "doctrine," as she herself terms it.[38] At this point, sor Andrea is asked to give detailed information—to provide the names of those present at the recreation when the story was told, to explain the form recreation took exactly in San José, to describe what she means precisely by "doctrine."[39] In this particular case, she seems simply to equate "doctrine" with "teaching." Sor Andrea says that the *gachupina* nuns do not understand the "doctrine" of Sta. Teresa on obedience but interpret it as applying only when they are subject to the rule of the order.[40] Significantly, Andrea de San Francisco emphasizes that these nuns not only say this but "practice" it. Clearly, this is the damning combination as far as "doctrine" is concerned. The conjunction of theory and practice confirms that the pro-Carmelite nuns are mistaken and conveniently provides the material evidence through which sor Andrea can unmask them not only as misguided but as malevolent. They, therefore, can be utterly condemned.[41]

These representations of the wicked convent community constitute a lively narrative picture built up around the genres of testimony, eye-witness account, and confessional letter and are strongly marked by the forensic rhetoric so much in evidence in Inquisition procedure.[42] As a result, we have a vivid impression of the discord in San José. We have transcriptions of the insults and dialogue bandied by nuns and prelates, details of people's family backgrounds and histories—all in all, an account of convent life far removed from the apologetic chronicle or hagiography. Nevertheless, the power of this genre as an archetype remains and is invoked particularly effectively by the pro-Carmelite nuns when they defend themselves against Andrea de San Francisco's charges. Hagiography provides them with a model against which to measure all of sor Andrea's failings, and the testimony of these nuns presents nothing less than a full-blown "antihagiography" in order to discredit their critic.

There are two communal letters from this group of nuns, defending themselves against the charges Andrea de San Francisco has made against them and, in turn, denouncing her as the cause of the convent's misfortunes.

In these writings, sor Andrea is the antitype of the virtuous and saintly nun. Other models of sinful womanhood are also evident. Perhaps a matter of surprise is that nuns should apply the misogynist topoi of the day so easily to one of their number, particularly since this was a trial and any accusations could very easily be used against them if they were to lose their case. From one perspective, however, the choice to pin the argument to a personal level is completely intelligible. These nuns wish to argue for the primacy of the Carmelite Order—a religious grouping that existed to enforce a rule that guaranteed to bring the individual salvation. Their example of what horrors can happen if the Carmelite rule is disregarded is clearly to be found in a fallen individual—in this case, Andrea de San Francisco. The gravity of the situation may be gauged by the apocalyptic terms employed by the Hijas de la Orden in their second communal letter to the Tribunal, in which they despair over ever reforming sor Andrea and invoke Sta. Teresa's warning that, in a year of "relaxed" government, even the most virtuous of convents can fall into an abject state and never be rehabilitated.[43]

The inversion of the hagiographic norm is extraordinarily rigorous in this letter. Andrea de San Francisco's childhood is described as one of wildness and turbulence of spirit. Significantly, her visit to a convent as a young girl, an erstwhile commonplace opportunity to describe precocious saintliness in hagiographies, is in her case a premonitory sign of the future disturbance she will cause in San José. She terrifies the nuns of San Jerónimo, whom her parents have taken her to visit on a Sunday outing, by pretending to be able to see fairies.[44] Not surprisingly, the mature nuns in San José detect this wild spirit in sor Andrea immediately and recommend she not be allowed to profess. Unfortunately, according to the letter, their advice is disregarded. The convent community is not pusillanimous, however, and tries to save sor Andrea by educating her unruly nature. She is represented as embodying a challenge to the Carmelite rule that is at once institutional and spiritual and that the nuns of San José must rise to.[45] The Carmelite discipline, described as a brake [*el freno*], is intended to hold sor Andrea's spirit within the strictures of the rule.

In the account of the chaos that they believe Andrea de San Francisco has brought to the convent, the Hijas de la Orden employ another inversion of a hagiographic commonplace: instead of silence, loquacity.[46] Logically enough, sor Andrea is represented as loose not only with her tongue but with all kinds of communication. She does not respect the cloister at all.

This disrespect ranges from her abuse of her position as doorkeeper (which she exploits in order to communicate with her family and other influential people—a charge she has herself made against others) to the worldliness of her desires as a nun. She is described in this letter as a "career" nun, wanting to be a great reformer like Sta. Teresa and planning it carefully with the support of her family and well-placed patrons.[47] Thus, she parades around the convent making gestures and holding little ritual ceremonies that disturb the peace of the cloister and draw attention to the persecution she imagines herself as suffering.[48] Sor Andrea also stands accused of deliberately corrupting the community by using dissimulation, *con modos y trucos,* an attribute more usually accorded to the devil. Moreover, her choice of victims is particularly contemptible. She chooses novices, who are the most vulnerable members of the community, as well as other nuns who are weak [algunas flacas y de menos observancia].[49] The Inquisitorial context of these declarations should not be forgotten. The description of this kind of theatrical and dissembling feminine piety, especially in a convent, would immediately have aroused the suspicion of the judges.[50]

The argument constructed on hagiographic lines, however, does not remain at this level of types and antitypes throughout the letter. At certain points, the effects of disunion are vividly represented in very practical and "naturalistic" terms. From the commonplace that sor Andrea should forget her worldly family and think only of her new religious family after her profession, the letter moves on to describe the hagiographically less formulaic, but utterly moving and convincing reason why. Andrea de San Francisco should remember that it is her brothers and sisters in religion who will accompany her in the hour of death [le han de poner la candela de bien morir en la manos] and not the acquaintances and patrons outside the cloister.[51] Apart from her fellow Carmelites, she is utterly alone and exposed in this world.

Similarly, the hagiographic commonplace of the convent hierarchy turned upside down by a rebellious nun is not devoid of a "naturalistic" and emotional dimension in these testimonies. The most obvious and startling departures from the image of the convent suspended in harmonious spiritual government and decorum are the gritty and prosaic references to birthplace and provenance that Andrea de San Francisco stands accused of making. The letter blames her for introducing this pernicious language of division into the convent, making a difference between *gachupinas* and criollas.

Moreover, apparently she does not limit herself to distinguishing between the two groups in this way but invokes the derogatory connotations attached to the terms. Thus, when her offer of forming an alliance is refused by a criolla nun, sor Andrea says the entire criolla community of the convent has failed to prosper because it has *ánimos apocados y de indias* [the weak will characteristic of people born in the Indies].[52] In María de San Cirilio's testimony, this charge is repeated. On this occasion, Andrea de San Francisco is accused of having said that a nun who did not stand her ground and who changed her mind during an election was an *india*.[53]

Although the Hijas de la Orden may have had as an ideal a saintly community in which birth and provenance had no influence, it is clear that this group of nuns also used the terminology of birthplace as a way to define and demarcate boundaries. As a result, the most obvious insult that could be made against Andrea de San Francisco is that her birth (rather than her virtue) makes her unsuitable to be a Carmelite. Effectively enough, she is eventually insulted in precisely this way, and in an impressively violent manner, by Catalina de la Cruz. In her letter of testimony to the Inquisition, sor Catalina complains that Andrea de San Francisco is ungrateful and that her behavior constitutes a reaction to the fact that the convent accepted her without a dowry, rescuing her from the "rubbish pile" [*el muladar*] from which she came.[54]

In many other accounts, however, this social explanation is abandoned for a more traditionally hagiographic one: Andrea de San Francisco is evil. The inversion of the hagiographic model is complete. Not only does the evil nun have an evil nature (over which she has no power), but she also has an active malevolence that involves her in particularly damnable activities marked by their artifice and calculation. Thus, Ana de San Bartolomé describes Andrea de San Francisco as having been adverse to the Carmelite rule from the day of her profession and as having a nature inclined toward excess and indulgence rather than the strictures of Carmelite life.[55] The final stroke to this damning picture is provided by María de San Juan's metaphor of the family. Andrea de San Francisco is described as a monster who, in her rebellion against the order, reneges on the most basic claims of family, rejecting her "mother," "brothers," and "sisters."[56]

There seem to be two independent rhetorical logics working in these testimonies concerning sor Andrea. In one, the convent really does exist as a "no place" of heavenly bodies possessing no culture, no family relations, and no language, and so constituting a place where Andrea de San Francisco's invocation of the world is particularly evil and unwelcome. Thus, in María de San Juan's testimony, sor Andrea rubs people's social and familial backgrounds in their faces [*sacándoles sus linajes*], introducing the language of place of birth into the convent. This is described as a revelation of unpleasant things, things that have been, or should have been, erased in the cloister.[57] This argument belongs to a very pure reading of hagiography, where Andrea de San Francisco represents the negative image of everything that constitutes the model. The second type of logic is concerned with a kind of reasoning and narrative substantially extraneous to the pure hagiographic model. It concentrates precisely on the details of *linajes* disdained by the first type of logic, examining the minutiae of social context. This version of events in San José relies on exempla and naturalistic narrative, both of which can be seen as connected to a notion of personal experience and subjective knowledge that is promoted by the Inquisition context, the structure of testimony, cross-examination, and so forth.

There is a proliferation of narratives telling the story of what brought San José to trial, each using a slightly different strategy and appealing to different generic forms for inspiration. There is, in fact, only one narrative moment at which all the stories of nuns in the trial react in the same way. This reaction, curiously enough, implies a reversion to the most archetypal of hagiographic commonplaces as far as women are concerned: the topos of *docta ignorancia*. Significantly, this compulsive narrative move made by every nun, disregarding the "side" they are on, is triggered when the women are pressed by the Inquisitors into describing what exactly constitutes the heretical behavior in San José. Describing doctrinal evil in their midst is not an easy task. There is no clear-cut hagiographic model to be followed, and suddenly the "sides" in the trial seem to be transformed from nuns against nuns into nuns against Inquisitors.

Toward the end of Andrea de San Francisco's testimony, she is asked directly what exactly are the doctrines that she alleges are not admitted in the convent because they are "secular" rather than "Carmelite."[58] In reply sor Andrea simply repeats that some of the nuns refuse to give obedience to the secular clergy, claiming they should be subject to the friars of their own order and not to strangers. Sor Andrea does not indulge in theory but states that the Hijas de la Orden have little respect for the archbishop and that they ridicule members of the secular clergy who come into the convent to confess them.[59] She has said this during her previous audiences, and the Inquisitors insistently ask for more details about the precise doctrine these pro-Carmelite nuns hold. Sor Andrea refuses to elaborate, referring them back to her audiences, saying that the "doctrines" are evident from the evidence she has given.[60] The only addition she makes is to emphasize that the Hijas de la Orden have been told that when confessing with the secular clergy, they should not divulge any breaking of the Carmelite rule because the secular priests will misunderstand and misinterpret it. Sor Andrea implies that this kind of advice had certainly been considered heretical by certain ecclesiastical authorities at one point, at least by some sections of the clergy. She recounts how, during one of the vicereine's visits, the Hijas de la Orden say such disrespectful things about the secular clergy that one of the persons present, the chaplain Cristóbal de Luna, is driven to pronounce that *esta doctrina es herética*.[61] Sor Andrea further consolidates her case by claiming that other Carmelite fathers have told her that such beliefs are erroneous and abominable.[62] She, of course, does not hazard a personal opinion.

The Inquisitors go on to pose the most crucial question: does sor Andrea consider what the Hijas de la Orden say about confession to be orthodox?[63] Given the exact wording of this question, Andrea cannot respond to it affirmatively. She is very precise and says she has not heard anyone express doctrinal opinions in the convent [sólo lo que tiene dicho de pedir confesores Carmelitas], only that, as she has said, these nuns ask to be confessed exclusively by Carmelites.[64] She continues to refuse to enter into a doctrinal discussion, or to offer a judgment, and stands by what she has already said. Sor Andrea reiterates that she definitely has not heard the Hijas de la Orden say that members of the secular clergy are unable to absolve them in confession. The same question is posed to several nuns who testify against the Hijas de la Orden. Given that every ordained priest has the power to absolve sins, the fact that the nuns seem to have placed this in doubt is, ultimately, the reason why the Inquisition is present in the convent. Without exception, the nuns reply with the same distance and refusal to engage with the precise terms of the question that characterizes Andrea de San Francisco's answer.

Thus, Clara del Santísimo Sacramento refuses to enter into a discussion about the possible issues of faith behind the behavior of the Hijas de la Orden, saying that she has not asked them the reason why they act as they do, nor have they offered to provide one. What does reemerge from sor Clara's reply is the gravity of the breach. The Hijas de la Orden say that confessing with a non-Carmelite is like trying to confess in Basque—completely incomprehensible.[65] Clara del Santísimo Sacramento also repeats—on firsthand evidence, since she was herself present—the claim that María de Sta. Inés said to the vicereine that she would rather confess with a lay Carmelite friar than with a secular priest. However, sor Clara mitigates the strength of this anecdote, which could be construed as containing some elements regarding doctrine, by saying that she is sure the comment was "only an exaggeration."[66]

While María de los Angeles makes no reply at all to the question, María del Niño Jesús' answer could be taken as emblematic of the hermeticism displayed by the nuns when asked about matters of doctrine. She claims only to be able to remember having overheard sor Francisca de San José (and this some two years before) declare on her way into a confessional inside which confessor Mercado, a secular clergyman, may or may not have been, that she could not confess with secular clerics, though she gave no reason for this that María del Niño Jesús can recall.[67] Any accusation contained here dissolves in the tentativeness and opacity of sor María's language.

The second question that is posed initially to Andrea de San Francisco and then repeated to various of the other nuns is also concerned with whether the Hijas de la Orden ascribe special priestly powers to the Carmelite fathers—a belief that could be condemned as heretical because of its implication that other religious orders were somehow less spiritually qualified.[68] Sor Andrea's answer to this question is in a similar vein to the one she gave to the previous question—a refusal to repeat its terminology and a reaffirmation of what she has declared in her previous audiences. On this occasion, Andrea de San Francisco is willing to offer only an observation, rather than an accusation, and uses different terms from those of the question. Thus, she claims that the Hijas de la Orden think that only the Carmelites are appropriate confessors because they keep the same rule, and also because they consider them to be the most spiritually perfect and saintly persons in the Church.[69]

Sor Andrea's curt reply is the most expansive; both María del Niño Jesús and María de los Angeles simply state they have never heard, understood, or known of any such doctrine being held in San José. It is again apparent that the nuns refuse to enter a discussion in the terms set up by the Inquisition. They are astute enough to know what heresy is, and thus they fall back on the supposed ignorance of women as a strategy. Their silence, however, is also eloquent—in part because it stems from a tradition that makes women's ignorance a sign of their intelligence and virtue. This tradition was, of course, governed by certain forms, and the answer to the question given by Sta. Teresa's namesake in San José is very interesting in this context because the Mexican Teresa de Jesús uses the well-established and widely diffused mystical lexicon pertaining to water and religious illumination. Such an idiom was clearly the legitimate one for a nun's spiritual expression and makes any declaration resonate profoundly. Thus, the powerful effect of the words of the New Spanish Teresa de Jesús when she says that she has heard the pro-Carmelite nuns claim that the Carmelite fathers are the "fountain" of true religion and that to learn from anyone else is to drink from dirty and muddied puddles.[70]

Teresa de Jesús' reply maintains a "distance" from the accusation implicit in the Inquisitors' question, both by using this specialized vocabulary and by replying in an anecdotal rather than substantial manner. She never hazards an opinion or interprets facts but instead attempts only to present them. Teresa de Jesús' statement is more about her own reaction than about the doctrinal correctness of the Hijas de la Orden—a move away from any pretense of possessing abstract knowledge to the assertion of subjective experience and sensation, which has been apparent throughout these replies. She concludes by saying that she has nothing further to add as she avoids all such conversations because they make her *inquieta* [ill at ease].[71] That the source of this disquiet is both very personal and spiritually entirely legitimate is clear from another comment in her statement. She discusses how the conversations she overhears about confession plunge her into doubt about the legitimacy of her own confessions, and at this moment, something of the genuine distress that this institutional wrangle has caused in the convent can be sensed in her words. This nun feels she tells her confessor simply and honestly about her faults, but these fights in the convent have made her come to doubt the validity of her own confessional practices.[72]

As in all the previous testimonies, the nuns are patently loath to accuse each other blatantly of heresy, though they are quick to levy charges of laxity and sinfulness. Teresa de Jesús, in her reply to the Inquisition's question on the teaching of heterodoxy in the convent refutes the idea that the nuns hold any doctrinal position whatever. In her opinion, their complaints about the secular clergy have nothing to do with metaphysics but concern solely practicalities; the nuns supporting rule by the Carmelites and confession by them do so only because they assume the Carmelite monks know what is required of Carmelite nuns better than any secular clergyman could.[73]

This concern to demote the terms of the debate from theory to practice and from doctrine to religious discipline is perhaps the only point in common between the warring factions in San José. As such, its significance should not be underestimated. It clearly unites the nuns in a representation of their convent and the spirituality within it as being removed from the theoretical qualifications of piety proper to the Inquisitors' terms of reference — and instead as inhabiting an enclosed feminine world where spirituality is experienced in a range of communal religious practices.

From these Inquisition records, it is evident that the convent is a site of conflict, both notionally and in reality. Sta. Teresa herself had divided her original convent through her insistence on reform, fulfilling her role as hagiographic *reformadora* perfectly. She also initiated the trope of the convent as a place of dissent.

One interesting facet of the transmission of this culture of reform is evident in Andrea de San Francisco's testimony. In her searing criticism of the activities of the *gachupina* nuns in the convent, Andrea de San Francisco alludes to this Teresian tradition of reform, representing the mundanity of the pro-Carmelite nuns as deflecting the reformed order away from its origins and into relaxed ways. She turns the usual categories inside out. In this version, the Old World women are "impure," and it is the transplanted religion, made vigorous by its American context, that is the true representation of the original Discalced rule. Sor Andrea can thus conveniently make use of the positive connotations of the New World on this occasion. The land of evangelical enterprise, she argues, is certainly not the place to re-create the sins of the Old World but one in which to extend the reformed "new" order. Thus, sor Andrea's comments throughout the trial can be linked very closely to principles of Teresian reform, but this reform should be understood to include even the dissent implicit in the concept. The New World Carmelites inherit a fractured tradition and reproduce it as fractured, but the terms of fissure are different and specific to New Spain.

The Inquisition records examined here provide a fascinating counterhistory to the chronicles of the convent that formed the basis of the previous chapter concerning New Spanish Carmelites. The fact that two such extreme versions of life in San José are available is extraordinary, and it highlights the uncertainty surrounding the traditional generic forms used to represent institutions and people in the Old World, when their transplantation to the New World confronted them with a different subject matter. Curiously, the breaking down of hagiography as the master narrative in which to tell stories of nuns and their convents, which happens both in the chronicles and in the Inquisition, results in similar rhetorical consequences: a greater degree of "naturalism" or "realism" in terms both of material detail and of psychology and emotions. And yet the main narrative axes, around which such representations are built, continue to be the same: the relation of the individual to the community and the New World social context that constructs these individuals and communities through specific cultural, racial, and social categories.

Cacique Nuns:

From Saints' Lives to Indian Lives

La divine Providence par ce en cecy s'est voulu montrer omnipotente, que depuis que la mere du monde Eve nouvelle nasquist, qui fut environ l'an de grace 1500 ans, elle ha plus descouvert le monde, & principalement des Indes, que par 5500 ans auparavant n'avoit esté faict. . . . pour attendre que la fontaine de l'esprit divin feust incorporée en generale maternité au monde.

GUILLAUME DE POSTEL, *Les très merveilleuses victoires des femmes du nouveau monde* (Paris, 1553)[1]

Hecha ya mención de la buena de Petronila [una india], no hay razón para no hacerla de otras humildes y pequeñitas que hoy en la corte del Supremo Rey de los Reyes serán muy grandes.

CARLOS DE SIGÜENZA Y GÓNGORA, *Parayso occidental* (Mexico City: Juan Luis de Ribera, 1683)[2]

Among the works of the prolific French humanist Guillaume de Postel is *Les très merveilleuses victoires des femmes du nouveau monde*, a book in defense of women. Postel's work, considered wild and heretical in its own time, is coolly descriptive about the worldly motivations driving the conquerors of America. In spite of this unpropitious background, he deems Providence to have been at work in the discovery of the New World and argues that the general coincidence of Columbus' voyage with the birth of Joan of Arc signals the global victory of an immanent feminine principle [*anime*] that will cure the world of its ills and prepare it for the Second Coming.

More than one hundred years later, Postel's radical optimism is notably absent from the writing of the Mexican humanist Carlos de Sigüenza y Góngora, though he too was engaged in a similar task of defending women's virtue in the context of the New World. Sigüenza y Góngora feels driven to justify his inclusion of the hagiographies of Indian women in the chronicle he is writing of the convent of Jesús María, the only religious foundation for women in the city to enjoy royal patronage. Even his recurrence to the topos of the meek inheriting the kingdom of heaven does nothing to dispel the genuine discomfort evident in the patronizing tone he employs.

That Postel's somewhat unusual stance toward the New World and toward women in general should have caused scandals in scholarly and theological circles is unsurprising. One facet of his thought, however, remained traditional: its cultural context. His curious reinterpretation of Neoplatonic and Gnostic notions of woman, though intellectually associated with and perhaps prompted by the discovery of the Americas, was still a European idea of femininity. When set beside Sigüenza y Góngora's pragmatic vindication of the real women of the Americas, that is *aboriginal* women, it becomes clear that these women, who literally embodied racial and cultural difference, posed conceptual problems considerably more difficult for traditional systems of knowledge to assimilate than any of Postel's exuberant theorizing.[3]

That Sigüenza y Góngora's attempt to rescue Amerindian women for European scholarly thought should be framed in the context of a convent chronicle is significant. It is as though the only possibility for women of another race to enter such conceptual schemes (which, insofar as they concerned themselves with women at all, were renowned for their misogyny rather than anything else) was as that ultimately exemplary woman, the nun. This chapter concentrates on the history of ideas surrounding both the notion of woman and of the Indian in the cultural politics of the imposition of the Spanish empire. It focuses more particularly on the idea of a *cacique* nun (a woman of the indigenous elite)—something that implied the revision of the debates mentioned above, forcing them to consider the gender dimension of the colonization and evangelization of the Americas. What was at stake, both materially and symbolically, in the project of founding a convent in Mexico City specifically for Indian women? In order to answer this question, the way in which the speculative debates on the nature of woman and of the Indian interacted with ecclesiastic policy and practice in the colonies toward Indians and toward Indian women in particular has to be examined.

The historical legacy of these debates consists primarily of the testimonies of certain priests asked to give their opinion on the feasibility of such a foundation. Hagiography was the genre most usually employed for the representation of female virtue in this post-Tridentine period. These testimonies, however, were written in terms drawn from speculative discourses, both Christian and classical, concerned with the nature of man and of civilization, rather than as saintly lives. What exactly did this change of genre imply in terms of defining the "subject" being written about? How did the novel rhetorical construction of these testimonies contribute to what is known about the place of Indian women in the actual practice and politics of evangelization and acculturation?[4]

The theological understanding that woman was inferior to man by nature, but his equal by divine grace, was largely uncontested in this period. Judged by this standard, women who professed as nuns were exceptional creatures who displayed an extraordinary degree of virtue that dispensed them from the usual frailties of their sex. The status of a nun as exceptional and in some sense outside the rule of nature meant that, on occasions, she could even be endowed with spiritual knowledge usually inaccessible to most men. In an analogous fashion, the New World itself provided a series of exceptional situations that confounded normative notions of spirituality by surpassing them. A land of erstwhile idolatry, it was ripe for conversion, religious conquest, and, in some accounts, the readying of humankind for the Second Coming. Given such circumstances, the paradox that the privilege of being considered capable of monastic profession should have first been accorded to Indian women rather than to Indian men is perhaps not so surprising. Though Indian men carried out certain basic religious offices as secular priests, there is no record of them having ever officially professed as monks, and no attempts were made to found monasteries specifically for them in this period. It is then with the philosophical and political debate surrounding the founding of the convent of Corpus Christi for noble Indian *women* in 1728 that this chapter is concerned.[5]

The idea of founding some kind of religious establishment for the female Indian population had been present from the beginning of the Spanish colonial enterprise in Mexico. In 1530 six Spanish nuns made the journey from the Peninsula to the New World to set up a school where young Indian girls would be taught. Four years later in 1534, Archbishop Montúfar brought eight *beatas* from Spain to be teachers, and in the following year Catalina de

Bustamante, one of the original eight, paid for three more *beatas* to travel to New Spain to set up another school. Simultaneously, schools were set up to educate young Indian boys, the idea being that the Indians educated in these establishments would marry one another and that the Spanish evangelical mission would be thus accomplished. This attempted incursion into the very heart of Indian culture, family structure, and social organization was a complete failure, and the schools lasted only about ten years. The girls who had been educated in them (when their parents could be coerced or convinced to allow them to attend) were considered unmarriageable by the wider Indian community. The Indian elite refused to send their eldest sons to the schools, fobbing the Spanish authorities off with second sons or even the sons of servants.[6] Clearly, though the educational route may have seemed to be the royal road to cultural and religious assimilation, it quickly revealed itself to be filled with unexpected difficulties.

The enterprise of founding another such institution had then to be carried out with care and after considerable research. All the priests who were asked to testify worked in a specific ecclesiastical area, the *jurisdicción* of San Pablo, and the Indian women who eventually became the four founding mothers of Corpus Christi came from precisely this area. From several of these testimonies, it is clear that building work for the convent was near completion (leading one to suppose that in certain circles the success of the initiative was a foregone conclusion) and that it enjoyed the backing of the Franciscan Order (to which the convent eventually belonged) and of the viceroy, the marquis of Valero. Considerable opposition to the foundation arose, however, based on practical grounds rather than any theoretical or philosophical argument, from the Consejo de Indias, the Cabildo of Mexico City, and from the Real Audiencia, the body that solicited the testimonies of the priests.[7] The professional opinion of the city's treasurer, for example, is very negative. He lists a number of previous foundations in other cities of a similar character that have been unsuccessful. The information he gives about the lack of adequate executive support and the poor supervision accorded them provides insight both into the critical financial situation of the city and into how the proposition to found another mendicant convent clearly presented considerable pressures for an already overextended administration. Corpus Christi, posing as it did both financial problems and what the treasurer called "formal" difficulties (an allusion no doubt to the theological and juridical implications of allowing Indian women to profess as nuns) was certainly not an immediately attractive proposal.[8] Here I will concentrate precisely upon the difficulties defined as "formal" by the city treasurer and on how the philosophical debate they gave rise to was represented, rather than on a detailed account of the material history of the foundation. Nevertheless, it is important to remember that the financial and political background exacerbated and influenced the political and theological debate.

The priests obliged to consider such a proposal embarked on a process of analysis and writing that led them into scholarly realms considerably removed from the traditional schema for expressing and conceptualizing female virtue in a conventual context—hagiography—and into more general and complex debates about human nature not only in the sciences of theology and medicine but also of jurisprudence.[9] Hagiography had always been connected to these disciplines, being in its inception a varied genre that encompassed writings of many kinds: from those of legal import designed to substantiate claims to sanctity, to stories conceived of primarily for liturgical purposes and to be read out during religious ceremonies, to accounts of *miracula*, the wondrous events connected to the saint's tomb or his or her relics. Nevertheless, as we have seen, the Counter-Reformation's use of hagiography as one of its principal tools in the battle against heresy meant that the genre became much more uniform and that any serious dialogue with other disciplines was reduced to formulaic references. After the Council of Trent, the hagiography, officially backed and vetted by the Curia, was intended for wide consumption and designed to be the most suitable and orthodox vehicle for representing spiritual virtues, especially those corresponding to a monastic context.[10] The step "backward" into a more speculative discourse made by the testifying priests who abandon the genre is an indication that the finely tuned and highly formal rhetoric of hagiography in this period was simply not adequate for conceptualizing the issues at stake.[11] In part, this speculativeness can no doubt be attributed to the continuing novelty of the question being posed. Though two hundred years might have passed since the "discovery" of the indigenous peoples of America, their "qualities" and their "nature" remained the subject of debate.[12]

Certain of these novelties, in relation to Indian women, could clearly be something of a shock for European men who had difficulty considering women outside the paradigm of marriage, even if they accepted the mystical doctrine of virginity as a divine gift. Although the Indian society that the Spanish colonizers encountered was organized through sexual divisions, these were clearly different from those of the Old World. Notably, the matriarchal systems of inheritance and of social organization of many of the peoples of the México empire were seriously disturbing to the conquistadores and missionaries alike, for whom marriage, not motherhood, constituted the chief relationship binding the sexes.[13] The tacit assumption was that the origins of civil society were to be found in the family and the sexual differentiation of roles that constituted the father as its natural ruler. This structure was reproduced in the metaphors used to describe the relationship to the Godhead of women who took religious vows. Nuns were not outside the paradigm of marriage; they, in fact, married the ultimate husband and became the brides of Christ. Unsurprisingly, the power enjoyed by Indian women in pre-Conquest family life and social organization made their distance from this model startlingly clear. How then was it possible to make of such a woman a nun?

For several of the testifying priests, the answer to such a question was self-evident; the attempt should not even be made, for to do so was to act counter to the weight of precedence and the Natural Law that it revealed. Their testimonies are a somewhat simplified and degraded echo of the great sixteenth-century theologian Francisco de Vitoria's classic exposition of the situation in his comments on why women should not be ordained as priests. Vitoria explains that what convinces him most of the unsuitability of women (he has previously cataloged a series of biblical and classical texts as well as the dictates of several church councils) is the fact that, "in all the long process of the years, and with all the abundance of good, wise women, the Church has never tried to raise any woman to ecclesiastical power or office."[14] It is precisely when there has been abundant opportunity for doing a thing and yet that thing has not been done, that it must be assumed to be neither lawful nor possible.

This debate about the scope of Natural Law is at the center of Vitoria's discussion of the legitimacy of the Spanish Conquest of the Americas in two lectures, *De Indis* and *De Indis relectio posterior, sive de iure belli.* The value of precedent, however, was clearly something radically challenged by the very existence of the New World. And the attractions for an evangelical mission of founding a convent for Indian women—however unprecedented an action—are all too obvious. The convent for Indian nuns would be of strategic use in restoring a degree of symbolic "order" to the disorder that New Spain, as a place, posed to two significant categories of difference: that of gender, dividing women from men, and that of politics, which divided civilization from barbarism. The journeys of male saints may certainly have been understood to imply an entry into a different world, an abandoning of the city for the desert, but the presence of convents and their inhabitants in the Indies was supposed to signify precisely the *imposition* of civilization.

The tradition of female asceticism that led to the establishment of the first Christian convents came not from the notion of removal from the city to the desert, as in the case of monks, but was based precisely on an idea of retirement *within* the city itself. More accurately, this was often conceived of as retirement within that civically significant institution: the household. By immuring themselves in the home, women were meant to bring down grace upon a community, and the withdrawal and immobility of virgin women was one metaphorically associated with the integrity of their bodies, an integrity that came to have an exceptionally charged significance. As Peter Brown writes, the female body was the most alien body of all for the male, and when consecrated to virginity, "it could appear like an untouched desert in itself: it was the furthest reach of human flesh turned into something peculiarly precious by the coming of Christ upon it."[15] The desire to name the convent for Indian women "Corpus Christi" resonates in this context; its foundation would signify in some sense that the incarnate Word had descended upon the doubly alien bodies of Indian women.

Such a foundation, however, required serious consideration of what or who this Indian woman was, and what or who she would become as a nun. The traditions that governed scholarly thought about women in the Early Modern period are generally recognized as having been the last to succumb to any kind of historical contextualization. Where woman was the subject of theological, legal, or medical discourse, the exegetical spirit continued to manifest itself in the kind of cross-referencing and commentary where language was assumed to have an objective status of truth.[16] Nevertheless, the fact that the female subjects of these New World testimonies on the nature of woman were also Indian, and lived in an acculturated world, seems to have meant that theoretical discourse about them ceded to historicism and its related demands: comparativism and relativism. In the particular case of Indian nuns, it appears that the paradigm governing the conceptualization of woman, which in other contexts thrived well into the eighteenth century, was challenged because it had to be considered along with a paradigm that proved to be marginally less powerfully embedded in Western thought—that governing the conceptualization of non-Europeans.

In the Early Modern period, Western ways of classifying human beings consisted both of physiological factors and of elements of social organization. The classifications that resulted from this amalgam of classical and Christian thought were complex and sexually differentiated. Any judgment on the nature of the Indian (man or woman) was, therefore, not only a matter of strategic expediency related to the political and economic stakes of the colonial context, but an issue of transcendental proportions that involved questioning both the classical and the Christian models of humanity. In this light, the fact that many of the testifying priests turn to somewhat fragmented but recognizable versions of the theory of Natural Slavery to discuss the spiritual potential of Indian women, rather than to the model provided by hagiography, becomes meaningful.[17]

Despite its universal embrace of humanity, the Catholic Church was no stranger, as an institution, to refined hierarchies and stratifications. The *congregatio fidelium* may have been open to all, but each occupied a defined place within it. As a result, any use of the topoi of Natural Slavery had to be careful not to endorse the theory completely. Such an endorsement would have meant that the Indians, as natural slaves, were inferior and incapable of change, and both of these premises were in direct contradiction with the evangelical teachings of the Church. The matter of whether the indigenous peoples were fully rational—and, therefore, admissible to the congregation of the faithful and eligible for eternal salvation—had been resolved favorably by the papal bull *Sublimus Deus* of Paul III in 1537.[18]

The fact that universalizing theories gradually ceded to a comparative spirit in the colonial context is a well-accepted notion in the intellectual history of the Americas. These "universal" theories were, however, always predicated on one crucial differentiation: that of sex. That this dichotomy, and the binary differences it gave rise to, was "natural" is best expressed by Aristotle, for whom:

> . . . wherever there is a combination of elements, continuous or discontinuous, and something in common results, in all cases the ruler and the

ruled appear; and living creatures acquire this feature from nature as a whole. . . . Again, the relationship of male to female is that the one is by nature superior, the other inferior, and the one is ruler, the other ruled.[19]

In the testimonies of the priests, this deep-seated acknowledgment of sexual differentiation is conjugated with the other manifold differences provided by the New World (of race, of culture, etc.).

The connections were easy enough to see.[20] Aristotle himself had made the analogy between the inferiority of women and children to adult males, on the one hand, and the inferiority of all barbarians to adult (Greek) men, on the other. Both women and children were in a sense incomplete men and, as such, considered as minors before the law because neither could fully exercise their reason (though male children were, of course, guaranteed a transition from this state if they grew to adulthood). Predictably, this analogy leads two of the priests who testify against the foundation to interpret a law designed to protect Indian landowners from losing their property by requiring that a qualified judge approve transactions over a certain given amount, as proof that the Indians were considered as minors by the Spanish authorities in juridical terms.[21] The wording of the statute referred to, drafted in 1571–1572, in which the judge is described as *mayor* [older/more experienced] certainly encourages the idea of the Indians standing in need of the paternal protection of Spanish law.[22]

If a person were a barbarian and a minor before the law, her also being a woman made her disenfranchisement from full rationality all too obvious. This "double" alienation of Indian women (by virtue of their sex and their race) from any place in the spiritual hierarchy, and particularly from such an exalted one as religious profession, appears frequently in the testimonies and in many guises. The significance of cities and communal life in the colonies has been emphasized before, and it is not surprising to find priests who are unsympathetic to the foundation of the convent using arguments about the barbaric past of the Indians to prove that they are incapable of the civility necessary for life in a Christian city, or in a Christian community. If this is true for the men, the reasoning is that it is doubly so for Indian women. In these arguments, the countless descriptions of the magnificence of the Méxica capital and the complexity of its metropolitan life are abandoned for a representation of the Méxica as pastoralists rather than agriculturalists. Evidently, the women of this nomadic people could not claim the honor of calling themselves the "daughters of Jerusalem"—to which all nuns living in convents were entitled.[23] Alejandro Romano derides Amerindian civilization as consisting mostly of persons living in the wild mountains or in "little farms." In Romano's experience, Indians have resisted living in the communities that missionaries established for them, a circumstance he ascribes to their uncivilized state, making clear that it renders them unable to govern themselves. Having proved how uncivilized Indians were, and largely remain, he asks if their women can in all seriousness be thought capable of living in community and of governing themselves.[24]

Both the arguments relating to civilization and to legal status are fairly refined discussions that attempt to analyze, and thereby prove inferior, indigenous culture and its people. The one difference that is so absolute it does not bare subjection to this reasonably sophisticated process of contextualization and comparison is somatic: the Indian woman's body is simply a female body, an inversion, exaggeration, or deformation of the male, depending upon which patristic or classical authority is invoked. For Felipe de Abarca, who pursues the idea that women present "extreme" incarnations of male qualities, this means that the noble Indian women admitted to the proposed convent (his neat collapsing of nobility, legitimacy, and purity is significant) will be doubly "Indian," that is, supremely docile and timorous.[25] In contrast, Diego de Moza uses the opposition male/female to argue that women's constitution is not the extreme but the inversion of its male correlative. Thus, the fact that all Indian men naturally incline toward evil means that all Indian women will equally naturally be inclined toward good, and should, therefore, be allowed to profess immediately.[26] He continues in this vein, pursuing a binary logic that allows him to condemn Indian men as lascivious, prey to the malign influence of the climate of the Americas, and to defend Indian women as chaste, their natural "opposition" to the male safeguarding them in this instance from the pernicious effect of the environment.[27]

In this context, the sacrament of communion becomes significant, having at this stage in Counter-Reformation thinking been transformed into a kind of litmus test of orthodoxy. In the Spanish colonies, the sacrament's materiality had become the subject of legislation, it being licit to make the Host out of only certain types of grain, European wheat in preference to Amerindian corn.[28] The Eucharist's materiality clearly posed questions of cultural specificity, and one would have expected the materiality, or rather the physicality, of the communicant's *body* to have posed them also. The controversy that had always surrounded excessively frequent communion and the attempts to limit access to the sacrament are evidence enough of how attention to the communicant's consumption of the divine body and blood highlighted anxieties about the human body that were not solely religious.[29] Hence, Antonio Pérez' lengthy discussion about the cleanliness of Indian women and the care they take in preparing themselves before communion. His defense of these women reveals how closely notions of purity, eating, and sexual continence were tied to the care of the body, and how this in turn was a sexually differentiated body. Indian women's chastity and their habit of fasting on Saturdays are thus judged as being consonant with the purest Hebrew tradition regulating the behavior of virgins. Their fasts are broken only because of sickness, thirst, or pregnancy. On the actual day of communion, they prepare their bodies, carefully cleanse the paths they will take to church by placing incense burners at the crossroads, talk to no one, and stay inside the church, their arms crossed and their eyes lowered, until midday.[30] In order to be received, the sacrament required a degree of inner and outer purity on the part of the communicant that *any* woman, traditionally considered to be more subject to her passions, would find difficult to achieve.

From these few examples of the meeting of Christian and classical thought, it becomes obvious that the exegetical spirit, and the hierarchical conception of society common to both, could result in impressive arguments alleging the inferiority and ineligibility to certain offices of indigenous peoples (and especially of their women). José de Guevarra is the most sophisticated in deploying the power of these two traditions. He exploits both to argue that certain Christians—the Indians—are indeed inferior, while simultaneously highlighting the providential base of his thought, thus avoiding the merest hint of any heretical belief in communities of the elect. Guevarra argues that God created human beings with qualities in proportion to their abilities, but this does not mean that their liberty is in any way affected, for they are completely free within this providential system. Nevertheless, it *is* a system that allows for inequalities. In it, some spiritual paths are more perfect than others, and some persons are more spiritually gifted than others. The force of Guevarra's argument is that of consonance and decorum; each person must follow the path most fitting for his or her abilities, which may of itself not necessarily be the most perfect one. Given the inconstant nature of the Indians (a *natural* failing that he attributes to them), it is clear that they are unfit for a religious vocation and will win their spiritual rewards following a different, more lowly, path.[31] The pragmatic conclusion to these arguments is given by Antonio Xavier García, who suggests that the Indian women should be made *beatas* or tertiaries of the Franciscan Order, instead of professing as full choir nuns.[32]

The kind of stratification of the *congregatio fidelium* being proposed by these priests, though in absolute philosophical terms quite a complicated stance to sustain, was in fact part of the very fabric of the everyday life of the Church, in the Old World as well as in the New. The Counter-Reformation's determination to "educate" the masses who had succumbed to superstition, and thus become vulnerable to heretical teachings, is the most patent example of a well-accepted notion of the spiritual "weakness" of certain members of the Christian community. The analogy between the barbarian and the ignorant peasant was widely used long before the "discovery" of America, but it clearly became politically more charged in the colonial context. The accompanying analogy between the rustic's privation of meditative powers and the woman's lack of deliberative faculties (which made both more suited to devoutness rather than to higher spiritual pursuits) could obviously also be used to organize misogynist thought more rigorously in relation to Indian women. If the range of spiritual capacities thought fitting for Indian man as a result of this syncretic analysis was limited, Indian woman was doubly barred by the classic misogynist logic that cast her as the weaker sex.

Thus, though proving the intelligence and rational ability and, therefore, the spiritual capacity of Indian men was a delicate conceptual task, proving that of Indian women was twice as difficult. Not only had their advocates to battle against the image of Indians as barbarians, there was also another traditional notion to contend with: that *all* women, regardless of race, were foolish and irrational. Those priests arguing against Indian women's spiritual capacity to profess as nuns had this impressive body of received knowledge to rely upon, and many of them exploited it with considerable skill. For example, José de Guevarra questions the talent displayed in painting by Indian men and declares he finds them incapable of the higher arts of theology, rhetoric, and philosophy where mimetic ability by itself is not sufficient.[33] Guevarra's comments connect to classical and biblical traditions that held that, as a group, barbarians and women of all races, along with idiots and some mythical creatures such as St. Anthony's faun, possessed a mimetic potential of the highest degree and could thus display great skill of the mechanical intellect. Nevertheless, they were considered incapable of totally autonomous thought and so unable to excel in the spheres of speculative intellect. Clearly, a judgment as severe as this about the intellectual capacity of the Amerindians places the whole educational dimension of evangelization in question. Guevarra's advocation of the fitting type of devotion of which Indians are capable is equally revealing. His description of their innocent piety is that of the devout fool, of the child, or—by logical extension—of the woman.[34] The feminization of the entire Indian spiritual potential means, of course, that Indian women are left with very little spiritual ability at all, victims once again of the double bind of sex and race.

Nevertheless, to avert accusations of heresy, any Christian proposal of a hierarchical ordering of the difference presented by the New World's original inhabitants had to avoid being too deterministic. In other words, whatever the hierarchy, divine grace had to be allowed to work in its mysterious ways, occasionally undoing what was most certain and astounding the mighty with the power of the weak. José de Acosta's (1540–1600) comments in book 1 of his *De procuranda indorum salute* (1596) illustrate how the analogy between Amerindians and Castilian peasants could be mobilized to recuperate the former for the educational mission so naturally extended to the latter. He argued that even in Spain itself, there were men born in villages who, if they remained among their own kind, made no intellectual progress. If they went to school, however, or to court, or even to an important city, they immediately stood out for their ingenuity and ability.[35]

In this respect, the misogynist logic casting woman as inferior to man could also be mobilized in her favor. In this scenario, woman becomes the perfect tool through which to show the miraculous workings of divine grace, whose power was so great it could even overcome the manifold weaknesses of femininity. Devotion, which was considered a particularly feminine quality because its virtue did not lie in any particular mental attribute but rather in its lack, meant that when divine grace worked upon it, it was paradoxically transformed into the gift of spiritual prophecy. Because of her "natural" passivity, Aristotelian thought confined women's virtue to those qualities as imperfect as she was herself (chastity, modesty, endurance) and the Christian reinterpretation of them occasionally allowed for the miraculous conversion of weakness to strength, women being understood to embody these virtues in a manner inaccessible to men. Antonio Pérez refers to the strong women of biblical tradition, arguing that Judiths and Deborahs abound in New Spain, and he cites Thomas Aquinas and Duns Scotus to emphasize the orthodoxy of his statements.[36]

The testimonies regarding the spiritual capacities of Indian women divide up neatly according to religious affiliation. Those opposing the foundation of the convent are written by Jesuits, while the favorable testimonies have Franciscan authors. As the convent was meant to be a Franciscan foundation, it is no surprise to discover that the Franciscans support it. Why all the Jesuits should be against the foundation is less evident, however. The position of both religious orders with respect to the acculturation of the Indians and their spiritual potential shifted throughout the period. Although the Franciscans were usually sympathetic toward the Indians and in the first years of evangelization were fiercely enthusiastic, even early works by Motolinía (1500?–1569) and his follower Jerónimo de Mendieta (1525–1604) put forward the view that the Indians were children and thus required perpetual tutelage, a condition making them unfit for the priesthood. In contrast, in the late eighteenth century, various Jesuits—notably Francisco Javier Clavijero (1731–1787)—wrote works in defense of the Indians and Creoles that refuted claims about the pernicious effects of the climate of the Indies on character.

The "rediscovery" of idolatry and the subsequently renewed attempts to extirpate it (a political and religious policy that took place primarily in Peru but also in New Spain in the early seventeenth century) highlight the different philosophies of acculturation espoused by the Franciscan and Jesuit Orders. This fact may be the key to understanding their radical disagreement over the foundation of Corpus Christi.[37] During the *extirpaciones,* the Jesuits revealed their skepticism about the Indians being able to be anything other than Indians (something that did not, of course, prevent them from being good Christians). The Franciscans, however, saw evangelization as necessarily involving the communication of a political and cultural identity. Thus, for the Jesuits, the notion of an Indian nun was a nonsense, something that would complicate their missionary goal, while for the Franciscans, the Indian nun symbolized the achievement of their several goals.[38]

Irrespective of the eventual aim of the testimony, and regardless of the religious affiliation of its author, the priests' accounts all share the characteristic of abandoning hagiography as an authoritative model of representation. Nevertheless, there does exist a significant difference in rhetorical approach between the favorable and the negative testimonies. The negative accounts tend to foreground their appeal to the authority of a universalist theory and its scholarly tradition, whereas the positive ones, while not ignoring this tradition, succumb quickly to descriptive and experiential terms upon which their claim to truthfulness is placed. These differences should not be over-emphasized, however, for what strikes the reader the most in the testimonies are the densely textured narratives produced, irrespective of their eventual conclusion. Testimonies forced, as in the nature of every legal document, one specific outcome; but the narratives that wind their way to these inevitable conclusions do so through extraordinarily complicated and crooked paths, filled with inconsistencies and characterized most faithfully by their confusion and profusion of facts, examples, and anecdotes.

In one sense, it is quite obvious why the "truth" of the evangelical mission should make such strong appeals to an extratextual confirmation of itself, however chaotic and disorganized, as it does in many of the testimonies in favor of the foundation. Though a religion of the Book, Christianity's community was one of belief, necessarily extendible and communicable—a community built on conversion not birth, radical change not kinship. Though intricately hierarchical and weighted with scholarship, it was obliged to allow space for dynamism and mobility. As a result, the very "difference" of the Amerindian peoples who came to be included in the *congregatio fidelium* could be interpreted as an unprecedented opportunity for proving the truth of the Word. The representation of such encounters produced narratives whose difference from the usual genres refracted the unusualness of the situation that gave rise to them.[39]

In such situations, only an eyewitness account could be considered an authentic one, and the missionary priests giving their opinions in this particular case are certain that this is precisely what is required of them: a *personal* account. Thus, Antonio Pérez contests the vulgar commonplaces spread by the ignorant about the Indians by saying that his own experience as a priest to these people has shown him how mistaken such opinions are.[40] A more sophisticated version of this authorizing strategy is apparent in his accounts of specific Indian women who have displayed their virtue by living like nuns without actually professing. Pérez describes a school for Indian girls that seems to be a de facto convent; but at the end of his description, he abandons the factual tone in favor of a strongly emotive account of how the Indian women's chaste behavior amazes him, leaving him at a conceptual loss. This comment, clearly directed at an equal (a man, a Spaniard) is meant to create a sense of complicity between Pérez and his reader, securing belief for the former's information.[41]

Clearly, this strategy can also be used to disqualify Indian women from profession as nuns. Having put forward the classic and philosophically respectable argument that Indians were inconstant and lacking in spiritual fortitude, José María de Guevarra caps his argument with an anecdote from his personal experience, moving the force of his reasoning from the general to the specific, and telling the story of an Indian woman who had put herself forward as a founding mother. She was placed by her confessor in the house of a devout woman, so she could live a retired life; but she proved unable to withstand even this degree of enclosure and left to return to her own home.[42]

In the testimonies, favorable judgment of the female sex does not usually signal any really radical thought about women's virtue but, in fact, involves a reinterpretation of various extremely traditional ideas of femininity. The most notable in relation to empire—and to the vulgarizations of the theory of Natural Slavery that have been discussed before—is the championing of the contractual nature of marriage. The analogy between a husband's role as steward of his wife—and the stewardship of all Indians that fell to the Spaniards as a result of the "natural" dependence of the Indians—meant that logically the Indian most easily maneuverable and open to conversion was the Indian woman. So, while the missionaries conceded that the Indian woman was virtuous, her virtue was tied to her submission within any contract.[43]

This very specific notion was complemented by more general ideas of the role of women in the household and in the education of children. Moralists of the period wrote at length on the importance of breast-feeding and considered maternal milk capable of transmitting religious values.[44] On the Peninsula, it was recommended that children not be given to wet nurses because the population was full of Jews and *moriscos,* and it was safer for a Christian mother to feed her own child.[45] The household, and Christianity itself, of course, was marked by a particular culture and this, in the colonial context, made it the obvious place upon which to build the foundations of a civil community. The priests in favor of the convent place great emphasis on the "double" mission that women's education in Christianity entails and the double profit it brings: both spiritual and political—a service to God and to the Spanish king.[46]

Once again, women's ability to learn and to transmit is tied to a conservative notion of femininity. That uncivilized persons were wholly the creatures of their passions was a commonplace, and their enslavement could only be remedied by education and environment. Women, of whatever race, were already a sex too closely tied to their passions and as such presented a particularly difficult case. The priests insist in these documents, however, that Indian women are receptive to their doctrinal teachings and are able to improve. In this case, the babbling barbarian and the querulous woman are doubly needy subjects for an education in rational speech. For Antonio Pérez, the ability of certain indigenous women, alienated as they were from the Logos because of their sex and their race, to learn Latin and to speak it "better than their natural language" was clearly a reason to celebrate the action of divine grace.[47] Indian women in their virtue were one of the true "marvels" of the New World. Their innate intellectual capacity is illustrated by their ability to copy actions and learn quickly from examples. These commonplace talents, cited by the priests, are ones that once again confine women to the lower faculties of the deliberative intellect. Thus, Antonio Pérez manages only partially to communicate the notion of sin to the female members of his congregation. They understand it to mean exclusively carnal sin and are incapable of conceiving its wider implications. Nevertheless, he claims that, in accordance with the accepted virtues of their sex, they are extremely zealous and devout and once informed of the evil of this sin, never fall into it.[48]

In all the accounts, the references to pagan history display the radical mobility of the Indian past in Spanish hands and show how, under the different requirements of each priest's political agenda, its degree of "civilization" and in fact its very nature as "past" could change. The strategic use of indigenous history in this way also, of course, indicates the centrality of the foundation of Corpus Christi in the debate as to whether the Indies were truly Christian (and civilized) or continued to be pagan (and barbaric). The fact is significant that both the positive and the negative testimonies break down into what could be termed broadly historicist accounts of this debate. To understand the implications of this historicist narrative turn, it is useful to return to the implications of the *extirpaciones de idolatrías* discussed earlier. The *extirpaciones* proper took place in Peru and were, overwhelmingly, a Jesuit enterprise. In Mexico the *extirpaciones* never spread so successfully, no doubt because of the stronger Mendicant presence and the fact that the evangelical mission had had more time to impose itself in New Spain. Nevertheless, the panic generated by the rediscovery of idolatry was shared by the two viceroyalties, and its management was not exclusively a Jesuit activity. Although there is clearly a political interpretation to be made of the Jesuit preeminence in at least the Peruvian *extirpaciones,* here I will concentrate on the effects the philosophical and religious mind-set of the *extirpador* implied for the representation of the colonial context, for the writing of its history, and for the way its future came to be envisaged.

Whatever the attitude to indigenous cultures, the rediscovery of idolatry was a moment for a kind of concentration upon them that had been abandoned since the first missionary efforts. The *extirpadores* were asked to write reports very much like the ones discussed here: first-person narratives that placed enormous value on empirical evidence and observation. The nature of the evidence and of what was observed also constituted a great innovation in the way of "thinking" the Indian people and their culture, the *extirpadores* becoming interested in how tradition was communicated and transmitted from one generation to the next.[49]

The testimonies about the foundation of a convent for Indian women form a body of texts that sheds greater light on the object of study of the *extirpadores.* Here the questions of how culture is transmitted, how the *habitus* in which religious practices are carried out is constructed, and of what the place of personal inventiveness and autonomy is in all this recover a gender dimension, precisely because they are asked in relation to women. The personal accounts of the priests concentrate primarily on the female reception of the Word in the New World, and on how this Word is interpreted and practiced by Indian women. The catalytic role women are seen to play in the process of transmitting religious (and by implication cultural) norms is eloquently described in Antonio Pérez' testimony. He claims that women have been quick to assimilate all the new religious practices, embracing them so fervently that they erase any past idolatrous customs, calling the "new" Christian practices their "customs."[50] Already in the New World chronicles, from Las Casas to Torquemada, the fear of an atavistic idolatrous historical memory can be identified, and the only solution to this cultural problem of accommodating a disturbing past is that of exchanging the old custom for a new one: straight substitution. Nevertheless, the field of custom was obviously a fluid one, and if it so readily changed from idolatrous to Christian, it might just as easily change back. This fear of the fluidity of the field of cultural practices and customs is in great part responsible for the obsession with purity that many of the writings of the period display. It is most certainly why the planned convent is reserved for "pure" Indian women and would not admit those of mixed race. Nevertheless, this purity was at odds with an evangelic mission that had by this point in the Conquest and colonization become synonymous with cultural negotiation.

The priests who were asked their opinion on the foundation of Corpus Christi acknowledge the presence of a racially and culturally heterogeneous society, a mestizo New World, however much they may have as a model the static victory of the Word that should have imposed its universal values throughout the empire. The plan to found a convent for Indian women unavoidably raised questions about the concept, direction, and success of the entire evangelical mission. It also required that the agents of the evangelizing project reflect on Indian society in ways that took into account issues of gender and that asked them to communicate their knowledge in a specific type of discourse that could claim the authority of truth. This they achieved not through the traditional rhetorical strategies usually associated with the defense of feminine virtue but instead through what could be described, not entirely inaccurately, as the provision of something approaching objective information.

In this sense, the testimonies provide magnificent examples of what Carlo Ginzburg, following Bakhtin, calls "dialogic" accounts.[51] They are representations of the colonial context that, when confronted with the absolute difference and reality of the New World, are unable to reproduce a "monologic" image of universality, be it theological, political, or cultural. Precisely because of this, they have a privileged access to this reality. Antonio Pérez' testimony provides a complete example of how complex these tensions can be. In his writing, they are resolved into a style of reporting that moves continuously from tradition to commonplace to personal experience in order to produce an authoritative opinion. Of course, in the moments of transition between these styles, the insights into the cultural context that Ginzburg attributes to the "dialogic" text can be glimpsed.[52] Pérez begins by generalizing about the Indian population of the colony and then moves swiftly on to the exceptions he has personally witnessed to these universal rules.[53] He goes on to allude to theories of bodily humors, as well as to the "strong women" of biblical tradition, and makes clear that he considers Indian women included in the grace God can dispense to the frailer sex to make it capable of heroic acts. The slippage between a scholarly disquisition on sexual difference, backed up by biblical precedents, and the examples necessary to promote the virtue of women who are racially different is evident in his writing.[54]

Another instance of this "dialogic" quality of description is provided by the discussion of alcohol consumption. The problem of alcoholism among the Indian population in New Spain was an acknowledged facet of late colonial reality and clearly was a consequence of the acculturation of the Indians.[55] In the testimonies of the priests, Indian alcoholism and the connection between its increase and the Christianization of the Indian population is presented as a fact. But significantly this is conceded only in order to emphasize the miraculous abstinence of Indian women from drink. Antonio Pérez' testimony provides an excellent example of this new narrative style. His general argument about the virtue of Indian men and women explodes in several directions at once. There is a historicist review of the traditional use of alcohol in Indian society and the changes wrought by contact with the Spaniards; a semiscientific account of the medicinal uses of alcohol considered to be licit; and a description of the violence Indian women were subject to from their husbands, who forced them to join in the drinking. This kind of narrative captures perfectly the transformation of intimate confessional knowledge into general information and of theoretical assertion into contextualized personal account.[56] Though the supporters of the foundation, in their enthusiasm, are quick to publish the success of evangelization, their accounts provide evidence of the uncomfortable realities that the evangelical mission created in its cultural interchanges.

Francisco de Vitoria argues for the need to assert the legitimacy of the relationship between the Spanish Crown and the Church, on the one hand, and between Spain and its newly acquired empire, on the other, in order to counter these uncomfortable realities of imperial rule. A curious aside on the legitimacy of marriage serves to illustrate his point:

> . . . Take the example of a man who is uncertain whether he is legally married to a particular woman. A doubt arises: is he bound to perform his conjugal duty with the woman? . . . He consults the experts; the answer is an emphatic negative. Nevertheless, the man decides on his own authority to disregard their verdict from love of the woman. Now in this case the man certainly commits a sin by having intercourse with the

woman, even if it is in fact lawful, because he is acting wilfully against conscience. It must be so, because in matters which concern salvation there is an obligation to believe those whom the Church has appointed as teachers, and in cases of doubt their verdict is law.[57]

The example establishes a clear hierarchy with the wife submitting to the husband, and the husband to the Church fathers. The lesson is clear: claims to property and authority over women, and by analogy over empires, have to be approved of by ecclesiastic learning and judgment. Vitoria uses this example of the legally dubious marriage later in the lecture to make the same point about the need to substantiate the legitimacy of relations of property and authority in the New World. He emphasizes that Tradition, in the guise of the experience of wise men, should be invoked as the ultimate authority in these matters. In very general terms, one could say that the novelty of the New World—and the intellectual and philosophical revolution and reevaluation it implied—lies behind Vitoria's anxiousness to secure its place within the familiar conceptual systems. Why, though, does woman and the correct legal and moral relationship to her appear at the heart of this worry in the guise of irrefutable example?

The testimonies of the priests concerning the foundation of Corpus Christi allow us to address this question from a very precise angle, examining how Tradition, embroiled in the practicalities of empire as well as the niceties of theory, attempted to legitimize its relationship with the real presence and symbolic significance of Indian women. The question of whether such Indian women were fit to become (Spanish) nuns prompted replies that abandoned the strictures of *any* tradition and its overarching or universalizing rhetoric. Although the accounts opposing the foundation of the convent do appeal in the first instance to scholarly authority and tradition, they also include narratives of lived experience and subjective perception to support their stance. The favorable accounts invert the importance of these techniques, giving prominence to personal testimonies that supply the empirical evidence for what can be deduced by induction from classical and biblical narratives about femininity within a colonial framework. In both cases, the affinities between the New World's novelty, the colonizing mission played out in it, and the narrative modes associated with each, may be interpreted as signaling the demise of grand narratives in this context and, paradoxically, to point to their resurrection and success as heterogeneous narrative forms. Writing, like other social practices in the colonies, both reflected the new reality and constructed it. The New World in this sense was less an imagined community (that is, a clearly defined and planned commonality) than an invented one: one made up on the spot and responsive to immediate demands and unavoidable circumstances. The Americas were a world in which rhetorically and theoretically decorous forms—and the complementarily civilized and harmonious society they were supposed to embody—were continuously fractured and reconstituted.

Afterword

*. . . estos santos caballeros profesaron lo que yo profeso, que es el ejercicio de las armas;
sino que la diferencia que hay entre mí y ellos es que ellos fueron santos y pelearon a lo
divino y yo soy pecador y peleo a lo humano.*

MIGUEL DE CERVANTES, *Don Quijote* (1615)[1]

Don Quijote's analogies between spiritual and chivalric quests and religious
and secular battles is comforting to the scholar studying Early Modern religious sources—an enterprise that is frequently justified by a similarly ana-
logic argument, claiming that religious sources constitute in some sense a
sacralization of the social cosmos. Analyses based on this type of approach
tend to concentrate on structural issues and broad description, but in *Colonial Angels* I have sought instead to look at the individual adventurers and
their stories. The spiritual adventures which these New World protagonists
attempt take place in an atmosphere of extreme religious upheaval. They are
stories born of extraordinary circumstance. It could be said that the evangelization of the New World was the Council of Trent's ultimate testing
ground, just as much as it was Catholic Spain's ultimate *reconquista*. As a
result, the narratives reveal not only the confrontation with the New but of
the Old with itself. They are both journeys to exotic lands and voyages of
return to origins.

The New Spanish convents and their pious heroines inhabit a universe
intricately patterned with tensions concerning gender and race, religious values and secular hierarchies, spiritual aspirations and mundane inducements.
The history of these convents and their inhabitants is multiplied into many
voices: the confessors, the nuns, the missionaries, the inquisitors. They prof-
fer a different history of empire to the familiar one—a history of the detail,
of the local, of the quotidian, perhaps even of the private—and certainly one
that embodies the tensions of center and periphery that were always inherent

in the imperial project. Subsequent philosophers of empire would confirm the impossibility, both practical and theoretical, of a hegemonic grip over something as extended and diverse, both geographically and culturally, as the Spanish empire. In the stories retold, we can see how attempts were made to hold all these contradictions together, at least at the level of narrative, and how such narratives did not necessarily define themselves through their opposition to or rejection of empire and cultural hegemony. Nevertheless, precisely because women and colonial society were their subjects, the narratives always in some way, in this case in their very heterogeneity, represented the margins of any project of transcendent union.

Not that rhetorical tropes could bring down the empire in any real political sense or liberate the women who wrote them. What they could do is create, and this book has sought to render some of this creative vitality back to both women as writers and to representations of them. Traditional confessional historians of the Mexican Church have, of course, been quick to dismiss the accounts of mystic trances, romantic stories, and the fantasies inspired by wicked Voltaire about colonial convents and nuns. Nevertheless, such fictions, as we have seen, had already crept into colonial accounts themselves. It was clearly impossible to maintain the purity of representations of the cloister when they were pressed into the transparently political and cultural uses we have identified.

The profound changes in European society in the period of the discovery and colonization of the New World were also, unsurprisingly, a moment for radical innovation in the narration of such changes. One could simply say, in narrative itself. The passage from *Don Quijote* makes clear how powerful such combinations of historical change and innovation in fictions and stories can be, pointing out that the difference between his own adventures and those of a saint is a question of ends rather than means; that the ironic and picaresque techniques of his antichivalric narrative are shared by innumerable hagiographies of the period. Naturally then, the difference that makes Don Quijote's adventures the first novel in Spanish and not another piece of baroque devotional literature is not purely a question of literary form but one of historical context too. It is also, of course, why the adventures of the women we have reviewed are not uncomplicated tales of angelic success or of imperial triumphs but instead are complex stories of personal experience and colonial realities.

por aberme ynquietado que conque nos en quieta la herma
na andrea de san francisco digo q̃ de de q̃ bine a este sto
conbento me ynquietado con lo muncho q̃ ablado en su
propia ada bansa y de su linage q̃ es contra Regla ablar
desto, y en el muncho ablar no faltara pecado, tanbien me
quietado la hermana andrea con ber q̃ es contra mi Reli
gion siendo mi propia ni ysuia y q̃ la esta persiguiendo no
quiriendo estar a la orden ni procurandolo sino estorban
dolo conquanto apodido no por q̃ no es bueno sino por q̃ no
selo Rueguen dando abiso al arsobispo si escribimos a nues
tro Rei para este fin de estar a nuestra orden sabiendo
q̃ para lo q̃ lo pretendemos no es para buscar nuestra co
modidad sino solo para ajuntarnos a nuestra obliga
ciones y guardar nuestra Regla y costitusiones y para al
cansar la persesion q̃ benimos a buscar, sabe dios nues
tro señor q̃ otra cosa no pretendo sino solo esto y sedasi
esto q̃ todas la q̃ lo pretendemos es a este fin y lo Jurare
y siendo esto asi abla esta Religiosa a los perlados mui
diferente de lo q̃ es y los Rita y dis fama a las q̃ mas
lo pretenden y aver mas diligencias como lo a echo con la
m̃ maria de santa ynes q̃ por q̃ meresa ser estimada y queri
da por su muncha birtu y Religion y prudencia la a per
seguido y dicho al perlado cosas y males de su Reberencia
q̃ no son para dichas ni oidas todo para desacreditarla y
ponella en mal con el abiendo sido dos beses su perlada
la tratata como si fuera una nobisia y a todo esto q̃ a echo
esta Religiosa con la m̃ m̃ de sta ynes esta nta la pasien
cia y prudencia de la m̃ q̃ sienpre a estado con un senbla
te con ella y asiendole el bien q̃ a podido y a consegado os
q̃ la amemos y perdonemos ynquieta nos tanbien ser q̃ sus
lenguages y sentimientos no son de carmelita descalsa
y si se trata de elecion de prelada dise q̃ mas quiere
burro q̃ cargue q̃ potro q̃ me derribe, y abla en si somos
criollas o gachupinas diciendolo a cada uno segun
su inclinacion, y en esta rreligion es mui dañoso es todo
la tierra por q̃ somos del cielo todos tanbien nos in
quieta con aberde conosido q̃ todo esto le nase de am
bision y deseo de ser tenida y estimada por mas de lo q̃
su partes merasen por q̃ no mira mas q̃ sus comodida des

Appendix 1

Confessional Letters of sor Sebastiana Josefa de la Santísima Trinidad. Circa 1744–1757. Biblioteca Nacional, Mexico.

Given constraints of space in the appendix, I have selected short excerpts from sor Sebastiana's letters rather than reproducing a single one. Although this practice, of course, obscures the form of her epistolary writing, what is lost in terms of integrity of the genre, I think is amply made up for in terms of communicating its variety and scope. As in the transcriptions throughout the book, I have modernized spelling and punctuation for ease of reading.

The Biblioteca Nacional in Mexico City has fifty-nine letters written by sor Sebastiana. On average, each has between five and seven thousand words. The excerpts in Appendix 1 total just over seven thousand words. I have divided the appendix into topics that reflect the general narrative movement of the majority of the letters; they begin with a reflection on the act of writing itself, then follow with a description of the spiritual experiences sor Sebastiana has undergone. Usually, both of these moments in the letters are interspersed with invocations to the confessor, or to God, or to herself, which I have gathered under the topic "Deseos/Desires." Finally, sor Sebastiana occasionally mentions the convent itself and the other nuns, sometimes even describing her relationship to them. These infrequent references clearly hold enormous interest for anyone concerned with the social and historical context in which sor Sebastiana wrote. They are reproduced in the section "La comunidad del claustro/The Convent Community."

La aventura de la escritura

Dulce Jesús ¿es posible que padezca tantas ansias, y para mayor tormento me mande la obediencia que escriba, y que lo haga a fuerza y con desconsuelo tanto que mejor tomara padecer un tormento, que tomar la pluma; y más experimentando tanto susto y embarazo que poniéndome a ello ni papel ni tinta; servía sólo para mancharme, y no parecerme que me convengan estas cosas? Pero por obedecer a Vuestra Paternidad me olvidaré de todo lo que me viene al pensamiento. (L6 f49)

Mi dulcísima madre y maestra María Santísima me facilite con su gracia lo que me manda la Santa Obediencia.

Sea todo lo que a mi pasa para gloria del Todo Poderoso, que es muy liberal para con todos y lo es conmigo, mereciendo menos; que tan mal me he sabido aprovechar de los bienes que me ha hecho [que] como ignorante, no los he sabido estimar. Me había parecido imposible volver a tomar la pluma, por muchos motivos suficientes, que me pusieron en mucho temor; a más de los muchos que siempre he tenido para escribir. Y de lo escrito tengo bastantes desconsuelos, que sabe Dios que ya lo hago por obedecer; venciendo todo lo mal que me parecen mis cosas, que es cierto, que en mí no hay cosa de provecho. Y si por beneficio de la bondad de Dios me da buenos deseos, no los ejecuto como debiera, para mayor vergüenza mía; que al presente me ocupa tanto, que mi alma esta tan encogida y el corazón tan atemorizado que no acierto a lo que tengo que hacer, que hasta de tratar cosa buena, me parece agravio por mi maldad; pero me veo precisada a obedecer, sin saber cómo. Que se haga la voluntad de Dios, y me reciba la amargura que me atormenta; que me tiene atontada para decir los admirables beneficios que obra Dios en esta miserable; deteniéndome mi cobardía y mucha ignorancia. Y por otra parte me mueve con suave fuerza su amor. (L22 f110–111)

Con tan bien ordenadas razones se manifiestan todas las necesidades que mi alma padece y unos amorosos sentimientos tan verdaderos y ardientes. Con tal abundancia de razones y todas tan acomodadas al intento y sin el uso de la lengua, se entiende en un modo claro muy diferente de éste que usamos; porque sin ver ni apercibir ninguna voz, es tan verdadero todo lo que se entiende, que es para alabar a Dios. ¡Qué enamorada queda el alma! ¡Qué firme en la sabiduría y Divino poder! Pero, ¡qué temor, qué vergüenza, qué conocimiento tan profundo para despreciar todas las cosas de esta vida como basura, como de verdad lo es, todo lo que en breve se ha de acabar por mucho que el mundo lo estime! (L51 f322)

Estando siempre con el desconsuelo de mi mucha maldad, y con un gran beneficio de llevarlo todo, por muy grave que sea, con paz interior, sin alborotarme, por más que me aflijan el corazón las amarguras, tristezas, y todo lo que se está ofreciendo, que a veces no se cómo entenderme en este laberinto de mi pensamiento, donde se me consume la esperanza de tal modo como si para mí no hubiera Dios, ni pudiera servirme. Son tan graves los pensamientos, que me acobardan para levantar el corazón, y por no dar gusto al Enemigo le digo: "Siendo tan gravísimas mis culpas, es más la misericordia de Dios. Y espero de su Divina Grandeza que me ha de perdonar y no ha de permitir que me engañen tus mentiras." Y haciéndole desprecio mi alma, con temor de ser tan miserable, le pido con vergüenza a Dios no me falte con su Divina Gracia, porque es cierto que me veo en evidente peligro por lo mucho que me persigue el Enemigo. Y más, turbándome los sentidos, mirando tanto enredo de cosas tan extrañas y otras tan penosas que no se pueden decir, ni entender cómo cabe tanto en el pensamiento que me revienta la cabeza, y pudiera perder la paciencia si la grandeza de Dios no me hubiera hecho el beneficio de no perder paz exterior ni la interior. (L42 f264)

La purísima luz de nuestra soberana reina María alumbre mi alma y me asista con todo. Con esta mucha tontera me suspendo, sin saber, ni entender lo que por mí pasa; y me ocupa la vergüenza, conociendo que de mi vida tan desbaratada no tengo qué poder decir, porque todos son disparates. Y Vuestra Paternidad me confunde, sabiendo las cosas que me está mandando que escriba, y teniendo tan perdida la memoria que por unas se olvidan otras, y siempre es lo menos de lo mucho que Vuestra Paternidad me apunta, que ponga lo más acertado. Me parece que todo se quemara para asegurarme de muchos peligros y mentiras, de malicia y de ignorancia; que de mi maldad todo puede ser para hallarme más cargada en la otra vida como lo estoy aquí, padeciendo sin provecho, como un bruto que estorba y le dan golpes y no entiende, y lo siente pero no aprovecha, como no entiende, se queda dando trabajo. (L57 f343−344)

Recogimiento y visiones

Y vi interiormente como una laguna que de las aguas salían unas manos muy feas y negras que me hubieran cogido porque yo estaba muy pegada a la orilla. A este tiempo vi a mi Señor, puesto en la cruz, y con mucho amor, bajó un brazo y abrazó mi alma que estaba en el lado del corazón, con mucha seguridad. Y el otro brazo le quedó pendiente de la cruz. Su amorosísimo rostro, muy humilde, inclinado a mi lado y muy lastimado pero muy lindo, y sus ojos bellísimos arrasados en lágrimas que le salían como hermosísimas perlas que causaban ternura y grande amor. (L24 f131)

Y la veo con la hermosura de reina y majestad de señora, ricamente vestida y también compuesta, y tal gracia que la hace más linda el bellísimo rostro, humilde y alegre, con un modo de mirar tan gracioso, modesto, y muy señor. El pelo muy lindo, que le adorna con mucho primor: unas hondas que le asientan por su divino rostro hasta bajo de los hombros con mucho lucimiento y todo recogido por el cuello. El pelo ensortijado todo; la hermosura y bizarría es admirable, toda linda, hermosísima y virtiendo alegría con algo de resplandor del blanco y nácar de su bellísimo rostro. (L24 f132)

Y no se cómo diga lo que siente mi corazón, que es un desfallecimiento, con suave aliento, que en el padecer hallo descanso. Pero conociéndome tan para nada, con gusto recibiera que a este cuerpo pesado Dios lo castigara con enfermedad que de ella muriera, que me atormenta vida mal empleada. Del parecer parece que hago y no se hace nada, las noches en miedos y fatigas y repugnancias las paso en el coro, que es una lástima, que pudiera hacer mucho y no hago nada. Cuando entro en el coro ¡qué pensamientos tan diversos, qué cosas pasan de perder la paciencia; con apariencia que dan espanto! Con los golpes son los sustos que entiendo no volver, porque temo que por mí se alborote el convento. Y porque me han visto; que es vergüenza. Los peligros de matarme cuando sin saber se acaba la vela y ando sin saber por donde. ¡Cosa temerosa! que me confunde. ¿Cómo será ésto? y lo que más siento es que sin luz, me estoy lo más de la noche, esperando que me cojan. Me asusto, pero no tengo alientos de pararme. Debo de ser una de día y otra de noche, según las [batallas] que padezco y la profundidad de allá dentro. A tiempos da Dios en estas noches unos tan conocidos movimientos que el alma y cuerpo se estremecen y hasta los pelos se erizan. (L15 f86)

En este conocimiento estaba cuando se armó tan espantoso ruido que toda me asusté y el corazón temblando. Daban unas carreras, como si se hicieran pedazos y tiraran con todo el coro bajo, dando unos tronidos como bombas que allí reventaban y como zastillos [*sic*] y salían unas voces o chillidos como de rabiosas monas (así me he querido explicar y digo cómo ello fué) que en el silencio de la noche sonaban con más espanto y congoja que me quedé espantada. (L25 f136)

Como me veo tan gravemente metida en pensamientos de mundo, como si me entrara en las casas de los ricos, así veo todo lo que hacen; cómo entran, y salen y cómo son servidos en el regalo de la mesa, con el gusto que viven y todo cuanto puede pasar lo estoy mirando y entendiendo con tanta viveza como si fuera cierto. Se me va la atención de lo que rezo. Que no me entiendo con tanto como se me pone delante, que sólo Dios me puede dar paciencia. (L33 f195)

Y así estoy, como con hambre de tratar con Dios y de tenerlo en mi corazón; y este deseo quita el amor a todas las cosas de esta mortal vida, envidiando muy diversas, a las que toda su vida han aprovechado en amar lo mejor y lo verdadero, que es la vida de mi alma, Dios, que no se cómo todos no le aman, y lo dejan todo, que no pierden nada. [   ] Y cómo quisiera decir esto; pero qué mal parece en mí, con mis locos pensamientos; tales que me sacan a las fiestas y plazas, comiendo de los puestos muchos que hay en tales funciones, que las veo y las tuviera por ciertas, sino me hallara en este coro. (L9 f72)

Halléme privada y ajena de todos los sentidos; andando por unas calles que no se podía dar paso, de un asqueroso lodo y arcos. Las paredes muy altas y negras, muchos hombres andaban y yo entre ellos, muy espantada y llena de confusión, sin saber lo que me había sucedido, ni esperanzas de salir de tan grave aflicción, que no es posible decir cómo yo estaba, y lo mucho que padecí. Cuando me sentí libre y me hallé en el coro, me parecía imposible. Con mucho encogimiento para mi alma y muy espantada (porque me había parecido muy cierto haber estado mucho tiempo) no me hallaba merecedora de estar libre, y con el sosiego y amor que mi alma tenía a mi Dios. ¡Qué ternuras, qué palabras, qué agradecimientos y alabanzas y dulzuras! Y más cosas, que ya Vuestra Paternidad puede conocer. (L23 f129)

Estando en este dilatado campo de dolorosas memorias, sin saber cómo, me vi en un lugar espantosísimo, como él era, no sabré decir, pero para darme algo a entender, sería como el más triste barrio de los más retirados; era muy grande, y habían muy pocas casitas que de verlas se arrancaba la alma [*sic*] de tristeza. Andaban unos que parecían hombres, muy zancudos, hablando en lengua que no se entendía. Vi una cosa muy alta que parecía torre que no se decir cómo era. Allá en lo último había como tabladito en donde estaban bailando y saltando que se quedaban en el aire. La luz era como cuando va llegando la noche, pero bastante para verlo todo, que había sombras que me asombraban. Lo que padecí en este desamparo, tan sola que ninguno se acercaba a mí, y todo lo estaba mirando y agonizando, con tan horrorosos tormentos y dolores tan intorelables que me parece imposible que los haya en esta vida. (L24 f134)

En una calle muy ancha había una fuente de agua en que estaban lavando (la luz era poca). Andaban unas mujeres, como que salían a misa. Iba una con su saya parda, toda tapada con su manto, y muy alta. Yo, pensando que era la que había visto lavando, la llamaba tres veces, por su nombre, y no me respondió, volvió la cara con mucha cólera y al verle tan espantosa y la nariz grande con punta dije: "Este es el diablo." Allí me hubiera caído muerta del espanto tan horroroso, que no se cómo decir los tormentos tan atroces. ¡Qué agonías tan mortales sentía en el corazón y con un pavor y miedo que me estaba sofocando sólo de lo que había visto! Que por no haberlo visto, hubiera padecido las penas del infierno. Estando con este mortal miedo y horrorizada de cara tan fea, que me parece imposible que pueda haber cosa tan espantosa, deseaba que en el mimso instante se me hubiera borrado del pensamiento tal cosa. (L25 f136–137)

DESEOS

¡Oh, cómo quisiera ser una santa! Con qué ansias me quisiera ver libre del pesado estorbo del cuerpo y de estos pensamientos mundanos que me aturden sin provecho, sin pensar en cosa buena. Sólo me quedo insensata y tan disgustada y sin esperanza de Dios que en nada hallo consuelo. La vida me es pensosa, la muerte, que se tarda, siendo breve. No me hallo con las gentes, y me alivio estando sola, que para pasar siempre sin consuelo es cosa dura. (L10 f74)

Con qué ansias desea mi alma infundir esta verdad a todas las gentes, y en especial a todas las religiosas, que me dan lástima verlas tan cuidadosas de que no les falten las cosas temporales, que parece les falta el tiempo para procurarlo y pedirlo a las personas de afuera, sujetándose a muchas penalidades, que todas se podían excusar dejándose a la providencia divina, con seguridad que no se puede olvidar un Padre tan poderoso que de verdad nos ama. (L31 f173)

Como soy tan ruin, no aguantan mis flacas fuerzas el mucho peso que me oprime con grande fatiga, que me veo en puntos de perder la paciencia y de hablar disparates y dejarme perder, porque nada me aprovecha. [Soy] tan furiosa en la rebeldía de todo lo malo que doy bramidos como si fuera el más rabioso bruto, padeciendo penosas ansias que me dejan como una simple. (L37 f221)

Se me ha dado tan claro conocimiento del fin de las cosas de esta mortal vida que todos lo saben, pero yo me pensé dueña de todas las estimaciones, hermosa con todos los adornos de la naturaleza y riquezas de la tierra, muy conocida y alabada, y todo muy al vivo me movió a entender la brevedad con que todo se acaba por mucho que dure. ¿Y de qué sirven las admiraciones de los primores y divertimiento [*sic*] si en un instante todo se acaba? (L6 f49)

Pocos dias me duró este alivio y paz, viniendo a mi alma tan horrorosa tempestad de congojas que no me entendía de desconsuelo, con un enojo con Vuestra Paternidad, como si tuviera la culpa de todo mi mal, estando inocente de lo que me pasaba. Yo no se decir las amarguras que mi alma padeció, que estaba traspasado el corazon de dolor sin poder más del ansia, tan suspensa que no podía hablar una palabra ni rezar, con un golpe en el corazón que bramaba, y conociendo que no me convenía que me confesara Vuestra Paternidad. Sentía mi bobera haber dicho los pecados y todo [lo] demás sin necesidad sino había de proseguir, y así tenía vergüenza, como también el que a Vuestra Paternidad le parecían muy mal mis cosas; y que si yo volviera, ya no había de tener consuelo y que sólo lo preciso diría que lo demás era peligroso. De repente me daba un aborrecimiento a mi padre de mi alma, que lo quería despreciar con malas palabras. Estaba como un gentil. (L26 f146)

La comunidad del claustro

Doy principio con lo que me manda la santa obediencia que presto, y al pie de la letra, deseo ejecutar sino fuera tonta, que apenas acierto como ha de ser; y por tener todas mis cosas aborrecidas. Que como sino fuera, quisiera estar olvidada y con mucha razón; que de nada sirvo, ni de tantito alivio a la comunidad porque de la celdita al coro no paso a más, y a lo sumamente preciso, sin ver ninguna cosa de lo que hacen en el convento de festejos, ni sé cómo es todo el convento, y lo preciso con muy poco cuidado, sin conocer a las niñas ni mozas, algunas y muy pocas conozco. Pero atiendo tan poco, que parece que no estoy en lo que veo, que me quedo como si no viera nada. Cuando me veo por cosa precisa con las religiosas, y que me hablan, no las entiendo de vergüenza que como no estoy hecha a hablar, estoy como extraña y siempre apresurada, que no puedo sosegar hasta estar sola, que me parece se pierde el tiempo; pero conociendo el favor que recibo de que me tengan en su compañía, igualándome en el hábito que traigo y en que me den lo que a todas, para mantenerme. Que me alegrara que para mí faltara, por no tener necesidad, que para lo que yo merezco de lo que desecharan tuviera bastante. Pero conozco que nada tengo, que el estar en el coro y pisar el convento es gracia, y lo agradezco. (L28 f154–155)

Y me veo muy fatigada, por no hallar salida para despegarme de las personas que tanto me atormentan, pues sin voluntad mía he tenido a esta hermana que habrá mas de diez años; y en ellos todo ha sido atormentarme con la continuación de muy graves enfermedades, dando con ellas bastante trabajo a la santa comunidad, y con la necesidad de haber de entrar padres a ayudarla a bien morir. Para mi mayor tormento, velándola todas las noches y dias sin más descanso que el tiempo que asistía con la comunidad a las horas y maitines; y así sólo podía cumplir con el oficio divino, por darme la Divina Majestad tan grande martirio en ver padecer a la enferma sin poderle dar alivio y estar todo a mi cuidado, que no podía faltar a lo mucho que se ofrecía de servir [   ] porque estoy en lugar de moza. Y lo hago con mucho gusto, pero con mucho trabajo, porque me faltan las fuerzas. Y lo que padezco con esta enferma es mucho más, por ser preciso que esta cruz sea de participantes, y haber de tolerar los diferentes pareceres y disgustos que me atarantan y no puedo entender cosas de sentimientos, y faltar a la paz, que es la vida del alma. (L55 f336–338)

Estoy sin poder sosegar con los temores de la enfermera, que ya no se cómo entenderme; y haber de tratar y contratar con las gentes, disimulando la profundidad de mi desconsuelo, tratándolas con amor y agradeciéndoles la caridad que me hacen. Pero el Enemigo las tienta con enojo y sentimientos de cosas, que yo ni se, ni entiendo. Dios lo permite para ejercicio de paciencia, que bien se ha menester, con las persecuciones y desabridas palabras que han pasado a decirme tan graves cosas delante de varias religiosas, que no me atrevo a decirlas, que sólo así se pudieran decir; que todo lo malo yo lo hacía. Y al entender de esta persona, no había cosa en el convento tan para nada, mentirosa, aulladora, puerca, inútil, engañando para que me tuvieran por santa. Decíame tanto, que pocas veces me decía mi nombre. Yo le procuraba dar gusto y servirla, sin darme por agraviada, mas no valían mis diligencias para contentarla, con grandes agravios me pagaba el amor que le tengo. No podía reprimir la cólera que le precipitaba. (L55 f339)

Estando en Betlém hubo grandes funciones de visitas de arzobispos y de virrey; que se aderezaba la casa de curiosas alhajas; de músicas, y graciosas loas y danzas y muchos divertimientos [*sic*] tan de gusto, que las mejores personas entraban que gustaban de la gracia especial que han tenido para todo. De todo, nada vi ni oí. Los alborotos, que por esto se ocasionaban, me disgustaban, pero me lo callaba; conociendo que yo estaba como si no estuviera; como inútil, que no servía para estar entre señoras. Poca cuenta se hacia de mí, que para mí era consuelo. Era tan poco lo que miraba; que muchas entraban y estaban bastante tiempo y se salían sin conocerlas, ni saber cosa, que me las mentaban pensando que las hubiera visto. Con la precisión de servir algunas pocas enfermas, a veces me salía sin ver lo que había; muy curiosos aderezos de casas, y me salí sin verlas, y muchas cosas se ofrecían; de donde se sacaba tener poco que hablar, como sucede hablar de lo que se ha visto, y notar algunas faltas. De no ver, se guarda mejor el silencio, que es muy importante para no pecar de muchos modos, y muy provechoso. (L22 f117)

The Writing Adventure

Sweet Jesus, is it possible that I should suffer so many anxieties and that for my greater torment I be commanded to write and obliged to do so, with such unwillingness that I would rather suffer another torment than endure the use of a pen? Especially as I feel so frightened and embarrassed that when I sit down to do it, the paper and pen only serve to stain me, and to confirm to myself that these things are not suitable for me? But in order to obey Your Grace, I will forget everything that comes to my mind. (L6 f49)

May the grace of Holy Mary, my mother and teacher, aid me to do what holy obedience commands.

May everything that happens to me be for the greater glory of the Almighty, whose liberality extends to everybody, and certainly to me, though I deserve less, not having profited from the favors He has shown me, my ignorance preventing me from recognizing their value. It seemed impossible to take up the pen again, having sufficient reasons to be very frightened, on top of the many that I have always had about writing, and I regret very much what has already been written. God knows I only do it in order to obey, overcoming how bad my things seem to me—which is true—for in me there is nothing worthy. If God's kindness allows me good intentions, I never fulfill them as I ought, causing me even greater shame. At present this preoccupies me so much that my soul is so withered and my heart so frightened that I am incapable of doing what I have to. Even having to do a good thing seems to exacerbate my wickedness, but I must obey, without knowing how. May God's will be done, and may He receive the bitterness that torments me and has me befuddled, unable to speak of the admirable benefits that God has wrought in this miserable one, my cowardice and great ignorance stops me, but at the same time, His love moves me with its sweet force. (L22 f110–111)

My soul's needs manifest themselves with such well-ordered reasons and such true and ardent loving feelings, with such an abundance of justifications and so fitted to the purpose, and all without using language, that everything is understood in a very clear way, far different to the one we use. For without perceiving a voice, everything is truly understood; praise be to God! How enamored the soul is! How solid in knowledge and divine power! And how great the fear and shame, how profound the knowledge that we should disdain the things of this life as if they were rubbish, as they truly are, for everything that exists will soon enough be finished, however much the world esteems it! (L51 f322)

[I am] still suffering from sadness at my great evil, and yet with the great benefit of being able to cope with it all, however grave, with interior peace, without becoming distraught, no matter how much bitterness and sadness afflicts my heart. With everything that is happening, sometimes I do not know what to make of this labyrinth of my thoughts where all my hope is consumed so completely; it is as if there were no God for me, and He could not help me. My thoughts are so grievous that they make me cowardly and unable to lift up my heart. But in order not to satisfy the Enemy I say to him: "Though my guilt is extreme, God's mercy is greater. I hope that His Divine Majesty will pardon me and will not allow your lies to deceive me." My soul thus dismissing him, fearful of being such a miserable thing, I shyly ask God that His divine grace should not fail me, for it is true that I am in real danger from the Enemy who persecutes me so much. Moreover, my senses are overcome perceiving such a confusion of very strange things, and others so sad that they cannot be expressed or understood. So much squeezes into my thoughts that my head feels as if it is exploding, and I would lose my patience had not the might of God given me this gift of not losing exterior or interior peace. (L42 f263–264)

May the pure light of our sovereign queen Mary illumine my soul and help me with everything: With this great befuddlement I find myself suspended, without knowing or understanding what is happening to me. Shame overcomes me, knowing that I am able to say little about my disorganized life, for everything in it is foolishness. Your Grace confuses me, you already know the things you order me to write and my memory is so bad that I have forgotten some and remember others. They are always only a part of the whole that Your Grace notes that I should write down accurately. I wish everything could be burnt to safeguard me from many dangers, lies, malice, and ignorance. Because of my wickedness, it is very possible that I should find myself more tormented in the next life than I am in this, suffering as I do like a beast that annoys and is punished with blows but does not understand; it feels them, but does not learn, and as it does not profit by them, not understanding, it gives only more trouble. (L57 f343–344)

PRAYER AND VISIONS

I saw in an interior mode something like a lake. From the water came ugly black hands that could have caught me because I was very near the shore. At that moment I saw my Lord on the cross, who with great affection lowered an arm and embraced my soul that was on the side of my heart, comforting me greatly. His other arm remained on the cross. His loving face, very humble, inclined toward me, was terribly injured, but very beautiful;

his wonderful eyes bathed in tears that fell like beauteous pearls, inspired tenderness and profound love. (L24 f131)

I see her with all the beauty of a queen and majesty of a great lady, dressed richly and so gracefully composed that her face appears more beautiful, humble, and happy, with a way of looking so charming, modest, and sovereign. Her hair was lovely, decorating her with great style, waves coming down her divine face just below her shoulders with much grace, and all tied back around her neck. Her hair was curled, its beauty and style admirable, she was completely exquisite, lovely, and gave off happiness with the resplendent white and pink of her beautiful face. (L24 f132)

I do not know how to express what my heart feels; it is a fainting, with a gentle sigh, so that in the suffering I find comfort. But knowing myself unworthy, I would willingly accept that this heavy body be punished by illness and die from it because nothing torments me more than my useless life. As far as appearances are concerned, it looks as if I do nothing; the nights in the choir pass amidst fear and fatigue and disgust. It is such a waste because I could accomplish many things and instead do nothing. When I go into the choir, I have so many different thoughts, so many things make me lose patience with their terrible apparitions, with blows causing me such frights that I resolve never to go back for fear of disturbing the entire convent. They have seen me, and it is shameful. The danger of killing myself, when the candles go out and I walk about without knowing where; it is terrible! I am confused at how this is so; all I know is that for the greatest part of the night I am without lights, worried that they will find me. I get frightened but I do not have the strength to stand up. I must be one person by day and another by night according to the battles I undergo and the depth there is inside there. Sometimes God causes certain familiar movements that make my soul and body tremble, and even my hairs stand on end. (L15 f86)

I was in this state when such a terrible noise began that I became terrified and my heart trembled. They ran about as if they were tearing themselves to pieces and bringing the lower choir down. Such groans like bombs exploding and like fireworks. Voices and screams like rabid monkeys (I have explained myself in this way and thus am telling how it was) that in the silence of the night they resounded with such fright and pain that I was terribly shocked. (L25 f136)

I find myself so utterly immersed in worldly thoughts it is as if I went into rich people's houses and saw all they did. How they come and go, how they are feasted at table, with what indulgence they live. Everything that happens I observe and perceive so vividly it is as if it were real, and my attention wanders from my prayers. I cannot cope with everything that is put before me, only God can give me patience. (L33 f195)

So I am like this—hungry to be near to God and to have Him in my heart. This desire takes away any love for the things of this mortal life, wanting very different things; things such as those cherished by people who have dedicated themselves to loving the best and the truest thing that is the life of the soul. I do not know how everyone does not love it, and leave the rest, for they lose nothing. I so want to say this, but it ill befits me, with my crazy thoughts that drag me out to parties and public squares, where I eat from the many stalls that there are on such occasions, and I see them so clearly that I would believe they were real if only I did not find myself in this choir. (L9 f72)

Stunned and lacking all senses, I saw myself walking through streets difficult to move through. There was disgusting mud. There were arches, the walls were huge and black. There were many men, and I walked among them, very frightened and confused, not knowing what had happened to me, and without any hope of getting out of such an affliction. It is impossible to say how I felt and how much I suffered. When I felt that I was free and found myself in the choir, it all seemed impossible. My soul was very cowed and frightened (for it seemed true that I had been there for a long time), and I did not think I deserved to be free and enjoying the comfort and love that my soul received from God. What tenderness, what words, what giving of thanks and showering of praises, what sweetness! And many other things that Your Grace may understand. (L23 f129)

Dealing with this extensive subject of painful memories, not knowing how, I found myself in a terrifying place. It is impossible to describe it, but to make myself understood I will say it was like the saddest, most remote quarter of a city. It was very big and there were very few houses, to see them pained the soul with sadness. What looked like long-legged men walked about speaking an incomprehensible language. I saw a very high thing that looked like a tower, I do not know how else to describe it. At the top there was something like a stage and they were dancing and jumping up in the air. The light was like when night is coming, but enough to see everything by, and there were shadows that amazed me. How I suffered in this desolation, so alone that no one came close to me, and I was looking and agonizing over everything, with such terrible torments and intolerable pains that it seems impossible that such things can exist in this life. (L24 f134)

In a very broad street, there was a water fountain in which some women were washing. The light was very dim. It was as if they had just come from mass. One wore a dark cloak, completely covered by her scarf. She was very tall. I thought she was one of the women I had seen washing, and I called her by her name three times. She did not answer me and eventually turned her head in anger. When I saw her terrifying face with a huge pointed nose, I said, "This is the devil." I would have fallen down dead there and then from the terrible fright. I cannot describe the dreadful torments. My heart felt such deadly agonies and such a shock and fear that I was suffocating only from what I had seen! I would have rather suffered the pains of hell than have seen it. Being thus mortally frightened and horrified by such an ugly face that it seemed impossible to me that a terrifying thing like that should exist, I wished that at that very moment the memory of it could be erased from my mind. (L25 f136–137)

Desires

Oh how I wish I were a saint! I desire so much to see myself free of the heavy distraction of this body and of all these worldly thoughts that assail me without profit, without a thought for anything worthy. I feel foolish and so displeased and without hope of God that nothing consoles me. Life is hard to bear; death though brief takes too long to arrive. I am uncomfortable with people and find ease only by myself, though to be like this, without succor, is a hard thing. (L10 f74)

With what yearning my soul wants to teach this truth to all people and especially to all nuns. I pity their concern and anxieties about being deprived of temporal things. It seems they never have enough time to search for them and ask for them from people outside, exposing themselves to many troubles that they could avoid by entrusting themselves to divine providence, in the certainty that such a powerful Father who loves us so truly could not forget us. (L31 f173)

I am so base that my waning forces cannot withstand the heavy weight that presses me down causing me such great tiredness that I am on the verge of losing my patience and saying foolish things and letting myself go because nothing is of any use to me. The rebellion of all evil things is so strong that I grunt like the most rabid beast and suffer such pitiful anxieties that they leave me like a simpleton. (L37 f221)

I have been given such a clear understanding of the end of all things in this mortal life, things that everyone knows. But I had thought myself the possessor of all admiration, beautified with all the decorations of nature and wealth of the earth, renowned and praised. And I was moved to understand very vividly that all this ends with extreme brevity, however long it might last. Of what use are admiration, courtly gestures, and enjoyment if in an instant all is finished? (L6 f49)

This peace and calm lasted only a few days, my soul entering such a storm of regrets that I could not understand my desolation. I felt so much anger against you, my Venerable Father, as if you were responsible for all my pains, though unaware of all that was happening to me. I cannot describe the bitterness that my soul suffered; my heart was pierced by pain so much so that I could do nothing because of the anxiety. I was so suspended that I could not say a word or pray, having such a wound in my heart that I cried out. I knew it would be better not to confess to you, Father, for I was sorry that in my foolishness I had told you these sins and everything else when there was no need as they were not to go on. So I was ashamed, and also of the fact that my things seemed wicked to Your Grace, and if I were to go back to you I would get no consolation, for I would say only what was necessary, the rest being dangerous. Suddenly I would feel such disgust for the Father of my soul that I would want to insult him with bad words. I was like a gentile. (L26 f146)

The Convent Community

I will begin what saintly obedience requires of me, and I want to do it quickly and to the letter, only I am stupid and can hardly accomplish it properly because I hold all my things in great disdain. I would want to be ignored as if I did not exist, and this would be fitting because I am good for nothing, not even being able to comfort the community just a little bit. I go out from my small cell to the choir only when necessary, without looking around, seeing none of the festivities they have in the convent. I am not even aware of what the convent is like, knowing only those bits that are absolutely necessary and even those not well. Of the little girls and young women, I know only a few. But I pay such little attention that it seems as if I see nothing. When I have to see the nuns for a specific thing, and they speak to me, I cannot understand them because I am so embarrassed and not made for speaking. I am like a stranger and always in a great hurry, and I cannot calm down until I am alone. But I am aware of the great favor they do me by having me in their company, raising me to the status of their order and that they give me the same things they give everyone else to nourish me. I do not need it all and am only worthy of the leftovers; that would be plenty for me. But I know I have nothing of my own and that to be in the choir and to step inside the convent is a gift, and I am grateful for it. (L28 f154–155)

I am very tired as I cannot find any way to free myself from the people that torment me. Without wishing it, I have had this sister with me for ten years, during which she has tormented me with continual serious illnesses that have also disturbed this saintly community because of the repeated need for priests to come and administer the last rites. For my greater torment, I have had to sit up with her every night and day, with no other break than when I went with the community to pray and to matins. Even like this, I could only recite the divine office, for His Divine Majesty had given me such a martyrdom of seeing the sick nun suffer without being able to ease her pain, and of being solely responsible so I could not fail to do the many things that were required. I am like a servant, and I do it with much pleasure but also with much trouble for I am very weak. What I endure with this sick nun is terrible because it is a cross I bear in which many participate. I have to hear and tolerate different opinions and preferences that confuse me, and I cannot bear these problems of favoritism and preference for they break the peace, which is the true life of the soul. (L55 f336–338)

The anxieties proper to being a nurse leave me without any moment of calm, and I do not know how to cope. I have to talk and deal with people while disguising the depth of my despair, treating them with love and thanking them for the charity they show me. But the Enemy tempts them with anger and strong feelings about things that I neither know or understand. God allows this in order to exercise my patience. I have really needed this, given the persecutions and ugly words that have come to be said to me in front of various nuns. I do not dare repeat them, they could only be said because of this (demonic inspiration); claiming I did every evil. In this person's opinion, there was nothing more worthless in the convent: a liar, moaner, dirty, useless, feigning so as to be thought a saint. She would call me so many things, she hardly ever pronounced my name. I tried to please her and serve her without letting it be understood that I was hurt, but my attentions did not please her, and she would pay back the love I feel for her with great insults, not able to contain the anger that I drove her into. (L55 f339)

While I was in Bethlehem, there were great ceremonies, visits by the archbishops and by the viceroy. The convent was adorned with elaborate decorations, music and gracious masques, dances, and many entertainments. All this was done with such good taste that the most noble people, who appreciated such graciousness, came to the convent. Of all this, I neither heard nor saw a thing. The disturbances that were caused by such things upset me, but I said nothing, knowing that I was there as if I did not exist; useless, not serving any purpose amidst these ladies. Little notice was paid me and this was a great comfort. I looked about me so little that many women entered (the convent) and were there for a long period of time and left again without my having known them. They would mention them by name, thinking I knew them, and I did not know them. Sometimes when attending to the sick I would leave (the cell) without having seen any of the rich decorations, I would go having seen nothing and noticed none of the many things that happened. Due to this, I have little to say in the usual way one sees things and talks about them, noting certain faults. By not seeing, one keeps a more perfect silence, which is very advantageous and is also necessary so as not to sin in many different ways. (L22 f117)

Appendix 2

Archivo General de la Nación. Ramo Inquisición. Vol. 581,
exp. 1. Autos hechos en el convento de San José de religiosas
Carmelitas Descalzas de esta ciudad sobre una carta escrita
a la superiora de dicho convento por el señor arzobispo don
Mateo de Buqueiro en que daba a entender se tenía por las
religiosas algunos errores y heregías, 1661.

ANDREA DE SAN FRANCISCO

07/feb/1661

Dijo que en estos dos dias de fiesta antecedentes ha encomendado a Nuestro Señor muy de veras este negocio. Y no quisiera en ninguna manera que se ofrecieran materias en que hubiese de tocar a las honras de nunguna persona, cuanto menos de prelados y de monjas sus hermanas, y de religiosos. Pero que como quiera que el Santo Oficio viene a inquirir; no es bien que la inocencia padezca, y los culpados queden con victoria; y así se ha determinado de decir [   ] en el Santo Tribunal todo lo que ha sabido y entendido desde que entró religiosa en este convento, segura de que todo quedará en secreto, y así dice:

Que cuando esta declarante entró en este santo convento, que a los nueve de enero próximo pasado de este año de 661 hizo 27 años, entendiendo que venía al cielo, o por lo menos a donde seguramente había de alcanzar la salvación; hallóle en grande alteración y bandos porque la madre Mariana de la Encarnación, [   ] fundadora de este convento que habrá trece años que murió, y la madre Inés de la Cruz, que fue la otra fundadora

[f88r]

que murió el año de 633, y vinieron del convento de Jesús María de esta ciudad a fundar este convento, movidas de Dios Nuestro Señor, se conservaron en suma paz y hermandad hasta que entraron estas madres gachupinas que fueron la madre Bernarda de San Juan, ya difunta, la madre María de Santa Inés su hermana, la madre Margarita de San Bernardo, y la madre Ana de San Bartolomé, y pusieron discordia entre esas dos madres fundadoras. Y la dicha madre Bernarda era mujer muy entendida y capaz, y se había criado en la compañía en el palacio de la condesa de Montalbán, y pasó a esta Nueva España en un navío con religiosos Carmelitas Descalzos que venían a ésta su provincia, de que cobró grande afecto a dichos religiosos, y ellos a la dicha madre Bernarda de San Juan y a la dicha su hermana, María de Santa Inés. Con que luego dichos padres estando ya en esta ciudad, trataron de que se les diese el hábito en este convento a las dos dichas hermanas; como con efecto se hizo por medio de la madre fundadora Inés de la Cruz, que pidió a Juan de Castillete que las nombrase por sus capellanas de dos [capellanías] que dotó perpetuamente en este santo convento. Y la dicha madre Inés de la Cruz, como era gachupina y natural de Toledo, les cobró grande afición. Y la dicha madre Bernarda de San Juan, que como ha dicho tenía buenas partes naturales y atractiva, ganó de manera la voluntad de la dicha madre Inés de la Cruz que acabada de profesar y muy joven la puso por tornera. Cosa que maravilló al padre fray María Calollete,

[f88v]

religioso Agustino y hermano de la dicha madre Inés de la Cruz. Y a la dicha madre de Santa Inés la hizo pedagoga de las novicias, siendo así que entró de catorze años de edad, y [   ] años en el noviciado, con que se hecha [*sic*] de ver qué edad tendría para ser pedagoga; y aún maestra de novicias, porque la dicha madre Inés de la Cruz, que era priora y maestra de novicias estaba muy enferma y no podía acudir al oficio. Y que las demás religiosas en que había muy grandes siervas de Dios que habían vivido como unas bestias sin discurso, sujetas a la obediencia, viendo lo que pasaba con dichas dos hermanas Bernarda de San Juan y María de Santa Inés, se comenzaron a inquietar y a tener envidia, y acudieron a la otra fundadora, la madre Mariana de la Encarnación, viéndose que no tenían cabida con la madre Inés de la Cruz. Y la dicha madre Mariana de la Encarnación, después de haber tenido grandes controversias con la dicha madre Inés de la Cruz con que se ha cavado la paz de las dichas madres fundadoras recurrió a [   ] Francisco Manzo, pidiéndole que quitase de maestra de novicias a la madre María de Santa Inés, porque [de] dos novicias que tenía sólo quería tener que la una, que era la dicha Ana de San Bartolomé, que por ser gachupina la querían mucho y hacían mucho por ella, y la otra que era Teresa de Jesús, que era criada de Querétaro, la querían echar del convento. Y dicho senor arzobispo quitó el oficio a dicha madre de Santa Inés

[f89r]

y puso en él a la dicha madre Mariana de la Encarnación, que lo había sido de todas las religiosas que había en el convento, menos [de] las dichas dos gachupinas hermanas Bernarda de San Juan y María de Santa Inés que las agregó así la dicha madre Inés de la Cruz. Y que desde entonces quedó esta comunidad partida y las cuatro gachupinas Bernarda de San Juan, María de Santa Inés, Margarita de San Bernardo, y Ana de San Bartolomé, por haber muerto en este tiempo la dicha madre Inés de la Cruz, publicaron y dieron a entender y lo dijeron al dicho Juan de Castillete que había muerto la dicha madre Inés de la Cruz, su hermana, la dicha madre Mariana de la Encarnación, por haberle quitado el oficio de maestra de novicias a la dicha María de Santa Inés. Y que así que tomó el hábito esta declarante, reconoció esta división. Y sucedió que dicho arzobispo Francisco Manzo quitó con deshonor el oficio de capellán de dicho convento al dicho don Alvaro de Cuevas, que fue después deán de la Iglesia Catedral de esta ciudad [   ], señor obispo de Oaxaca, cuya virtud y espíritu es bien conocido en este reino. Y que la causa está [   ] para Dios, aunque tuvo de ella noticia esta declarante, y fue el evitar una grande ofensa de Dios Nuestro Señor, que estaba para suceder en este convento, la cual noticia le dieron a esta declarante la dicha madre fundadora Mariana de la Encarnación y las madres Catalina de Cristo y su hermana Francisca de San José. Y puso en su lugar el señor arzobispo Manzo, [   ] F [   ] Miranda, grande aficionado

[f89v]

de las cuatro gachupinas, que de mercader que había sido en la ciudad de la Puebla se ordenó, e hizo mucha las partes de las dichas cuatro madres con dicho señor arzobispo Manzo. Y que sucedió que la dicha madre Catalina de Cristo escribió una carta al dicho don Alvaro de Cuevas, significándole el sentimiento con que estaban la dicha madre fundadora Mariana de la Encarnación, ella, y Francisca de San José su hermana, y las demás religiosas de lo que le había sucedido; y que el dicho don Alvaro Cuevas escribió otra en respuesta a la dicha madre Catalina de Cristo, diciéndole, entre otras cosas, que como dicho señor arzobispo Manzo le había quitado la ocupación que tenía en este convento sin interés alguno, le había de quitar Dios a dicho arzobispo su mitra. Y que teniendo noticia las cuatro madres gachupinas de esta respuesta, que paraba en poder de la madre Leonor de San Diego, religiosa del convento de Santa Isabel, Franciscanas de esta ciudad, le escribieron un billete contrahaciendo la letra de la dicha madre Catalina de Cristo; en que le decía que dicha Catalina de Cristo y Francisca de San José su hermana estaban en la reja del coro bajo de la iglesia aguardando la dicha respuesta que tenía en su poder, con que la dicha madre Leonor de San Diego se la envió y paró en poder de las dichas cuatro madres gachupinas, que dieron con dicho papel en manos del dicho arzobispo Manzo;

[f9or]

que viendo lo que contenía y escribía el dicho don Alvaro de Cuevas, concibió grande ira contra él, y contra las religiosas que le comunicaban, y dentro de breves dias comenzó dicho señor arzobispo a tener la visita de este convento, la cual fue muy larga y con toda contra dicha madre Mariana de la Encarncación. Y puede esta declarante certificar de sí que siendo novicia entonces, le insistieron el principal el dicho padre Miranda (por cuya boca hablaban las dichas cuatro gachupinas, y la madre Inés de la Madre de Dios, cuñada de las dichas Bernarda de San Juan y María de Santa Inés que iban haciendo gente, y dicho padre Miranda las confesaba) y no podía esta declarante hablar a las religiosas por [ser] novicia; que levantase falso testimonio a la santa madre fundadora, Mariana de la Encarnación, entrando pidiendo a dicho señor arzobispo maestra de novicias, porque la dicha fundadora era una relajada que no guardaba en nada la regla, ni trata[ba] jamás que de regalarse y quebrantar el silencio, poniéndole grandes premios en esto el dicho padre Miranda. Y aunque esta declarante le decía que esto no era así verdad; le decía que aquello no importaba, pues así era, y que él había dicho a dicho señor arzobispo Manzo que esta declarante le había de dar noticias de la dicha fundadora y maestra de novicias. Y cuando llegó la vez de que entrase esta declarante a visitar [   ]

[f9ov]

el señor arzobispo, con mesura, a que dijese todo lo que había visto de su maestra, y con verdad, mirando a Dios, le dijo lo que había de verdad, y las faltas que había advertido en otras religiosas, y que después de esto le inquietaron el ánimo a esta declarante dichas gachupinas (conviene a saber, Bernarda de San Juan, María de Santa Inés, y Margarita de San Bernardo, y la dicha madre Inés de la Madre de Dios, y el dicho padre Miranda) diciéndola que se había excomulgado por no haber declarado ante el dicho señor arzobispo todo lo que ellas y él querian. Y la absolvió el dicho padre Miranda. Y que acabada la visita se hizo elección de priora y salió la madre Beatríz de Jesús, natural de esta ciudad, y pusieron por su priora, sin votos, a la madre Bernarda de San Juan. Y tuvieron el dicho señor arzobispo en lo interior del convento, [   ] los dos capellanes, dicho padre Miranda, y [el] licenciado Manuel Téllez, un capítulo que duró cuatro horas, a que mandó que asistiese la novicia (que era esta declarante) y en él discurrió con grandes palabras sobre la pretensión de dar la obediencia a los padres Carmelitas Descalzos, y trujo aquel lugar de los, [   ] cuando los israelitas pidieron [   ] que le había mandado Dios a Samuel [   ] les dijese que no le habían despreciado a Samuel sino del mismo Dios, y sacó los [   ] la carta de respuesta de dicho don Alvaro de Cuevas, y jurando por su [   ], dijo que había estado por llevar [   ]

[f9ir]

[   ] quemarle en las espaldas de la carta. Y después se siguieron entre la dicha su priora Bernarda de San Juan, y las dichas dos hermanas Catalina de Cristo y Francisca de San José, y Mariana de Santa Leocadia (que está al presente tullida), grandes recensiones por haber dicho de la dicha su priora que la habían puesto en un oficio siendo tan recién profesa, y que no sabía ni había leído latín ni romance, y sólo deletreaba; porque cuando entró monja, ni aún el abece sabía, ni ceremonias del coro, y se lo escribieron a dicho arzobispo. Y era el que enandra [*sic*] el fuego el dicho padre Miranda, y dicho arzobispo puso reclusas en sus celdas a la madre fundadora y a las dos hermanas, y a la madre Santa Leocadia, más tiempo de dos meses, que

fue en cuaresma, sin que oyesen misa ni sermón ni se confesasen, con censura para que ninguna religiosa las comunicase. Y después las sacó de la reclusión y a larga penitencia. Y que antes de pasar un año quitaron el oficio de priora a al dicha madre Beatríz de Jesús, desacreditándola con el arzobispo, y una de las culpas graves que le pusieron fue que había escrito un papel al padre fray Alvaro de Jesús, Carmelita Descalzo de esta ciudad, preguntándole algunos particulares de observancias de la orden, en que era muy nimia [   ];

[f91v]

lo cual supo el señor arzobispo por medio de dichas madres gachupinas, y como le cogió desabrido al dicho arzobispo de la resistencia que la dicha madre priora Beatríz de Jesús hizo sobre no admitir un breve de Su Santidad el que trujo la marquesa de Cadereita (entonces virreina), para poder entrar en los conventos de religiosas, viniendo en ello los prelados y los conventos, le quitó el oficio de priora a la dicha madre Beatríz de Jesús, y puso por presidenta a la madre Bernarda de San Juan. Y que es de notar la astucia de dichas madres gachupinas, que dieron cuenta a dicho señor arzobispo de este papel escrito a Carmelita Descalzo para derribar a la dicha madre priora, como la derribaron, y por otra parte estaban tratando de que se les diese la obediencia, pues en la crónica manuscrita (cuyo autor es fray Antonio de la Madre de Dios), tocante a las fundaciones de conventos de Carmelitas Descalzos de esta Nueva España, que se trujo a este convento y se le leyó a la comunidad de dos a tres de la tarde por lección espiritual, como se acostumbra, se pone la larga vida de la dicha Bernarda de San Juan (por ser ya difunta). Se dice de ella que cuando le propusieron los padres Carmelitas el que entrara monja en este convento, preguntó si estaba sujeto al ordinario o a la orden, y diciéndole que al ordinario, le dio gran disgusto. Y desde entonces había tenido en su mente hacer cuanto pudiese porque estuviese a la orden, como lo hizo siempre

[f92r]

hasta que le cortó la vida, como se puede ver. Y que así que se vio por presidenta la dicha madre Bernarda de San Juan, comenzó a entrar la dicha marquesa de Cadereita, porque como se había criado en el palacio de la condesa de Montalbán, era amiga de cosas de palacio, y [de] dar gusto a dicho señor arzobispo. Y que de las venidas de la dicha marquesa de Cadereita a este convento resultaron graves escándalos en este convento, por la mucha comunicación que en él tenía dicha señora marquesa con el dicho señor arzobispo, tanto que obligó a esta declarante a decirle a su confesor, el dicho padre Miranda, que ¿cómo las dichas madres gachupinas, por ganar la voluntad del prelado, venían en una cosa tan fea como que en este convento tuviesen tanta comunicación entre dicho arzobispo y la señora marquesa de Cadereita? Porque apenas venía dicha señora marquesa de Cadereita a este convento, cuando luego a [   ] se venía el señor arzobispo, y que por eso había quitado dicho señor arzobispo del oficio de priora a la dicha madre Beatríz de Jesús y puesto por presidenta a la dicha Bernarda de San Juan, que por ser mujer de poca obligación y de menos religión venía en un caso tan feo como en lo de dicha comunicación. A que le respondió el dicho padre Miranda que a un prelado no se le podía ir a la mano, ni estorbárselo. Y que ha dicho que dicha madre de San Juan era de poca obligación porque su padre, Pedro Bermudo o Bermudes, siendo obligado de la carnicería Gabriel [   ] de la Cruz, tuvo a su cargo en Tacuba la carnicería

[f92v]

y casaba las vacas. Y lo mismo hizo su hijo Cristóbal de la Casa, que allí ganó dinero. Y su madre doña Ana de Lima, que todos eran de España, vendía velas en Tacuba en una puerta de su casa. Y que lo supo por la comunicación que su padre de esta declarante, Francisco Fernández de Segura, y toda la gente de su casa (que vivían en una estancia de la jurisdición de Tacuba) tenían con el hijo de Cristóbal de la Casa [y] con su madre. Y los esclavos de su padre de esta declarante iban a comprar carnes y velas. Y que así que se fue a España el dicho señor arzobispo Manzo, por haber quedado por vicario entonces de todos los conventos de monjas el doctor Luis de Sifuentes, hizo elección de priora en la madre Francisca de San José; y que con esta ocasión de ausencia del señor arzobispo, escribió la dicha madre Catalina de Cristo a la dicha su tía Leonor de San Diego, que ¿cómo había dado la dicha carta del doctor don Alvaro de Cuevas? Y lo mismo [   ] hizo para que el padre Manuel Téllez también se lo preguntase. Y ella dijo que por un papel de su misma letra de Catalina de Cristo, en que decía las razones referidas, que había enviado carta; con que se descubrió el enredo. Y esta vez trató con esta declarante con harto sentimiento de este sujeto. Y que habiendo acabado su tiempo de priora la dicha madre Francisca de San José con hartos trabajos

[f 93r]

y contradicciones y una continua guerra con dichas madres gachupinas Bernarda de San Juan, María de Santa Inés, Margarita de San Bernardo, y Ana de San Bartolomé; que en este tiempo trajeron a los padres Carmelitas a este convento, porque en tiempo de dicho señor arzobispo Manzo había más de 6 años que ni aún en la iglesia entraban. Se trató de elección de priora siendo vicario el deán don Diego Guerra, que por estar muy al cabo de su vida dio comisión para ello al doctor don Pedro de Solís Calderón, canónigo de esta santa iglesia. Y pretendió mucho ser priora la dicha Bernarda de San Juan, y viendo que no podía salir, echó la elección por su cuñada, la madre Inés de la Madre de Dios. Y en tiempo de esta priora se hicieron dueñas las madres gachupinas de este convento, y se trató con viveza y atrinco [*sic*] el que se diese la dicha licencia a las [   ], y se hiciesen los informes de que trató en su primera [   ]. Y que en tiempo de la dicha madre priora Francisca de San José, como tiene ya dicho, comenzaron a venir los dichos padres Carmelitas Descalzos. Y entre ellos un fray Andrés de los Santos, que fue bien conocido en este reino, que hacía pláticas al convento, siempre ensalzando a las Hijas de la Orden, que eran y son las dichas madres gachupinas, que siempre se intitulan las Hijas de la Orden y que no lo diesen [   ] a la madre fundadora

[f 93v]

Mariana de la Encarnación, llamándola "aquella vieja endemoniada" porque no la tenían por afecta a estas pretenciones, si bien hacía lo que podía, que tenía ojos, firmando lo que daban a firmar. Y que de ver que dichos padres Carmelitas apoyaban a unas por Hijas de la Orden y a otras las afrentaban, se le crecieron muchos bandos en este convento. Y el dicho padre, fray Andrés de los Santos, trataba con grande desprecio a las dichas Catalina de Cristo, y Francisca de San José, y a esta declarante, y a Teresa de Jesús, y a Beatríz de Santiago, porque obedecían al prelado ordinario. Y que al acabado su trienio la dicha madre Inés de la Madre de Dios, el señor obispo don Juan de Palafox, que era gobernador de este arzobispado, volvió a elegir a la dicha madre Beatríz de Jesús. En la plática que hizo al capítulo que tuvo interior, volvió a tratar con el mismo lugar de la escritura que trajo el señor arzobispo Manzo, de que le había de pesar de andar en estas pretenciones. Y visitándose esta declarante se acuerda que le dijo dicho señor don Juan de Palafox, tratando de esta pretención de dar la obediencia a la orden, y de las grandes inquietudes que causaban en las almas de las religiosas, le dijo estas razones: "Mi hija, que éste ha sido ardid del demonio para, [a] título de perfección,

[f94r]

destruir lo espiritual y temporal de esa casa." Y que luego al primer año quitaron el oficio de priora a la dicha madre Beatríz de Jesús el dicho canónigo doctor don Pedro de Solís, que era vicario de este convento, por orden de dicho don Juan de Palafox que estaba en la Puebla. Y movió esta quitada el padre fray Juan de los Reyes (que le parece era provincial de dichos padres Carmelitas, y era muy amigo de dicho don Juan de Palafox), a petición de dichas madres gachupinas, y lo sabe porque así se trata la voz pública entre las monjas de este convento. Y aún a esta declarante le habló sobre ello la madre Ana de San Bartolomé, pidiéndole el voto para priora para la dicha madre Bernarda de San Juan, que de allí a tres meses la eligieron por priora. Y que siendo priora vino por arzobispo de esta ciudad el doctor don Juan de Mañozcar [*sic*], y en este tiempo de este priorato fueron los informes tan sangrientos que tiene dicho en su primer año. Y por ser muy tarde se cesó.

ANDREA DE SAN FRANCISCO

She said that in the feast days immediately preceding this, she offered this business up to Our Lord very fervently. She hopes that in no way will anything touching on the honor of any person, and especially not that of priests or of her sister nuns, or of friars come up. However, if the Holy Office is investigating, it is not good that innocence suffer and the guilty remain victorious, and so she has determined to tell this Holy Tribunal everything she has known and understood since she became a nun in this convent, certain that it will remain secret, and so she says:

That when this witness entered this holy convent, which on the ninth of January of the next year following this year of 1661, will have been twenty-seven years ago, she believed she was entering heaven, or at least somewhere

where she was sure to find salvation. She found it in great division and disunion as Mother Mariana de la Encarnación, the founder of the convent
who died thirteen years ago, and Mother Inés de la Cruz, the other founder

[f88r]

who died in 1663 (both of whom came from the convent of Jesús María in
this city to found this convent, moved by God our Lord) kept themselves in
complete peace and sisterhood until these *gachupina*[1] Mother Bernarda de
San Juan (deceased), Mother María de Santa Inés her sister, Mother Margarita de San Bernardo, and Mother Ana de San Bartolomé, came into the
convent and sowed so much discord between these two founding mothers.
The said Mother Bernarda was a very clever and capable woman and had
been brought up in the courtly company of the palace of the countess of
Montalbán, and she traveled to New Spain in a ship with Discalced Carmelite friars who were coming to their province; as a result of which she
became very attached to the said friars and they to her and to her sister, the
said Mother María de Santa Inés. So much so that later, when they were in
this city the said friars tried to get this convent to admit the two said sisters,
which in effect was done through the intervention of the founding Mother
Inés de la Cruz, who asked Juan de Castillete to name them as beneficiaries
of two grants that he gave in perpetuity to this convent. The said Mother
Inés de la Cruz, as she was a *gachupina* born in Toledo, became very attached
to them and the said Mother Bernarda de San Juan who, as she has declared,
had such an appealing nature and was so attractive, won over the will of the
said Mother Inés de la Cruz so completely that though she had just professed and was very young, she was put in charge of the gate—something that amazed Father María Calollete,

[f88v]

an Augustinian friar and brother of the said Mother Inés de la Cruz. She
also made the said Mother de Santa Inés adviser of the novices, even though
she entered being only fourteen years of age and with only [   ] years of
novitiate, from which one can see what kind of age she had to be an adviser,
or even a teacher of novices, because the said Mother Inés de la Cruz, who
was prioress and teacher of novices, was very ill and could not do her job.

The other nuns—among whom there were some very faithful servants of
God—had lived like beasts without reason, subject to the vow of obedience,

witnessing what was happening with the said two sisters Bernarda de San Juan and María de Santa Inés. These nuns became disruptive and were envious, appealing to the other founding mother, Mother Mariana de la Encarnación, as it was clear they could not get anywhere with Mother Inés de la Cruz. And the said Mariana de la Encarnación, after having great arguments with the said Mother Inés de la Cruz that shattered the peace between the founding mothers, appealed to Francisco Manzo, asking that he remove Mother María de Santa Inés from the post of teacher of novices as of the two novices they had she only really wanted to have one, the said Ana de San Bartolomé, to whom they were very attached and for whom they did a lot because she was a *gachupina,* while they wanted to throw the other novice, Teresa de Jesús, who had been born in Querétaro, out of the convent. The said archbishop took the post away from the said Mother de Santa Inés

[f89r]

and appointed the said Mother Mariana de la Encarnación, who had been teacher to all the nuns in the convent except the two said *gachupina* sisters Bernarda de San Juan and María de Santa Inés, who had been introduced into the convent by Mother Inés de la Cruz. From this moment, the community was divided. When the said Mother Inés de la Cruz died, the four *gachupinas* Bernarda de San Juan, María de Santa Inés, Margarita de San Bernardo, and Ana de San Bartolomé said publicly and let it be known, telling the said Juan de Castillete, that the said Mother Mariana de la Encarnación had killed the said Mother Inés de la Cruz, their sister, by taking away the post of teacher of novices from the said María de Santa Inés. As soon as she took the habit, this witness was aware of this division.

It so happened that the said archbishop, Francisco Manzo, dishonorably dismissed the chaplain of the said convent, don Alvaro de Cuevas, who afterward became dean of the cathedral church of this city and bishop of Oaxaca, and whose virtue and spirit is well known in this kingdom. The reason for this, which this witness learned, was in order to avoid a great injury to God our Father that was about to take place in this convent; this information being given to this witness by the said founding Mother Mariana de la Encarnación and the Mothers Catalina de Cristo and her sister Francisca de San José. Archbishop Manzo put in his place F. Miranda (who had been a merchant in Puebla before taking orders) and who was a great devotee

[f89v]

of the four *gachupinas* and who recommended the said four nuns highly to the said Archbishop Manzo.

It chanced that the said Mother Catalina de Cristo wrote a letter to the said Alvaro de Cuevas, telling him of the feelings of the said founding Mother Mariana de la Encarnación, herself, her sister Francisca de San José, and the other nuns with regard to what had happened, and the said don Alvaro Cuevas wrote in reply to the said Mother Catalina de Cristo saying among other things that as the said Archbishop Manzo had taken away from him the unsalaried post he held in the convent, God would take away his miter from the said archbishop. The four *gachupina* nuns, having learned of the existence of this reply, which was in the keeping of Mother Leonor de San Diego, a nun in the Franciscan convent of Santa Isabel in this city, wrote her a note, forging the said Mother Catalina de Cristo's handwriting, in which they said that the said Catalina de Cristo and Francisca de San José, her sister, were at the grille of the choir under the church, waiting to receive the said reply she had in her keeping. With this, the said Mother Leonor de San Diego sent it, and it ended up in the power of the said four *gachupina* nuns who delivered the said letter into the hands of the said Archbishop Manzo.

[f90r]

Seeing what it contained and what the said don Alvaro de Cuevas had written, he became furious with him and with the nuns he corresponded with, and in a matter of days the said archbishop organized an ecclesiastic visit of the convent that was very long and mostly directed against the said Mother Mariana de la Encarnación.

This witness can declare from firsthand experience that when she was a novice, Father Miranda insisted (speaking for the four *gachupinas* and Mother Inés de la Madre de Dios, sister-in-law of the said Bernarda de San Juan, and María de Santa Inés, who were gathering people to their side and whom he all confessed) that she give false testimony about the saintly founding Mother Mariana de la Encarnación, and this witness could say nothing to the nuns because she was a novice. She was to go in and ask the archbishop for a teacher for the novices, saying that the said founding mother was relaxed in her mores and did not keep the rule, being only concerned with indulging herself and breaking the vow of silence. The said Father Miranda insisted on this, even though this witness told him that this was not true. He said that that was not important because that was the way things were, and that he had told the said Archbishop Manzo that this witness would give him news about the said founding mother and teacher of novices. When the moment came for this witness to inform

[f90v]

the said archbishop, she told him everything she knew about her teacher in measured tones and with complete truthfulness, aware of God's presence. She told him what was true and what were the faults she had noticed in the other nuns. After this, the said *gachupinas* destroyed this witness' peace of mind (that is, Bernarda de San Juan, María de Santa Inés, Margarita de San Bernardo, the said Mother Inés de la Madre de Dios, and the said Father Miranda). They told her she had excommunicated herself by not telling the archbishop everything they, and he, wanted. The said Father Miranda absolved her. The visit having finished, there was an election for prioress, and the Mother Beatríz de Jesús, of this city, was elected, but they put Mother Bernarda de San Juan in the position, without having another election. The said archbishop and the two chaplains, the said Father Miranda and the licenciado² Manuel Téllez, had a chapter inside the convent that went on for four hours and where they ordered the novice—meaning this witness— to attend. In this chapter the archbishop spoke with passionate words about the attempt to submit the convent to the obedience of the Discalced Carmelite fathers, invoking the commonplace of when the Jews asked [   ] God why He had sent them Samuel, they had not shown disrespect toward Samuel but toward God Himself. He took out don Alvaro Cuevas' reply, swearing by his [   ] that he had been on the point of [   ]

[f91r]

burning the letter upon his back.

Thereafter, there were enormous arguments [*recensiones*] between the said prioress Bernarda de San Juan and the two said sisters Catalina de Cristo and Francisca de San José and Mariana de Santa Leocadia (who at present is disabled) about their having said that their said prioress had been given a position when she had so recently professed, and did not even know how to read Latin or Castilian and could only just write; for when she became a nun she did not even know her alphabet or any of the ceremonies of the choir. They wrote all this to the said archbishop, and the one fanning the flames was the said Father Miranda. The said archbishop sent these nuns, the founding mother and the two sisters and Mother Santa Leocadia, into isolation in their cells for more than two months during Lent, preventing them from hearing mass or any sermon, and not allowing them to confess, with a further order that no nun communicate with them. Afterward he took them out of isolation and into a long penitence, and before the year was out they took the priorate out of the hands of the said Mother Beatríz de Jesús, discrediting her with the archbishop. One of the grave faults they attributed to her was that the said Mother María de Santa Inés had written a letter to Friar Alvaro de Jesús, a Discalced Carmelite of this city, asking him some details about the duties of the order of which she was very observant [*nimia*].

[f91v]

The archbishop learned of this through the said *gachupina* nuns, and as he was displeased by the resistance the said prioress Beatríz de Jesús had shown over not accepting a letter from His Holiness that the marchioness of Cadereita (vicereine at the time) had shown in order to be admitted into convents, and that had been accepted by the prelates and the convents, he took away the office of prioress from the said Mother Beatríz de Jesús and replaced her with the Mother Bernarda de San Juan. The cunning of these *gachupina* nuns is remarkable; they notify the archbishop of this letter addressed to a Discalced Carmelite friar in order to topple the said prioress as they did, and at the same time they themselves were trying to get themselves considered as subject to the Discalced Carmelites.

In the manuscript chronicle about the foundation of Discalced Carmelite convents in New Spain, written by Friar Antonio de la Madre de Dios, which was brought to this convent and read aloud to the community between the hours of two and three as a spiritual lesson as is customary, there is an account of the long life of the said Bernarda de San Juan, deceased. This says that when the Carmelite fathers offered her entry to this convent, she asked if it were subject to the secular clergy, or to the order. Having been told it was subject to the secular clergy, she was very displeased, and since then had had in mind to do as much as she could so as to subject it to the order, which she did always

[f92r]

until her life was cut short, as can be seen.

As soon as the said Mother Bernarda de San Juan was prioress, the said marchioness of Cadereita started coming to the convent; as she [Bernarda de San Juan] had been brought up in the countess of Montalbán's palace, she liked all things courtly, and also liked to please the said archbishop. The visits of the said marchioness resulted in serious scandals for this convent due to the excessive encounters that the said marchioness and the said archbishop held in the convent. So frequent were these, that this witness was forced to comment to her confessor, the said Father Miranda, on how it was possible that in order to win over the archbishop the said *gachupina* nuns had fallen into accepting such an ugly thing as was the immoderate communication that took place in the convent between the said archbishop and the marchioness of Cadereita. No sooner did the said marchioness of Cadereita come to the convent when immediately the archbishop arrived, and it was for this reason that the said archbishop had removed the said Mother Beatríz de Jesús from the office of prioress and replaced her with the said Bernarda de San Juan, [for the latter was] a woman of little discipline and less religion, who fell so easily into tolerating such an ugly thing like the said communication. Father Miranda replied to this saying that one could not stay a prelate's hand nor hinder him. And what she has said about the said Mother de San Juan being of little discipline was because her father, Pedro Bermudo or Bermudes, who worked for the butcher Gabriel [   ] de la Cruz, was in charge of the butcher's shop in Tacuba,

[f92v]

and he herded the cows, as did his son Cristóbal de la Casa, who earned his keep there. They were all from Spain, and his mother, doña Ana de Lima, sold candles from the door of her house in Tacuba. This witness knew all this from conversations her father, Francisco Fernández Segura, and all the people from her house (they lived on a farm in the jurisdiction of Tacuba) had with Cristóbal de la Casa and his mother. Moreover, the slaves of this witness' father would go there to buy meat and candles.

As soon as this said Archbishop Manzo went to Spain, Dr. Luis de Sifuentes, having been elected as vicar of all the convents, held an election for prioress in which Mother Francisca de San José was elected. Taking advantage of the archbishop's absence, the said Mother Catalina de Cristo wrote to her said aunt Leonor de San Diego asking how it was that she had given over the said letter from don Alvaro de Cuevas, and she also arranged for Father Manuel Téllez to ask her. Leonor de San Diego said that she had sent it because of the note in Catalina de Cristo's handwriting that gave the reasons already referred to, and so the riddle was resolved. On this occasion, she spoke very angrily about this subject with this witness.

The term of office of the said Mother Francisca de San José's priorate came to an end amid many troubles

[f93r]

and arguments, and continual war against the said *gachupina* Mothers Bernarda de San Juan, María de Santa Inés, Margarita de San Bernardo, and Ana de San Bartolomé. During this time, they brought Carmelite fathers into the convent, for while the said Archbishop Manzo had ruled, more than six years had passed since a Carmelite father had so much as entered the church. Being near the end of his life, Dean don Diego Guerra acting as vicar, charged Dr. don Pedro de Solís Calderón, canon of this holy church, with holding elections for prioress. The said Bernarda de San Juan was very keen to be elected prioress, and seeing that she would fail, she voted for her sister-in-law the Mother Inés de la Madre de Dios. During this priorate, the *gachupina* nuns made themselves owners of the convent, and a great deal of energy and resourcefulness was devoted to gaining the license for the [ ] and to getting the reports which she spoke of in her first [declaration].

In the term of the said prioress Francisca de San José, as she has already declared, the said Carmelite fathers began to come to the convent. Among them was a certain Friar Andrés de los Santos, who was well known in this kingdom and who preached in the convent, continually praising the said Daughters of the Order who were and are the said *gachupina* nuns; they always call themselves "Daughters of the Order" but never called the founding mother

[f93v]

Mariana de la Encarnación by this name, instead calling her "that possessed old hag," for they believed that she was not in favor of this project, even though she did what she could while she could still see, signing what they gave her to sign. Given that the said Carmelite fathers supported some nuns as Daughters of the Order and insulted others, many factions grew in the convent, and the said priest Friar Andrés de los Santos treated the said Catalina de Cristo and Francisca de San José, this witness, Teresa de Jesús, and Beatríz de Santiago completely disrespectfully because they obeyed the secular prelate.

The three-year term of the said Inés de la Madre de Dios being over, Archbishop Juan de Palafox, who was governor of this archbishopric, reelected the said Mother Beatríz de Jesús. In the speech he gave to the private chapter, he again used the same reference from Scripture that Archbishop Manzo had used, warning that they would pay heavily for persisting with their project. This witness remembers during her interview with the said don Juan de Palafox that she mentioned the great anxiety that the project to submit the convent to the obedience of the order was causing many of the nuns' souls, and that he replied with the following: "My daughter, this has been a ploy of the Devil in order to

[f94r]

destroy this house spiritually and temporally under the guise of a search for perfection."

In the first year the said canon Dr. don Pedro de Solís, who was vicar of this convent, removed Beatríz de Jesús from office under orders from the said don Juan de Palafox, who was in Puebla. It seems that Father Friar Juan de los Reyes, who she thinks was provincial governor of the male Carmelites and a great friend of the said don Juan de Palafox, engineered this removal at the request of the said *gachupina* nuns. She knows this because it was spoken of publicly among the nuns of this convent. Even Mother Ana de San Bartolomé talked to this witness about it, asking for her vote in favor of the said Mother Bernarda de San Juan for prioress. Within three months they elected her as prioress, and being prioress, Dr. don Juan de Mañozcar became the archbishop of this city. During this priorate, the very bloody events happened that she has declared as taking place in her first year. It being very late, the court adjourned.

ANA DE SAN BARTOLOMÉ

Lo que siento y he conocido siempre de la hermana Andrea de San Francisco es un natural inquieto, poco humilde, inclinado a vanidad, presumiendo de sí, muy pagada [*sic*] de su gran capacidad y juicio, haciéndose reformadora cuando con ella no han podido todos los prelados y preladas que han tenido que corregir su natural travieso; porque de las nuestras más correcciones [*sic*] saca quejas y agravios que las preladas le hacían, que todas la querían mal porque ella procura o quería lo más perfecto. Con esto inquieta a la comunidad que la tiene bien conocida, y saben todas las religiosas su modo de proceder tan contrario a la religión del Carmen. Está tan ciega con sus pasiones que no conoce los daños tan grandes que ha causado y está causando a este convento, desacreditando con su lengua en cuanto puede la buena opinión y fama de las religiosas. Y esto en particular con la madre María de Santa Inés, de quien toda esta ciudad tiene grande estima y veneración por las muchas partes y capacidad que Dios ha puesto en esta religiosa; por lo cual he conocido en la hermana Andrea de San Francisco una envidia, notable en todo el convento, y esto da a entender a los de afuera, que la tienen conocida por sus palabras poco recatadas y mal consideradas, sin atención a Dios y a sus obligaciones. Ha llegado a tanto la inclinación y mala voluntad que esta hermana nuestra tiene a esta madre, poniendo lengua con infamia en su honor, levantándole graves testimonios con que la tiene desacreditada con el prelado, a quien tiene tan ciego y engañado que en todos sus sinietros informes le ha dado crédito, con que se ha hecho a sí mismo mucho daño en haberse dejado engañar de un mal juicio. En otra ocasión supe y oí de boca de la madre Mariana de la Encarnación, fundadora de este convento, lamentándose de la mala conciencia y poco temor de Dios con que esta hermana hablaba de la madre María de Santa Inés, me dijo estas palabaras: "Mis dos manos meteré en un fuego por ella." También me dijo en esta ocasión: "¡Ay hija! qué dolor sería que saliese de entre nosotras presidenta, no lo permita su Divina Majestad, encomiéndele a Dios muy de veras que le dé luz para que se salve." En otra ocasión oí de tan inquieta a esta hermana y indignada con la

[f 180v]

madre priora, que era entonces María de la Encarnación, religiosa nuestra y observante de sus leyes. La causa de su indignación no fue más que mandar la prelada que acudiese a la misa conventual en ocasión que estaba hablando en el torno con una hermana suya seglar, a quien dijo la esperara o volviera después, mas la prelada no le consintió volver. Causóle esto muy gran pesadumbre e inquietud, que mostró por las palabras que le oí decir, que Dios la vengara, que a su Divina Majestad pedía justicia y venganza, que el prelado los había todos amenazado, al convento y a la prelada, y a las que lo habían sido, encaminando estas palabras a la madre María de Santa Inés, con quien ella muestra tan declarada aversión que siendo dos veces priora, le dio harto en qué entender con su natural inclinación a conversaciones de seglares, con que anda esta hermana inquietando a las preladas y a la comunidad. En cuanto quiere, hace su voluntad, sin tener quien la corrija. Al prelado tiene engañado; hace más de lo que ella manda; de la prelada es ella prelada; con esto anda todo al revés. A estas hermanas legas las tiene engañadas y opuestas a la comunidad que, siendo como son de profesión humilde, las ha hecho capitulares, sacando leyes contra las de la religión, que prohíbe y manda que estas hemanas no puedan dar voto ni tener voz ni consejo en nada. Y siendo esto así, las ha inquietado y metido en cuantos males procura hacer al convento. Con esto las trae turbadas, y sin atención a sus leyes y obligaciones que les prohibe y hace exentas de estas inquietudes en que esta hermana las mete, causando con esto notable inquietud a toda la comunidad. Todas sus trasas y afán de todad su vida es en orden de huir de la observancia y estrechura de la orden de su religión, que tanto ha repugnado, y cada día la contradice más, sabiendo lo que a Nuestra Santa Madre le dijo Cristo Nuestro Señor de un sólo convento que tenía al

[f 181r]

ordinario; que si no procuraba ponerlo a la orden, vendría presto en relajación. Pues, ¿qué se puede esperar de éste donde está la hermana Andrea de San Francisco sino que está en gran riesgo de perderse? Si Dios, quien es por su infinita misericordia, no se compadece de estas almas y pone este convento a la orden, no hay duda sino [que] enflaquecerá y descaerán las almas por falta de la doctrina y pasto espiritual de nuestra sagrada religión, que tanto hace esta hermana por desterrarla de esta casa; pero no se matará por conservar las penitencias de la orden, y a las asistencias del coro, que más inclinada es su naturaleza a blandura y regalo que a aspereza y rigores. Esto vive muy satisfecha de sí y de su desahogo, y no tan sólo es anojada [*sic*], sino temeraria en sus palabras, pues se atrevió a llamar al confesor que nos confiesa (que es un clérigo muy ajustado y temeroso de Dios) [y] le reprehendió, diciéndole que cómo nos absolvía, con otras cosas que callo, porque lo es mucho. El cuanto asombrado [*sic*] de ver tal osadía en una religiosa con hábito de Carmelita. Todo esto no es nada para lo que sabe y conoce la comunidad de esta hermana. Dios la reduzca a la verdad y conocimiento de ella. En dos ocasiones he procurado hablar a esta pobre hermana con amor y hermandad, compadecida de su desbaratamiento, por ver si la podía reducir a la unión y paz; con que la he convidado dos veces. Le dije, "Hermana Andrea de San Francisco, mucho me pesa de sus desconsuelos. Por amor de Dios, que se aquiete." Apenas me dejó decir la palabra cuando volvió a mí con una resolución, y me dijo, "Dios volverá por mi" o "me vengará," no me acuerdo bien cuáles de estas palabras dijo. Como la vi de tan enconada impenitencia, que hiciera un acto de humildad y mortificación en el refetorio, la cojí [a] solas y le pedí con las manos puestas, por Jesucristo y Santa María, que hiciera aquella mortificación delante de la comunidad, [que] quedaría edificada si mostraba rendimiento y humildad. A ésto me miró con inclinación y nada le ha aprovechado. Aprovéchele la gracia de Jesucristo. Y por ser verdad, lo firmo de mi nombre.

Ana de San Bartolomé

ANA DE SAN BARTOLOMÉ

What I feel and have always known about the sister Andrea de San Francisco is that she has a turbulent nature, lacking in humility, inclined to vanity, proud of herself, and very convinced of her great capabilities and intelligence, making herself out to be a reformer when not a single prelate or prioress who has had to correct her unruly nature has been able to cope with her. For from all of our corrections, she infers complaints and grievances done to her by the prioresses, saying that they all disliked her because what she wanted or tried to obtain was utmost perfection. With this she disturbs the community who knows her inside out, and all the nuns know her way of going about things—so contrary to the Carmelite religion.

She is so blinded by her passions that she ignores the huge damage she has caused and is causing in this convent, discrediting with her tongue whenever she can the good opinion and name of the nuns, and in particular that of María de Santa Inés, who is esteemed by all in this city and is venerated for the many qualities and capacities that God has given her. For this reason I have noted in sister Andrea de San Francisco an envy that is evident to the whole convent. She tells these things to people outside the cloister, who have come to know her by her unguarded words, ill-considered and heedless of God and the obligations owing to Him. The bad propensity and wicked intentions that this our sister feels toward this nun María de Santa Inés have reached such a point that she has spoken infamously of this mother's honor, raising grave and false testimony against her. Using this she has discredited María de Santa Inés with the prelate, whom she has so utterly blinded and deceived that he believes all her sinister reports, doing himself much harm by allowing himself to be taken in by such wicked opinions. On another occasion I understood and heard from the mouth of Mother Mariana de la Encarnación herself (founding mother of this convent) complaints about the wicked conscience and little fear of God with which this sister talked about Mother María de Santa Inés. She said these words to me, "I would put both my hands into the fire for her," and she also said to me at this time, "Oh, my daughter, how painful it would be if she among all of us were to be elected prioress, may His Divine Majesty prevent it. Pray to God very fervently that she may be given light in order to save herself."

On another occasion, I heard this sister to be very distraught and indignant with María de la Encarnación, who was the mother prioress at that time and very observant of the rule. The cause of her indignation was nothing more than that the prioress had ordered that she attend mass in the convent when she was at the grille talking to a secular sister of hers whom she told to wait or to come back later; but the prioress did not allow her to come back, and this made her (Andrea de San Francisco) very unhappy and distraught, which was clear from the words I heard her say. She invoked God to revenge her and demanded justice and vengeance from His Divine Majesty, saying that the prelate had threatened the entire convent and the prioress, and those who had been prioress (meaning by these words Mother María de Santa Inés). She has such an open aversion for María de Santa Inés that, the two times the latter was prioress, she gave her much trouble with her natural predilection for conversation with secular people—a thing with which this sister disturbs the prioresses and the community.

She does what she wishes whenever she wants, having no one to discipline her. She has deceived the prelate so utterly that he does most of what she wants; she is the prioress of the prioress, and so everything is upside down. The lay sisters have been deceived by her and set against the community. Their profession being a lowly one, she has raised them to the status of chapter nuns, inventing laws that are against the rule, which prohibits and bars these sisters from voting or giving an opinion or any advice on anything. She has stirred them up in this way and involved them in all the evils she plans for the convent, so making them turbulent and inattentive of their laws and obligations that prohibit them from the concerns in which this sister embroils them. With all this she causes an incredible disturbance to all the community.

All her work and the whole purpose of her life is dedicated to escaping the observance and strictness of the order of her religion, which she has so repudiated and which every day she contradicts more, though she knows what Christ Our Lord said to Our Holy Mother about a convent that was subject to the secular prelate. He said that if she did not try to put it under the authority of the order, it would soon fall into relaxed ways. Well, what hope can there be for this one where sister Andrea de San Francisco is? Nothing but certainty that it is at risk of damning itself. If God through his infinite mercy does not have pity on these souls and puts this convent under the authority of the order, there is no doubt but that it will weaken, and the souls will fall off through lack of the spiritual doctrine and nourishment of our Holy Religion that this sister does so much to exile from this house, though she would be incapable of exerting herself [lit. killing herself] to conserve the penitences of the order and the attendance at choir, for her nature is more inclined toward softness and ease than toward hardness and rigor.

She lives very contentedly with her lack of inhibition, and not only is she angry but also bold in her words. She dared to summon the confessor who confesses us all and who is a very upright and God-fearing cleric, reprehending him, asking how could he absolve us, and other things that I will leave in silence, they being too much. He was amazed to see such boldness from a nun wearing the Carmelite habit, but this is nothing in comparison with what this community knows and has experienced from this sister. May God reconcile her to truth and to knowledge of herself.

On two occasions I have tried to talk to this poor sister with love and sisterliness, full of sympathy for her ruinous state to see if I could reconcile her to union and peace. Thus I have approached her twice, saying "Sister Andrea de San Francisco, I am very sorry about your afflictions, for God's sake calm down." She hardly let me say a word when she turned toward me resolutely and said "God will return for me" or "God will revenge me"—I cannot remember accurately which of these words she said. As I saw her so intent on not repenting, I came up to her when she was alone and asked her with my hands uplifted, and for the sake of Jesus Christ and his Holy Mother, to do an act of humility and mortification in the refectory in front of the community. I said she would be edified if she showed abjection and humility. At this she looked at me irately, and told me that what I said was of no benefit to her. May the Grace of Jesus Christ be of some benefit to her. In proof that this is true, I sign my name.

Ana de San Bartolomé

María de San Juan

[f 181v]

Digo como religiosa Carmelita Descalza, que preguntada en qué manera nos inquieta o ha inquietado la hermana Andrea de San Francisco, respondo que ha 14 años poco más o menos que estoy en este convento, y en dicho tiempo he experimentado por experiencia propia, como diré después, y por haberlo oído decir a religiosas antiguas y que desde su noviciado conocieron dicho sujeto, que es una religiosa de espíritu muy inquieto y poco acomodado al estilo de Carmelita Descalza, antes en todo contrario. Y ésta juzgo es la causa de haberse opuesto a la pretención que todo este convento tiene de dar la obediencia a su religión para su mayor observancia y reparo de los daños que todas experimentamos el día de hoy por haber el señor arzobispo quitado la doctrina de nuestros religiosos Carmelitas en púlpito, confesionario, y pláticas espirituales; con tanto extremo que hasta en artículo de muerte los ha negado, con notable daño de nuestra mayor perfección, e inquietud y desconcierto de toda la comunidad, experimentando y sabiendo por evidencias ciertas que todo ha procedido de temerarias y siniestras relaciones que esta religiosa ha hecho al prelado. Y de lo mismo el haber el señor arzobispo quitado a la madre superiora que por muerte de la prelada (originada de pesadumbres que por abusos de dicha religiosa le dió el señor arzobispo, como es notorio a este convento), y puesto en su lugar contra el gusto de la comunidad, y sin votos, a una religiosa que aunque buena no [era buena] para prelada, por ser muy tímida e inabilitada con la cortedad de vista, que es tan grande que ni registrar papel ni escribir puede, siendo especial punto de nuestras leyes para las preladas el registrar todas las cartas y papeles que se traen al convento. Esto nos sirve de inquietud y desunión con dicha religiosa, como lo es también la oposición que ha tenido siempre con sus preladas, detrayendo [sic] de todas sus acciones, y publicando entre las cuditas [sic] para malquistarlas, que procedían con pasión y ambición, sacándoles

[f 182r]

sus linajes, cosa tan indecente y aborrecible en nuestra religión; introduciendo en este convento las oposiciones de mujeres de España y de esta tierra, poniendo malos ánimos y de unas con otras, con que ha causado muy poca unión en algunas, hasta que se reconoció ser demasías de este sujeto. Y esto no ha sido con dos o tres preladas, sino con todas las que en discurso de 14 años he visto. Y esto mismo le dije en una ocasión a ella misma, porque me molestaba sobre que dijese a un prelado que una religiosa estaba enferma de pesadumbres que la prelada le había dado. Todo era en orden a malquistar dicha prelada, y no constándome a mí que aquello fuese así, y que no admitía las excusas que yo le daba, en 3 o 4 ocasiones que en la materia me habló, le dije con enojo, "Hermana Andrea de San Francisco, por amor de Dios que se vaya y no me venga a dar tales consejos, porque es una religiosa que de cuantas preladas ha alcanzado, de todas la he visto decir mal. Y no puede ser que todas sean malas, y use caridad buena y no al contrario. Y así no me venga jamás con más consejos de esos, y Dios me libre de religiosa que todas las preladas son malas de su boca." Fuese muy colérica, diciendo algunas palabras que por no alargarme no digo. Y entendiendo esto le sirviera de escarmiento, no lo fue, antes en otra ocasión que estando yo con necesidad de hablar al prelado le escribí un papel, enviándolo al torno con una religiosa para que lo despachase, y sabiendo que ella lo había abierto y escrito en él, [se] lo pedí a Pedro de Vig [   ] que lo llevaba. Y abriéndolo, hallé que le escribía en mi mismo papel al prelado el daño de la prelada, diciéndole que por allí me ganaría. Y yo hice pedazos dicho papel, no queriendo se llevase, de que ella se enojó mucho con el dicho Pedro de Vig [   ], que ¿por qué me había dado el papel? Y en otra ocasión me habló con tanta temeridad de un prelado y prelada, que espantándome yo de lo que me decía, si bien no creyéndolo, me dijo otro día, "Hermana María de San Juan, aquello que le dije ayer, claro está que no sería tan malo como pareció, y así no lo piense. Use caridad." Respondíle yo, "Hermana Andrea de San Francisco, no tiene que decirme, que yo nunca lo creí, y esa religiosa de quien me habló tiene muy asegurado su partido, y así no tiene que darme satisfacción." Concluyo con decir que rara ha sido la vez que me he puesto a hablar con ella que no haya salido con menoscabo de mi alma y detracción de la prelada. Y por último, la presidenta que hoy tenemos, habiéndola hecho el señor arzobispo (por consejo de la hermana, y siguiéndose

[f 182v]

en todo por sus órdenes, aunque sea con menosprecio propio) la trata con la indecencia que es notorio a la comunidad. Esto y mucho más que pudiera decir en esta materia me ha sido causa de poca unión con esta religiosa. Y también la oposición y poco amor a nuestra sagrada religión del Carmen [en] palabras y obras, como lo experimenta hoy este convento. Y esto mismo ha procurado sembrar en las demás, y hablo por experiencia propia, que en conversaciones le he oído. Y no habiendo hallado en las religiosas coristas quien la siguiese, sino ha sido la hermana Teresa de Jesús, y la madre presidenta, se ha metido con las hermanas de velo blanco, queriéndolas introducir a que asistan en las reprehensiones y visitas que los prelados hacen a la comunidad, no dándoles nuestra religión sagrada más facultad que de meras sirvientas; no dándoles para nada más que para el ministerio a que vinieron del servicio de la comunidad. Y para ésto se ha valido de aparentes obras de caridad, aunque contra nuestras leyes, y también con los consejos del doctor Serna, que juzgo ha sido la causa, porque antes que le comunicaran estaban tan deseosas de nuestra religión y hacer las diligencias que las demás hacemos, que con sumo gusto firmaron cartas que en orden a este intento se escribieron a nuestro Rey y Señor. Y la hermana María de los Angeles dijo una y muchas veces que ella diría al señor arzobispo, como la primera del convento, las diligencias que de sus principios habían hecho nuestras fundadoras de ponerlo a la obediencia de la religión, para su mayor perfección, y otras muchas cosas en orden a esto. Y lo mismo la hermana María del Niño Jesús, y la hermana Bernarda de la Presentación, de que hoy las vemos tan contrarias con la comunicación de la dicha Andrea de San Francisco y de Serna, que entrando en las recreaciones cuando se junta la comunidad [y discute] de los provechos del alma y mayor perfección nuestra que nos será el estar a nuestra religión, enmudecen y no hallan qué decir las que solían hallar tantas conveniencias en ello. Y no me espanto, porque quien da oído a la dicha hermana Andrea de San Francisco, siempre sentirá mucho que decir en esta parte. Y por no repetir cosas de un mismo género, no lo hago. Como es Dios testigo de ello, y que en esta materia ni en otras no digo más que lo que ha pasado por

[f 183r]

mí con esta religiosa, pudiendo decir lo que he visto con otras. Y lo dejo porque cada una dará cuenta de sí, y todas estas cosas fuerza [   ] que nos causa desunión e inquietud, viendo un mostra [*sic*] que es contraria a su misma madre la religión, y a sus hermanos y hermanas, y a nuestra santa madre Teresa de Jesús, que nos dejó por palabra y obra tantos ejemplos en esta materia. Pues un convento sólo, no paró ni cesó, siguió hasta que le hizo dar la obediencia a la religión, y esto con particular mandato de Dios, que le dijo se relajaría sino se unía con los demás que estaban sujetos a la religión. Y a todo esto adelante, la hermana [ordena] sus dictámenes mirando al interés propio, y no al común, y mayor gloria de Dios. También he experimentado en esta religiosa un espíritu tan inquieto, así en las eleccíones o recenciones de novicias y visitas de prelados, que causaba en las demás desasosiego, porque andaba de unas en otras inquietando de tal manera que en una ocasión de elección de prelada, estando ya para elegir, aguardando el prelado en el coro bajo, a mí y a otra religiosa nos puso en aprieto de echarnos por una ventana porque se puso en el cabo del dormitorio, aguardando que saliésemos de las celdas, nomás que para inquietarnos. Y como tiene tanta eficacia en lo que habla, nos restamos [*sic*] a salir de las celdas, viendo que ya no podía ser menos, sin responderle a palabra que nos dijera. Y así lo hicimos. Muchas cosas que pudiera decir de este género dejo, y sólo digo que habiendo la madre superiora llamado al Santo Tribunal de la Inquisición, por escrúpulos que le causó una carta del señor arzobispo, diciéndole una nochea la hermana Teresa de Jesús que "¿no sentíamos el haber traido la Inquisición a casa?" Y respondiendo yo, que lo oí, "[que] el convento no ha perdido nada en que el Santo Tribunal haya venido, y harto trabajo fuera que tuviéramos que temer," tomó la demanda la hermana Andrea, y respondiéndome muy colérica dos o tres veces, "no ha perdido nada, pues aguarde que yo los llamaré." Respondíle yo, "llámelos muy en ora buena, que yo soy cristiana y no tengo qué temer." Ultimamente, digo que Dios es testigo que cuanto ha que he dicho va sin encarecimiento, y que no lo dijera sino fuera para que se conozca lo que este convento pasa y ha pasado.

María de San Juan

Being asked in what way sister Andrea de San Francisco disturbs us or has disturbed us, I reply as a Carmelite nun that I have been in this convent for about fourteen years and during that time I have experienced for myself, as I will declare later, and I have heard from nuns who have been here a long time and have known her since her novitiate, that said subject is a nun of very turbulent spirit, little accustomed to the style of the Discalced Carmelite, but instead contrary to it in everything. I judge this to be the reason for her opposing the project that the whole convent has to subject itself to the order, for the good of its greater observance and repair of the damage that all of us experience at this time due to the archbishop having deprived us of the doctrine of our Carmelite priests in the pulpit, confessional, and spiritual lectures; so extreme is this ban indeed that even for the administration of the last rites he has forbidden their coming. This has caused notable damage to our greater perfection, as well as the distress and bafflement of the whole community that has experienced and knows by undeniable proofs that all this comes from bold and sinister reports that this nun has given the prelate. Moreover, the archbishop removed the mother superior from her position that she held due to the death of the prioress (which itself was occasioned, as is well known in this convent, by the troubles the archbishop caused her, misled by the abuses of the said nun) and replaced her against the will of the community (and without an election) with a nun who, though good, was not fit to be prioress as she was too timid and lacking in skill, and so short-sighted that she could not even read or write a letter. It is a particular point of our laws that the prioress should check all letters and papers that are brought into the convent, and so this disability causes us distress.

All of this sets us against the said nun, another reason being the opposition she has always manifested against her prioresses, belittling their actions and making public among [   ] in order to discredit them by saying that they were guided by passion and ambition, invoking their family background—a totally indecent thing and completely alien to our religion—introducing the opposition between women from Spain and women from this land into this convent, setting one against the other in such a way as to cause divisions among some, until it was realized that these were the excesses of this particular nun. She has done this not only with two or three prioresses, but with all those I have known in my fourteen years of experience. I said this to her on one occasion when she was insisting that I tell a certain prelate that a nun had been made sick by the troubles a prioress had given her, in order to discredit the prioress. As I was not at all sure that this was true, and as she would not accept the excuses I gave her on the three or four occasions she talked to me about this, I said angrily to her, "Sister Andrea de San Francisco, for God's sake go away and don't come and give me such advice, for I have seen that you are a nun who speaks badly of every prioress she has known, and it's not possible that they are all bad. You should be more charitable and not the opposite, so don't come to me anymore with such council, and God save me from a nun in whose opinion all prioresses are bad." She left very angry, saying some words that I will not repeat in order not to go on for too long, and I hoped this would serve as some warning to her. This was not so. Instead, on another occasion when I needed to talk to the prelate I wrote him a paper and sent it to the gate with a nun so that she could send it off. I knew that Andrea de San Francisco had opened it and written on it, and so I asked for it from Pedro de Vig [   ] who was delivering it, and opening it I saw that she had written damaging things about the prioress in my own letter, saying that that was the way I could be won. I ripped the said paper to shreds, not wishing that it should be delivered, at which she was very angry with the said Pedro de Vig [   ] because he had given me the paper. On another occasion she spoke to me so boldly about a prelate and a prioress that I was totally shocked by what she said, even if I did not believe it. Next day she said to me, "Sister María de San Juan, what I said to you yesterday is of course not as bad as it seemed and so don't think it is so; be charitable." I replied, "Sister Andrea de San Francisco, you don't have to tell me as I never believed it and that nun you spoke about can be very sure about having support so you don't have to convince me of anything." I will end by saying that few have been the times I have spoken to her when I have not come off with some damage to my soul and some detraction done to the prioress.

Finally, the prioress we have now (who was appointed by the archbishop on the advice of the sister, her orders being carried out in every respect) is treated shamefully by her in a way that is well known to all the community. This and much more that I could say on this matter have been the cause of my little alliance with this sister. Another reason is the opposition and scant affection she has shown toward our sacred Carmelite religion, both in words and in deeds, which even up until this day the convent community experiences. She has tried to foment this opposition and lack of love in the other nuns, and I know this from my own experience, as I have heard her say as much in conversations. Not being able to find anyone among the choir nuns who would follow her except for the sister Teresa de Jesús and the mother superior, she got involved with the lay sisters. She wanted to make them part of the disciplinary audiences and inspections that the priests carry out in this community when our sacred religion does not allow them this function, only that of being servants, banning them from anything other than what they came to do which is minister to the community. In order to do this, she has used apparent acts of charity that are against our laws. I judge this and the advice of Dr. Serna to have been the cause of their change, for before they communicated with Dr. Serna they were as impatient for our religion and to do the necessary things that all the rest of us did, that they signed all the letters that were written to the king, our lord, for this purpose, with great delight. Sister María de los Angeles said not once but repeatedly that she, as the oldest nun in the convent, would tell the archbishop of the things that had been done from its foundation by our founding mothers in order to submit it to the obedience of the order so as to bring it to greater perfection, as well as about other matters pertaining to this. The sisters María del Niño Jesús and Bernarda de la Presentación agreed with this, and now we see them so set against it, no doubt due to the dealings they have had with the said Andrea de San Francisco and Serna. This is so much the case that when they come into the informal meetings in which the community gathers to discuss the benefits to the soul and the greater perfection we will attain if we have our religion, they are silent and find nothing to say in its support when before they found so many benefits. This does not surprise me, for whoever has listened to the said sister Andrea de San Francisco will always feel strongly about this. But so as not to repeat the same kind of thing I will not continue.

As God is my witness, on this matter and on others I say nothing except what has happened to me personally with this nun, although I could say what I have seen happen with others. I leave this so that each one can give her own account. Undoubtedly these things have brought about disunion among us, and it distresses us to see a monster who is opposed to her own mother religion, her sisters and her brothers, and Our Holy Mother Santa Teresa de Jesús, who left us in words and deeds so many examples in this matter. She did not stop or desist in her efforts for one sole convent, she carried on until she made it submit to the obedience of the order, and this was with the specific command of God, who warned that it would become relaxed if it did not join the others that were subject to the order. In every-thing I have described beforehand, the sister's opinions were formed on the basis of self-interest, rather than on the good of the community or the greater glory of God. I have also known this sister to have a disruptive spirit during elections, examinations of novices, and inspections by prelates; on all these occasions she caused great unease in the other nuns, for she would go from one to the other troubling them to such a degree that on one occasion, when elections were held for prioress, just when the votes were about to be cast and while we were waiting for the priest in the lower choir (myself and another nun) she importuned us so much that we thought of escaping through a window, as she was lying in wait at the end of the dormitory for us to come out of the cells. This was in order to upset our peace of mind, and as what she says is so persuasive we had no choice but to leave the cells, deciding not to reply to whatever she would say to us. And so we did.

I could say many other things of this kind, but I leave them, and say only that the mother superior having called in the Inquisition because of doubts that a letter from the archbishop had caused her, Andrea de San Francisco had said one night to sister Teresa de Jesús if we were not sorry for having brought the Inquisition into the house. Having overheard this, I replied that in my opinion the convent did not lose anything by the Holy Tribunal's coming, and that it would hardly be necessary for us to be frightened. Sister Andrea took up the question, and she answered me very angrily saying two or three times, "Well, so it hasn't lost anything then; well, wait and see because I'll call them." I replied, "Call them as quickly as you like for I am a good Christian and have nothing to fear." Finally, as God is my witness, nothing I have said has been elaborated, and I would prefer not to have said anything except that what has happened and happens in this convent should be known.

Appendix 3

*Archivo General de la Nación. Ramo Historia. Vol. 109,
exp. 2, ff. 8–56 (1723). Diligencias ejecutadas en virtud de la
real cédula de su majestad sobre la licencia pedida por el
excelentísimo señor marqués de Balero, virrey y gobernador y
capitán general que fué de este reino, para la fundación de un
convento para religiosas de San Francisco en esta ciudad.*[1]

MANUEL PÉREZ

Mándeme Vuestra Alteza le informe qué inconveniencias o conveniencias
pueden seguir de la nueva erección del convento de religiosas [   ] que se
ha labrado junto a la alameda de esta ciudad para indias caciques que quieran
tomar el hábito. Por razón de la experiencia que me asiste de la naturaleza,
propiedades, y costumbres de las indias y obedeciendo tan [   ] digo:

Lo primero, que no sólo no le hallo inconveniente para que las indias puedan
ser religiosas, pero le hallo muchas utilidades. Que no tenga inconveniente
consta porque el que pudiera haber (y es el que se pretexta para pedir este
informe) es lo rudo de su naturaleza y la inconveniencia que en ella se infiere.
A lo primero digo que más difícil y más perfecto es el estado de sacerdocio
que el de la monja y estámoslo en lo [*sic*] muchos indios en esta ciudad,
sacerdotes y muy perfectos, luego en su proporción, no estorba su [   ] a
ellas para los menos [*sic*] que en efecto que el sacerdocio, pues a ellos no se
les estorba ser sacerdotes [   ]

Lo segundo, que tan no es vileza la que se les nota que en esta jurisdicción de San Pablo tengo dos de las que están ya admitidas para dicho convento que a la fecha de ésta saben rezar ya el oficio divino, que me consta; luego, no es su vileza tanto como se quisiera ponderar por quien quisiera impedirles este bien.

Lo tercero, en ellos lo más de su vileza depende de su malicia [   ] del vicio de la embriaguez a que están connaturalizados, y vemos que muchos de ellos lo deponen [   ] que llegan al estado de sacerdotes. Y la experiencia de veinte y siete años me lo ha mostrado que en este vicio en que ellos son tan fáciles y que éste usa de su vileza, ellas son tan no fáciles, puede decirse que por doscientos indios suele embriagarse una, y esta una nunca es de las doncellas, porque éste no es caso [   ] verlas ebrias, y habiendo de ser de este estado las que se eligen para religiosas, por ningún modo puede temerse la embriaguez. Luego, ni por ese comino puede no dárseles [   ] dicho fin.

Lo cuarto, el recién conquistado este reino estando ellos tan toscos y rudos como se deja entender, tanto que hubo de expedir una bula el señor Paulo V en que mandó los tuviesen por racionales, que era porque llegaron muchos a dudar si lo eran. Y entonces dice el doctísimo padre fray Juan Bautista de la religión de mi reverendo padre San Francisco, en el cómo de ser monjes [advierte] que en el colegio de Sta. Cruz (hoy es Santiago de Tlatelolco) había indios que llegaron a saber perfectísimamente latín y a ser muy doctos. Después de doscientos años de cultivo, y mucho más los de esta ciudad con el mucho comercio de españoles, ¿por qué no creeremos que hayan ya desterrado su natural ignorancia y rudeza? Y si ellos la han desterrado siendo (como es cierto) más inclinados que ellas a embriaguez y a otros muchos vicios, ¿por qué no creeremos que ellas, que no son tan inclinadas, tengan menos rudeza y mucha habilidad?

Lo segundo que puede pretextarse es su inconstancia o poca perseverancia, y si es esto, no tome el hábito en ningún convento ninguna española, pues hemos visto muchas que han salídose en el año de la aprobación o noviciado; porque no debe reputarse inconstancia de la india que se saliere pues no se reputa de muchas españolas que se salen. Digo más, que aún más debiera temerse esta poca perseverancia de las españolas que de las indias. Para esto hay todas estas razones: la primera, que el no perseverar, si era porque extrañaran en el convento la falta del regalo del siglo, las españolas por pobres que sean tienen sin comparación más regalo en sus casas que las indias aunque éstas sean ricas, porque las indias rara es la que come pan sino tortilla, carnero muy pocas, gallina aunque tengan muchas en sus coradillos [*sic*] jamás las prueban, chocolate es muy difícil sino sólo su bebida de atole. Luego, si vemos que muchas españolas perseveran y profesan en conventos de instituto muy estrechos sin echar [de] menos el regalo de sus casas, las Indias que no tienen regalo que echar [de] menos, ¿cómo no perseverarán?

La segunda razón, si el no perseverar es por lo rígido de la clausura, más clausura tienen las indias (mayormente las doncellas) que las más encerradas españolas, porque me consta que se suelen (si no hay permiso a qué salir) estar dos y tres y más días sin salir de sus casas sin haber hecho voto de clausura; pues éstas ven [que] a lo que entran es a estar encerradas como las religiosas en otros conventos, ¿por qué negaremos que puedan hacer el ánimo, pues ven que tan religiosas han de ser éstas como las que ven en los demás conventos?

Mírase (que ya yo lo he oído) que ¿qué entienden ellas [de] el voto solemne de castidad, pobreza, obediencia y clausura? Respondo dos cosas; la una que ¿qué entienden ellos, o qué entendían de los demás misterios de nuestra santa fe? Y no obstante se les ha explicado por los ministros evangélicos y ya en su [   ] lo perciben (que esto es innegable) luego con la explicación podrán percibirlo. Lo segundo, que yo conozco indias que en el modo que pueden percibir y explicarme, han hecho voto de perseverarse doncellas y no casarse, y mostraré en caso necesario indias de dicha jurisdicción, doncellas viejas que nunca se han casado. Luego, si sin el cultivo y explicación de lo que es voto hacen esto, con su explicación, harán aquello.

Por último señor, yo no hallo inconveniente alguno en dicha erección, antes sí la utilidad del bien que a muchas de ellas se les hará, pues si es cierto que muchas son malas o no son muy buenas, es porque no han tenido esta ocasión que ahora se les ha ofrecido, y lo que muchos dirán que es inconveniente, no es sino no estar en uso. Pero las cosas, mucho más las buenas, merecen principio; puesto lo que en el mundo hay [de] bueno [en] algún principio parecía difícil y hoy está ya fácil. Sólo lo hacerlo y [   ] proseguirlo.

Además que ellas son por su naturaleza humildes, obsequiosas, y trabaja-doras, y creo que estas tres cosas y las demás virtudes las conservarán con gran facilidad. Esto es lo que según la experiencia me ha enseñado puedo decir de tan buenas obras, que creo que será muy del servicio del Señor, salvo se puede tener otro motivo que yo no lo alcance. Porque aún el de que no puedan guardar el voto de la castidad, que es el que pudiera pretextarse, según mi larga experiencia es para ellas el más fácil, pues en el fuero sacra-mental doy gracias a Dios de ver lo difícil que son en su fracción, y no sólo difícil pero las más de las doncellas, aunque tengan ya edad capaz de malicia, parecen incapaz de impuridad; con que por camino alguno yo no hallo in-conveniente en el que han de ser muy perfectas religiosas y que sea el con-vento que se ha erigido en pocos años un emporio de virtudes. Esto es lo que me parece. Vuestra Alteza determinará y mandará como siempre lo mejor.

Manuel Pérez

Your Highness commands that I inform you of what disadvantages or ad-vantages can result from the new convent recently built on the main avenue of this city for noble Indian women who want to take the habit. Given the experience of the nature, qualities, and customs of Indian women, which aids me in this task, and obeying such an order, I say:

First, that not only do I not find any inconvenience in Indian women pro-fessing as nuns; rather, I find many benefits. That there is no inconvenience is evident, for the only one there could be (which is the one given in order to solicit this report) is the rudeness of their nature and the disadvantage that is inferred from it. To this, I say that the priestly calling is much more difficult and perfect than that of the nun, and that many [   ] Indians in this city are priests, and with utmost perfection. Therefore, proportionately, their [nature] cannot prevent the women from taking a calling that is less than the priesthood, for Indian men are not prevented by it from becoming priests.

Second, what is manifest in them is so unlike lowness that in this jurisdic-tion of San Pablo, I have two who have already been admitted into this convent, and who at this moment know how to recite the Divine Office, and

I can vouch for this. Therefore, their lowness is not such as those who would like to refuse them this privilege lead us to believe.

Third, in them (the Indians) the worst of their lowness comes from their wickedness [   ] of the vice of drunkenness to which they have become accustomed, and we see that many of them overcome it [   ] reaching the priesthood. Twenty-seven years' experience has shown me that this vice into which Indian men fall so easily and which exploits their lowness, Indian women do not fall so easily into. It can be said that for two hundred Indian men that get drunk, there is only one Indian woman, and this one is never a virgin,[2] for these are never to be seen drunk. And as the women chosen to be nuns will be from this unmarried estate, there is no reason whatsoever to fear drunkenness. Thus, it is impossible to deny them said aim for a reason not worth peanuts [lit.: a cumin seed].

Fourth, when this kingdom was first conquered, the Indians were very un-couth and rude, as is well known; so much so that Paul V had to expedite a Bull in which he ordered that they be considered rational because many had begun to doubt that they were. And so the very learned Father Fray Juan Bautista, of the order of my Reverend Father St. Francis, in this matter of becoming monks, reports that in the school of Sta. Cruz (today Santiago de Tlatelolco) there were Indians who came to know Latin perfectly and be-came very learned. After two hundred years of cultivation, and more so, of the Indians of this city, and because of the great commerce with Spaniards, why are we not to believe that they will have exiled their natural ignorance and rudeness? And if they have exiled it being (as is true) more inclined to it than the women, and to drunkenness and many other vices, why are we not to believe that the women, who are not so inclined, will be less rude and more talented?

The second objection possible is their inconstancy or little perseverance, and if it is this, then no Spanish woman should take the habit in any convent, for we have seen many who have left in the first year of trial or novitiate. Then Indian women who leave should not be reputed inconstant if the many Spanish women who leave are not reputed so. I add that in fact this lack of perseverance should be feared more in the Spanish women than in the In-dians. For this, there are all these reasons: the first, that of not persevering, if caused by missing the comforts of the world in the convent, the Spanish women, poor as they may be, have incomparably more comfort in their homes than the Indian women, even if these be rich, for it is rare for Indian women to eat bread, instead they eat tortillas; very few of them eat lamb, and though they may have chickens in their yards, they never taste them; they drink chocolate very rarely, having instead their drink of *atole*.³ Therefore, if we see that many Spanish women persevere and profess in convents with very strict rules without missing the comfort of their homes, how will Indian women who have no comfort to miss fail to persevere?

The second reason, if the failure to persevere is because of the strictness of the cloister, the Indian women (especially those unmarried) are more cloistered than the most locked-up Spanish women; I can vouch that if they have no permission to go out, they can be inside their houses for two or more days, without having taken a vow to live encloistered. As they understand that they are entering the convent to be encloistered like other nuns in convents, how can one deny that they have the spirit, for one can see that these women will be as religious as the women in other convents?

It is said (and I have already heard it), what do they understand of the solemn vow of chastity, poverty, obedience, and cloister? I have two replies. The first, what do they understand, or what have they understood of the other mysteries of our Holy Faith? Nevertheless, it has been explained to them by the evangelical ministers and already in their [   ] they perceive it (and this is irrefutable), then with explanation, they will be able to perceive it. The second, that I know Indian women who in their own way of understanding and explaining to me have already made a vow to remain virgins and not marry. And I can, if necessary, point to old women in this jurisdiction who have remained virgins and never married. Therefore, if they do this without the meaning of the vow being cultivated in them or explained to them, then with the relevant explanation, they will do the latter (profess as nuns).

Last, Sir, I find no disadvantage whatsoever in such a foundation, rather the usefulness of the benefit that it will bring to many (is apparent to me), for if it is true that many Indian women are bad or not very good, it is because they have not had the opportunity that is now offered to them, and what many deem to be unfavorable is only in fact unfamiliar. But all things, and especially good things, deserve a beginning, for what there is in the world that is good, in its beginning may have seemed difficult, but today is easy. One need only do it and [   ] continue it.

Moreover, they are by nature humble, submissive, and hardworking, and I believe that they will keep these three things and the other virtues very easily. This is, according to what experience has taught me, what I can say about such good works, for I think it will be to Our Lord's honor, unless there is some other reason that I have not understood. Even the one of their not being able to keep the vow of chastity, which could be alleged, according to my long experience, is in fact the easiest one for them to keep. In the Holy Court, I thank God that one may see how they break it with difficulty, and not only with difficulty, but in fact the majority of the virgins, though they are of an age to be capable of malice, seem incapable of impurity. So saying, I find it in no way inconvenient that they become very perfect nuns, and that the convent that has been built become an emporium of virtues. This is what I think. Your Highness will determine and order, as always, the best thing.

Alejandro Romano

Me mandó Vuestra Alteza, por auto de vuestro Real Acuerdo, que expresase mi parecer en orden a una fundación de religiosas caciques que se intenta en esta imperial ciudad de México, y obedeciendo como debo a este mandato, digo que no hallo disposición en las indias, antes sí positiva ineptitud, para ser religiosas, por las razones siguientes:

son las religiosas unas señoras cristianas, que deseando conseguir la perfección de todas las virtudes, profesan de vivir en comunidad y en perpetua clausura debajo de la obediencia de una prelada que las obligue a guardar los tres votos comunes a todos los religiosos, y otras reglas y estatutos que se juzgan ser medios eficaces para conseguir su fin. Para nada de todo ésto yo veo disposición en las indias.

Primeramente, no tienen natural para poder vivir en comunidad, como lo manifiesta su modo antiguo y presente de vivir, pues antes de la venida de nuestra Santa Fe a estas tierras (quitados los que vivían

[folio not numbered]

en compañía de sus reyezuelos), los demás moraban en los montes y en rancherías pequeñas como aún acostumbran los gentiles, los cuales, aunque después del santo bautismo, a costa de mucho trabajo de sus ministros se hayan reducido, se vayan reduciendo a pueblos, siempre han conservado y conservan en gran parte su natural disposición a la vida asociable e incivil. Pues cada uno fabrica su casa bien distante de la del otro, lo puede haber de una de estas dos razones: o porque no tienen paciencia y providencia para sufrir y [disimular] alguna molestia de vecino, o porque no sean notadas sus acciones. O por lo uno, o por lo otro, que es lo más verosímil. Y si el natural de los indios es tal que no pueden sufrir el vivir uno al lado de otro ¿cómo podrán acostumbrarse las indias a vivir juntas en una casa expuesta cada una a la vista de todas que le noten sus acciones para que se las corrija su prelada, y obligada a asimilar y a sufrir las molestias de todas?

Falta también, generalmente hablando de los indios, la constancia de ánimo en sus buenos propósitos, como nos enseña la experiencia, y aunque ésta faltara, no lo hiciera manifiesto la razón porque la facilidad en mudar de parecer y de voluntad se origina, como enseñó Sto. Tomás, de la imperfección del entendimiento en conocer los objetos. Por esta razón los ángeles

[f33r]

clara y perfectamente conocen las cosas, son muy tenaces en sus juicios y afectos; y por la misma razón vemos en los hombres que los más cortos de entendimiento son también más expuestos a mudar de parecer y de voluntad. Siendo pues notoria la suma cortedad de entendimiento en los indios, a la cual se sigue como su propiedad la inconstancia. ¿Quién no ve la ineptitud que tienen las caciques para el estado religioso, el cual dice perpetuidad en el ejercicio de virtudes muy arduas y repugnantes a la humana naturaleza?

Confirma este discurso la experiencia, porque no hay duda que es más fácil y menos repugnante a la humana flaqueza el cumplir con las obligaciones de casado que con las de religioso, y con todo, apenas se hallará india casada que no se haya arrepentido de serlo. Y muchas de ellas se arrepienten tan de veras que dejan para siempre a sus maridos. Por lo cual yo no veo como pueda dictar la prudencia que mujeres tan inconstantes profesen estado de religión y de clausura perpetua, el cual pide mucha constancia de ánimo y no menor fortaleza que falta también generalmente en las indias, por cuya causa son ineptas para el estado religioso, pues éste es estado de mortificación de todas las pasiones, y de un continuo anhelo a la abnegación de la propia voluntad; lo cual no se puede conseguir sin una gran fortaleza de ánimo, efecto en gran parte del entendimiento, que descubre

[f33v]

a la voluntad lo honesto de las virtudes, escondida a los sentidos, y con éso la alienta y esfuerza a mortificar sus apetitos desordenados. Por esa razón todos los padres y directores de espíritu encargan tanto la meditación de las verdades eternas a los que tienen en su cuidado; porque sin ésta no puede haber fortaleza en el alma; sin fortaleza no puede haber mortificación, y sin mortificación es locura el pretender alcanzar virtud alguna. Siendo pues notorio que el entendimiento de las indias es cortísimo, es también manifiesto que son incapaces para bien meditar de sí mismas las verdades eternas y consiguientemente que les falta la fortaleza de ánimo tan necesaria para mortificar las pasiones y para llevar no solamente la cruz que el Señor mandó cargar a todos los cristianos como medio necesario para alcanzar el cielo, mas también la más pesada y más difícil para llevarse (y por éso no quiso que fuese obligatoria sino de consejo) cual es la de los religiosos, que por más agradar al Señor prometen con voto varias cosas muy arduas y difíciles de ejecutarse. Que las indias sean de entendimiento tan corto que no puedan meditar y discurrir seriamente sobre las verdades de nuestra fe, me lo ha enseñado la experiencia de treinta años que las manejo; pues por diligencias que he hecho para enseñarlas el modo de meditar, todas han salido vanas y sin fruto.

Dudan los doctores [de la Iglesia] si sea válido o no el voto de castidad que hace quien es sumamente inclinado a la incontinencia

[f34r]

y muchos de ellos, muy graves, afirman que no, fundados en que este voto respectivo a tal persona *non est de meliori bono* [sic], ni puede ser sacrificio agradable al Señor por faltarle la sal de la prudencia. Yo no quiero que estas razones valgan para probar en las indias la incapacidad de ser religiosas, por la suma dificultad que han de hallar en cumplir con todas las obligaciones de este estado, pero ¿quién podrá negarme que dichas razones a lo menos convencen que no se les debe permitir el que profesen dicho estado, que les puede ser ocasión más de tropiezo que de provecho espiritual?

Ni a esto satisface con decir que la gracia divina y no la luz de nuestro discurso es la que enfrena y sujeta nuestras pasiones; porque la gracia no solamente obra en nosotros, mas también con nosotros, y ordinariamente se acomoda a la naturaleza, como nos enseñan los doctores [de la Iglesia], los cuales también afirman que de los talentos naturales que el Señor ha dado [　] alguna persona, se puede elegir el empleo a que le destina en su Iglesia. Constándonos pues el corto alcance de las indias para conocer lo honesto de las virtudes propias de las personas religiosas, no debemos esperar que el Señor supla su falta natural con luz extraordinaria, sino juzgar que no las quiere para tal estado, supuesto que les negó el talento del entendimiento y discurso tan necesario según el orden de su providencia ordinaria para alcanzar las virtudes religiosas.

Pero sobre todo yo no veo en las indias rastro tampoco de aquella gran prudencia y cordura que se requiere en una superiora para gobernar a una comunidad

[f34v]

de mujeres incapaces y en las súbditas para obedecer a una prelada de la misma calidad. Porque para bien gobernar a gente incapaz, se necesita en quien gobierna de gran conocimiento de las inclinaciones y disposiciones del ánimo de cada una de sus súbditas, como también de mucho disimulo, paciencia, y destreza, llevando a cada una por su camino, sufriéndole muchas faltas sin perjuicio empero del bien común; calidades que no se pueden esperar sino casi milagrosamente en una superiora india de poquísimo alcance. Y menos se puede esperar en las súbditas incapaces aquella heroica humildad, paciencia y obediencia ciega que se requiere para sufrir a una superiora ignorante y consiguientemente indiscreta.

Este pues, muy poderoso señor, es mi parecer en orden a la nueva fundación que se intenta, y creo que del mismo parecer han sido y son cuantos superiores de religiones han habido hasta ahora y hay en este inmenso reino, porque siendo los indios capaces de ser religiosos, siendo también naturalmente tan humildes, con todo, ningún superior los ha querido ni los quiere admitir aún por legos en su religión, por ser mucha su incapacidad, inconstancia, y flaqueza de ánimo, razones que deben tener más fuerza hablando de las indias, por ser de sexo más imperfecto.

También juzgo que este parecer es conforme al juicio que de esta gente han hecho los supremos gobernadores de ella, así eclesiásticos como seglares, porque aquellos considerando su gran flaqueza

[f35r]

en vencer sus pasiones, nacida en gran parte de su poco alcance, los han eximido de la obligación de guardar algunas leyes eclesiásticas que obligan a todos los cristianos, y esto por la misma razón, considerándolos como a pupilos y menores, dan por nulos sus contratos hechos sin consentimiento de quien está en lugar de su tutor. México, 20 de mayo de 1723.

ALEJANDRO ROMANO

Your Highness, through your Royal Act, ordered that I should give my opinion about the foundation of a convent for noble Indian women that is planned in this imperial city of Mexico, and obeying this command as I must, I say that I find nothing that predisposes Indian women to become nuns. On the contrary, I find them positively unfit for the following reasons:

Nuns are Christian ladies who, wishing to achieve perfection in all the virtues, profess that they will live in a community and perpetually encloistered under the obedience of a prioress who will oblige them to keep the three vows common to all religious, and other rules and statutes that are deemed effective means of achieving this end. I see nothing predisposing Indian women to any of this.

First, they do not have the right nature to live in communities, as is apparent from their ancient and present manner of life, for before the coming of our Holy Faith to these lands (not counting those who lived

[folio not numbered]

in the company of their little kings), the rest lived in the mountains and in small farms. And the gentiles continue like this, even though after Holy Baptism and thanks to the enormous hard work of their ministers, they may have begun to conform to living in towns. For the most part, they maintain their natural proclivity for asocial and uncivilized life. For each one builds his house very far away from any others. For this there may be one of two reasons; either they have no patience or faith in being able to suffer and pass over any irritation from their neighbor, or they do not want their behavior to be observed—one or the other, whichever is truer. And if the nature of the Indians is such that one cannot bear to live next to the other, how will Indian women get used to living together in a house where each one is exposed to everyone's gaze, and where all their actions will be observed so that the prioress can discipline them, and where they will be obliged to accept and suffer all the vexations of the other women?

Generally speaking, constancy of spirit in their good intentions is also lacking in Indians, as experience teaches us. And even if this were lacking, reason cannot compensate for it as the facility to change one's mind and wishes comes, as St. Thomas taught, from the imperfect understanding of things. For this reason angels

[folio not numbered]

know things clearly and perfectly and are very certain in their judgments and feelings. For the same reason, we see that those men who lack understanding are also more likely to change their minds and wishes. As the Indians' grave lack of understanding is well known to all, it naturally follows that they will also be inconstant. Who cannot fail to see that the noble Indian women are unfit for profession, which requires that very arduous virtues, alien to human nature, be exercised constantly?

This argument is supported by experience, for there is no doubt that it is easier and less alien for weak human nature to fulfill the obligations of a married person than those of a religious. Despite this, it is almost impossible to find a married Indian woman who does not repent being so, and many of them repent so sincerely that they leave their husbands forever. Due to this, I cannot see how prudence will allow that such inconstant women profess as religious and vow eternal cloister, things that require great constancy of spirit and no little strength—something that is also generally lacking in Indian women. For this reason, they are unfit for the religious estate, as this requires the mortification of all passions and the continual desire to abnegate one's self-will. This cannot be achieved without great strength of spirit, something that is in large part a consequence of understanding, for understanding reveals

[f33v]

to self-will the value of virtues that are hidden from the senses, and so encourages and urges self-will to mortify its disorderly appetites. For this reason, all priests and spiritual directors strongly recommend that those in their care meditate on the eternal truths, for without this meditation there can be no strength in the soul, without strength there can be no mortification, and without mortification it is madness to pretend to reach any virtue at all. It being well known that the understanding of Indian women is very limited, it is also manifest that they are incapable of meditating by themselves on the eternal verities; consequently, they lack the strength of spirit so necessary for the mortification of passions and for carrying not only the cross that Our Lord commanded all Christians to carry as a necessary means of reaching heaven, but also the most heavy and most difficult cross to bear, the cross borne by religious (who in order to please Our Lord promise solemnly many hard and difficult things) which Our Lord did not wish to make obligatory but discretionary. Thirty years' experience of dealing with them has shown me that Indian women have such little understanding that they are unable to meditate or reason thoughtfully on the verities of our Faith. Every effort I have made to teach them meditation has been in vain and without success.

The Doctors of the Church doubt whether a vow of chastity made by a person extremely inclined to incontinence is valid

[f34r]

and many of them, all very grave, affirm that it is not, basing (their judgment) on the fact that such a vow, in relation to such a person *non est de meliori bono* and cannot be a pleasing offering to Our Lord because it lacks seasoning [lit.: the salt of] with prudence. I do not wish that these reasons be used to prove that Indian women are incapable of becoming nuns because of the extreme difficulty that they will find in trying to fulfill all the obligations of that estate, but who will deny that these reasons at the very least convince one that they should not be allowed to profess, for it will certainly rather be the occasion of spiritual misadventure than benefit?

It is not enough to say that it is Divine Grace and not the light of our reason that reigns in and subjects our passions. For Grace does not only work within us but also with us, and usually it molds itself to Nature, as the Doctors of the Church teach us, also affirming that of the natural talents that God has given a certain person, choosing how one is destined to serve in His Church is one. The little understanding that Indian women can have of the honest virtues appropriate to religious persons is evident to us, so we should not hope that the Lord will compensate for their natural lack with extraordinary light; instead, we should interpret that He does not mean them for this estate given that He denied them the talent of understanding and reason usually so necessary for achieving religious virtues according to the system of His ordinary providence.

But above all, I do not see in the Indian women any sign of that great prudence and rationality that is needed from a mother superior in order to govern a community

[f34v]

of incapable women and that is in turn needed from these women when under the authority of a similarly incapable mother superior. In order to govern incapable people well, the person governing must know the inclination and disposition of each of her subjects thoroughly and must have much discretion, patience, and skill, leading each one in the most appropriate path and suffering many injuries without sacrificing the common weal. These qualities are not to be hoped for, except perhaps miraculously, from an Indian mother superior of little understanding; and even less can it be hoped for from her nuns, incapable as they are of that heroic humility, patience, and blind obedience which is required to suffer an ignorant and consequently indiscreet mother superior.

This then, most powerful Sir, is my opinion with regard to the new foundation that is planned, and I believe that every superior of every religious order that has ever existed in this immense kingdom has been and is of my opinion. Although Indian men are capable of being religious (being naturally humble), despite this, no superior has wanted to admit them or wants to admit them—not even as lay brethren of their orders, principally because of their great incapacity, inconstancy, and weakness of spirit; all of which reasons should bear more weight in relation to Indian women, they being of a less perfect sex.

I also judge this opinion to be in accordance with the verdict passed by the supreme governors of this people over them, both ecclesiastic and secular, for considering their (the Indians') great weakness

[f35r]

in overcoming their passions (this being the fruit of their lack of understanding), they have exempted them from the need to keep certain ecclesiastical laws that bind all Christians, and for this same reason, judging them to be youths and minors, they consider as null any contracts they make without the consent of the person who acts as their tutor. Mexico, 20th of May, 1723.

Notes

Preface

1. Sahagún (1988, 2:629).

2. On ecclesiastical reform in Mexico, see Lavrin (1965).

3. My thanks to Stacey Schlau for sharing this anecdote with me.

4. Kathleen Ross' (1993, 4–7) discussion of what constitutes Creole literature is interesting in this context because it tries to see what role women (nuns) and writing by and about them played in creating a literary tradition.

5. Of course, Sta. Teresa is herself the inheritor of a tradition of writing by women. See Surz (1995).

6. Sor Juana Inés de la Cruz (1648–1695), called by contemporaries "the tenth Muse," poet, playwright, and leading intellectual figure, first entered the novitiate of the Carmelite convent of San José. She withdrew, however, and eventually professed in the convent of San Jerónimo. See Lavrin (1991) for a discussion of sor Juana's "originality" in relation to the didactic models of the period. For an attempt to trace sor Juana's literary sisters in colonial America, see Monguió (1983).

7. A great deal of interesting work has been done on the female writing tradition in the Hispanic world. The foundational study remains *Untold Sisters* by Arenal and Schlau (1989) with its concept of the "mother tongue" and its tracing of genealogies linking women writers across cultures and time. Kathryn Joy McKnight's book on the Bolivian mystic, Madre Castillo, *Mystic of Tunja* (1997), follows in this tradition, invoking communities of female readers and writers in order to situate her subject. My work is slightly different in emphasis from these two books, as I seek to see how women writers and readers participated in a broader colonial cultural and intellectual world. I do not intend by this to erase differences of gender, but instead to see how they worked in practice in the period, affecting what *both* men and women could do. See Ross (1993, 152–153) for a similar position.

8. Arenal and Schlau (1989, 351) discuss the need to investigate the particularity of colonial Latin American texts but offer only analogies to painting in the period, which

according to them incorporates "indian elements." In relation to the particular social context of colonial society, they describe this as both more unsettled and more rigid than that of Spain. McKnight (1997, 83) takes up this point, suggesting that the "relaxation" of convent government is perhaps a specifically colonial issue and may be linked to the peculiar material situation of most New World convents, which meant they could not live up to ideals of absolute poverty. McKnight (1997, 156) also argues that the Teresian models of righteousness and persecution had an especially strong attraction in the New World, where she maintains the Counter-Reformation took place in an atmosphere of heightened intensity.

Chapter 1

1. Letona (1662, 86–87). [Suffice it to say that impelled by her ardent fervor for the salvation of souls and zeal to see the Faith spread and by her desire for martyrdom, she traveled by sea and land for six thousand leagues, a thing most wondrous for a woman and a nun]. All translations are mine. The punctuation and spelling of both printed and manuscript sources has been modernized for ease of reading.

2. Quoted in Caro Baroja (1978, 190). [From pilgrim woman to prostitute there is but little distance.]

3. A version of this chapter first appeared in *History and Anthropology* (1996).

4. Pardo (1676, chap. 3).

5. Salmerón (1675, chap. 4, 16).

6. Castillo Graxeda (1692, chap. 27, 125).

7. See le Goff (1981, 311).

8. Le Goff (1981, 311).

9. Pardo (1676, 121).

10. Pardo (1676, 77).

11. For the ossification of hagiography as a literary form, see Vauchez (1981).

12. Anon., *Vida de la venerable virgen sor Ana María de San José* (1641, 82v) [Sometimes I felt I was lifted up; I do not know by whom, and being in ecstasy I could see myself, dressed in the habit and in the way I usually am. I could see how they lifted me, as if I were someone else. This happened to me many times, traveling through the air as if flying, and sometimes I find myself among a multitude of Indians of various nations, and I have the Christian doctrine in my hand, and they are on their knees, listening].

13. This discussion may principally be traced in the analogies continually drawn by Spanish jurists from Vitoria to Francisco de Ugarte between the pagan ambition to civilize the world and the Christian dream of an empire of the converted.

14. See Anthony Pagden (1991, 148) on this logic of substitution: ". . . the process of reducing distance by direct substitution was an enduring feature of most early European efforts to steady the initially vertiginous experience of being in a (new world)." Cf. also

the idea of the "place" in hagiography as *non lieu* in Certeau (1977, 287). "Il renvoie les lecteurs à un (au-delà) qui n'est ni un ailleurs ni l'endroit même où la vie de saint organise l'édification d'une communauté."

15. Sta. Catalina, "Crónica" (Manuscript chronicle kept between circa 1620 and 1663, 127). [Who can imagine that passengers traveling light to their destination should seek comfort in hotels and inns? Well, our house is an inn on our way to our destination which is eternity.]

16. Certeau (1977, 285): "L'histoire du saint se traduit en parcours de lieux et en changements de décors; ils déterminent l'espace d'une (constance)."

17. Flores Valdés (1707, 246r).

18. Peña (1728, 24). The "strong woman" is a particularly resonant and apposite symbol for these nuns, whose evangelical and "political" role in Spain's empire building finds an ennobling model in the biblical *mujeres varoniles*, Judith and Deborah. The comparison also makes the male author's interpretation of the Spanish mission in the Indies transparent: the chosen people being led to wildernesses they then evangelize.

19. Cf. also the ability of the very presence of the nuns to "neutralize" the stereotypically lewd masculinity of sailors, thus making the ship less of a ship and more of a continuation of the cloister. Anon., *Relación histórica de la fundación de este convento de nuestra señora del Pilar . . .* (1793, 79). The events recounted take place in the early 1700's.

20. See Vauchez (1981) for an explanation of this change in the official review of requests for beatification and canonization.

21. See Pagden (1991, 152). See also Ross' (1993) extensive discussion of Carlos de Sigüenza y Góngora's attempt to secure an authoritative narratorial voice for his writing on two "illegitimate" subjects—women and the New World.

22. Rosa Figueroa, "Crónica sucinta del Convento de Sta. Clara de México" (1755, manuscript, unpaginated). [What we see is always associated with Truth and what antiquity or distance sees of our news is always sublime in its grandeur—a saying which wise Horace used in his *Ars Poeticae*, adding that admiration was more easily conceded when the eyes were witnesses than when only the ears had heard.]

23. A difference that also largely corresponds to the sex of the author, most printed works being by men, the manuscript writings by women.

24. *Vida*, Agustina de San Juan, in Sta. Catalina, "Crónica" 48v–49.

25. Salmerón (1675, chap. 16, bk. 3, 103). [The day of the Holy Innocents, 1630, Mother Isabel de la Encarnción was very tired from her torments and pains, especially the one in her side. At ten o'clock at night, the nurse went in to see her . . . on this occasion, the prioress arrived. She was there in the cell along with two other nuns keeping the patient company when the latter sat up in the bed as if she were well, leaned against the pillow, and remained entranced, with her face and eyes so beautiful and illumined that she seemed an angel.]

26. Peña (1728, 29). [Those who have traveled and experienced the dangers of the sea,

consider this! And those who have not, marvel at what these poor nuns suffered, for if the inconveniences and troubles of an ocean voyage are great, so much the greater those undergone by the nuns because of the strictness of their rule and the excessive enclosure of their cloister.]

27. Salmerón (1675, Postscript 123).

28. Sta. Clara, "Crónica" (1755, unpaginated).

CHAPTER 2

1. [Mexico: a city honorably deserving that her name has reached the remotest parts of the universe on the echoes of Fame. She has become the head and metropolis of America not so much because of the wonderful pleasantness of her location nor for the incomparable beauty of her spacious streets, nor the opulence and courage of her ancient kings, nor the number and gravity of her courts, nor the gifts that heaven has benignly distributed to her sons, but thanks to this and innumerable other temples with which her expansive area is adorned and could thus easily be mistaken for the empyrean heaven, both because of the sacrifice and tribute owing to God, which are sent continually to Him from them in the form of praises and because they are inhabited by those who live in celestial purity] (Sigüenza y Góngora 1683, conclusion to bk. 1).

2. [Having arrived at the house, we went into a courtyard. The walls seemed to me to be falling down, but not as much as they proved to be when daylight came. I did not know what to do, as I realized it was not a suitable place in which to erect an altar. We looked for nails in the walls, and finally, after much work, we found enough. Some people fitted hangings, we cleaned the floor, and we were so quick that when dawn came the altar was in place, the bell hanging in a corridor, and mass was immediately sung] (Teresa de Jesús, *Libro de las fundaciones*, García de la Concha, ed., 1982, chap. 3).

3. Cf. Arenal and Schlau (1989, 303) for the centrality of Sta. Teresa as a validating model for writing/founding activities.

4. The most significant of these writings are transcribed and translated in Arenal and Schlau (1989).

5. Avendaño, "Crónica" f1. The manuscripts are to be found in the Archivo Histórico del Convento de San José, hereafter AHCSJ. My thanks to Manuel Ramos Medina, who made transcriptions of various documents available to me.

6. See Inés de la Cruz, "Fundación"; Mariana de la Encarnación, "Fundación"; and Avendaño, "Crónica" AHCSJ.

7. Mariana de la Encarnación, "Fundación" (63). This argument is reproduced by Méndez with a long comment on how the only perfection possible is the perfect observance of the rule professed, thus attempting to avoid any insinuation that the nuns consider the Conceptionist rule as in some way less holy than the Carmelite one. Méndez, "Historia de la Fundación" (46v, AHCSJ).

8. Mariana de la Encarnación, "Fundación" (75, AHCSJ).

9. The relics of Gregorio López were paraded through the streets during the ceremony of the taking of legal possession of the new convent. (Méndez, "Historia de la Fundación" 22, AHCSJ). The continued ecclesiastical and political favor shown toward San José should be noted. As abbess, Bernarda de San Juan enjoyed the patronage of Archbishop Palafox. (Cf. Méndez, "Historia de la Fundación" 72, AHCSJ). On the political and cultural value of the Carmelite Order, see Olwen Hufton (1995, 370). "It may be that the order was regarded as intrinsically Spanish, the product of a proven saintly mystic [. . .] To put a daughter in the Carmelites was then a political statement, one of allegiance to a country and its cultural creations."

10. *Relación,* in Ramos Medina (1990, 197). This rather elaborate reading of the deployment of the image of Santiago is encouraged by the text itself, which describes how such images should be interpreted. The importance of the intellectual explanation of such visual displays in the period is discussed at length in Maravall (1990, especially sec. 4, "Los recursos de acción psicológica sobre la sociedad Barroca"). And Mexican examples come easily to mind: the texts of sor Juana Inés de la Cruz and Sigüenza y Góngora explaining the respective triumphal arches they designed for the entry of a viceroy, or that of Cervantes y Salazar for the funerary ceremonies on the death of Charles V. For an account that questions monolithic theories of the power of the image in the period, such as those of Maravall, and concentrates on the colonial context, see Taylor and Pease, eds. (1993).

11. The Teresian voice differs in emphasis in both these texts. See McKnight (1997, 148) on how, given the changes in female enclosure after Trent, the Teresian voice of *Libro de las fundaciones* (1982), with its independence and often its disregard for ecclesiastical authority, is impossible to imitate faithfully. In some sense, Sta. Teresa contributed to these changes in enclosure and could thus be seen as proscribing for others the powers she herself enjoyed.

12. See the anonymous "Relación de unas cositas, . . ." (194, AHCSJ). Reading was a process fraught with moral dangers, however. Juan Luis Vives (1492–1540) wrote worriedly about the untrammeled fantasy such an activity could cause and about the impossibility of punishing the type of sin that was experienced in the very act of reading. See Ife (1985) for a review of contemporary attitudes to the process of reading.

13. Critical appreciation of this style ranges from the patronizing—praising Sta. Teresa's "delicacy"—to works that attribute considerable rhetorical dexterity and strategy to her.

14. For a discussion of the Teresian text's multiple narratives, see Weber (1990, 128–134).

15. *Libro de las fundaciones,* García de la Concha, ed. (1982, chaps. 15, 19, 25).

16. Mariana de la Encarnación, "Fundación" (82, AHCSJ).

17. Sigüenza y Góngora (1683, 44v).

18. Sánchez Llora (1988, 372). Raquel Chang Rodríguez (1982, xii) claims the early autobiographies in chronicles, reports, and letters to be the foundation of a distinctive Latin American novel that she characterizes as: "una escritura transgresora y a la vez participatoria de diversos modelos historiográficos y literarios" [a writing that at once transgresses and participates in various historiographic and literary models]. More specifically, see Ross (1993, 112) on historical/fictional approaches to narration in the convent chronicle, in particular how female subjects eliminate the need for documentation and so, paradoxically, because the narrative is about nuns "it can stretch into the realm of profane discourse."

19. [As a novice she was in charge of the chicken run, and one day as she gave them bran, the bell rang for communion. As she was meant to be praying at the service, she hurried in order to finish, but the cockerel ran into the sack of bran, preventing her from closing it. Anxious, she hit him on the head with the ladle, and he dropped down dead. The poor novice stuck his head in the bran and went to communion, asking God for the life of the cockerel, with great faith that she would be granted it. When she came out of the choir, she went to see her deceased and found him strutting spiritedly the length of the run] (Méndez, "Historia de la Fundación," marginal note to f81v, AHCSJ). Cf. Bennassar (1982, chap. 11) for an account of the relation between oral and written culture in the period.

20. Certeau (1977, 278).

21. Certeau (1977, 283).

22. Cf. Weinstein and Bell (1982, 141).

23. Ross (1993) concentrates on this issue, investigating how Carlos de Sigüenza y Góngora attempted to write a decorous New World history out of the *vidas* of nuns.

24. St. Augustine (1978, 14).

25. St. Augustine (1978, 34).

26. Maclean (1980) provides an overview of theological, ethical, and scientific texts of the period.

27. [I will have to make use of some comparisons which, being a woman, I would prefer not to do and to write simply what I am ordered to, but this spiritual language is so difficult to speak for those who like myself have no learning, that I will have to find some way and probably the greater part of the times the comparison will not fit; at least such clumsiness will serve to amuse Your Grace] (Sta. Teresa de Jesús, *Vida*, Chicharro, ed., 1990, 192–193).

28. The exempla used by Mendicant preachers (whose sermons Sta. Teresa confesses a penchant for) were frequently condemned for their lack of decorum in this period. Cf. Chicharro (1989, 52). See also sor Juana Inés de la Cruz' description of the kitchen as a philosophical and scientific classroom in "Respuesta a sor Filotea" (an autobiographical text modeled on hagiographic forms) for an instance of how such extrascriptural ex-

amples could be manipulated—in this case in order to reevaluate the feminine domestic sphere. Sor Juana Inés de la Cruz (1989, 827–847).

29. Vauchez (1981, 41).

30. Cf. Diane Purkiss' (1992) argument (indebted to Lacan's interpretation of Sta. Teresa).

31. The importance of interpreting marginal spiritualities such as that of women or that of the ignorant "mass" as creative rather than simply as deviations from the norm is emphasized by Ruggiero (1993, 89).

32. [Her understanding rose to such heights on such occasions that she herself marveled at what she reasoned (which was usually in the most gentle and elegant verses), exclaiming she would say, "What is this! Who has made of me a poet? Who illuminates my simple understanding and suggests such words to my clumsy tongue?"] (Sigüenza y Góngora 1683, 88). Later, there is another description of Marina de la Cruz' "possessed" speech that emphasizes its elegance and order, a rhetorical dexterity that leaves even the learned *letrados* silent with amazement. Her speech is clearly far removed from the "nonsense" of mystical transport (Sigüenza y Góngora 1683, 93). See also Inés de la Cruz' ability to understand Latin through divine intervention though she can normally neither read nor speak it.

33. Méndez, "Historia de la Fundación" (55v, AHCSJ).

34. Lavrin (1993).

35. For an eloquent explanation of the "risks" involved in representing such spirituality for apologetic purposes, see Peña's (1728) comment in *Trono Mexicano:* "Aunque lo substancial de la virtud no consiste en visiones, raptos, revelaciones y profecías, porque siendo sentimientos extraordinarios puede mezclarse en ellos algún engaño, y fuera liviandad de corazón el dar luego crédito a esas cosas, también es temeridad el condenarlas sin suficientes indicios y despreciarlas, cuando los efectos que dejan y causan en el alma son virtuosos y humildes, y los fines son santos." [Though what is substantial in virtue does not consist of visions, raptures, revelations, and prophecies, these being extraordinary feelings and liable to become mixed with some falsity and it would be superficiality of heart to give credit to such things, it is also weak to condemn them without sufficient reason and to dismiss them when the effects that they have and cause on the soul are virtuous and humble and the ends are saintly] (Peña 1728, 197).

36. The Teresian tradition would have presented an inspiration in this respect, for Sta. Teresa had modified hagiographic form in all her writings, thereby creating "mixed" genres.

37. This inversion where the saintly nun is tortured by her companions is a commonplace of conventual literature. Authors such as Sta. Teresa clearly manipulated the figure for their own benefit.

38. Anon., *Regla y ordenaciones* (1635, unpaginated).

39. The issue of reform and laxness must not be seen as confined to these two convents or to the Franciscan and Carmelite Orders in particular, however, but as part of a larger social and religious crisis that was to lead to extended ecclesiastical reform in the eighteenth century. Asunción Lavrin's (1965) summary of the main causes of this crisis make apparent how deep-rooted the problems revealed in this particular instance were. See Anthony D. Wright (1982, 142): "The integration of religious and civil life was predictably clearest in the case of female convents in Mexico where, by the eighteenth century, nuns retained personal incomes, and convents employed lay agents to manage their property and made loans at interest; a return to truly communal living was resisted."

40. For an orthodox opinion on the pernicious effects of the world for the nun, see Méndez, "Historia de la Fundación" (62, AHCSJ): ". . . porque más fácil es hacer un milagro que remediar el daño que al religioso de la comunicación secular [*sic*] puede provenir" [because it is easier to do a miracle than to salvage the damage that a monk or nun can suffer from communication with lay persons].

41. Margarita de San Bernardo, "Escritos" (143, AHCSJ).

42. Sigüenza y Góngora (1683, *vida* of Marina de la Cruz, unpaginated). Cf. Poutrin (1987) for an attempt to read the history of childhood and its emotions from hagiographic narrative while respecting the genre's symbolic structure.

43. Méndez, "Historia de la Fundación" (2v, AHCSJ). See also Méndez' (4v) description of the friendship between the two founding mothers as disembodied: "De dos instrumentos unísonamente templados (dice Plinio) sin que los toque la mano, el aire basta para que ambos suenen con melodía uniforme" [Of two instruments tuned together (Pliny says) without a hand touching them, it is enough that the air (touch them) for them both to sound with the same melody] (Méndez, "Historia de la Fundación" 4v AHCSJ).

44. For an example of how elite families and convents formed a complex social network in New Spain, see Loreto López (1991).

45. Inés de la Cruz, "Fundación" (46, AHCSJ).

46. Sigüenza y Góngora (1683, 172, *vida* de Petronila de San Hildefonso).

47. Mariana de la Encarnación, "Fundación" (73, AHCSJ).

48. I use *honor* here in the global sense ascribed to it by Maravall (1990) when he discusses *honor* as being the defining characteristic of Spanish preoccupations with sexual, cultural, political, and social orthodoxy in the period.

49. [. . . Virgin Capuchin ladies, Creoles, legitimate daughters of the spirit and breath of the first Capuchin mothers, so that Europe might see that there are fitting vocations in America, because even though the influences, the food and the air can debilitate strength to such an extent that the complexions of bodies become more delicate, Grace is powerful enough to form gigantic spirits] (Peña 1728, 253). The theory of the climate of the Indies affecting its inhabitants was articulated as early as 1570 by Bernardino de Sahagún.

50. See Pagden (1987, 85).

51. Sigüenza y Góngora (1683, 75). For a similar complication of theoretically transcendental narrative values by very worldly concerns, see McKnight's (1997, 73) description of how Madre Castillo's *vida* describes cultural practices that contradict the dominant prescription for holy femininity.

52. Mariana de la Encarnación, "Fundación" (73, AHCSJ).

53. Mariana de la Encarnación, "Fundación" (70, AHCSJ).

54. Mariana de la Encarnación, "Fundación" (92, AHCSJ).

55. [Arguing about the Indies and Spain, setting one country above the other, is to fulfill to the letter what the mystical Doctor of the Church Sta. Teresa says: that it is like arguing over whether one soil or another is better for making sun-dried mud or simple mud. Let us try and forget countries—I speak to every monk and nun, those of us who have promised to crush and stamp beneath our feet the world and its vanities] (Méndez, "Historia de la fundación" II, AHCSJ).

56. "Sobre cuál es la mijor tierra, que no es otra cosa sino debatir si será para lodo bueno u para adobes" [about which is the better soil, an argument that is nothing other than to debate what soil is better for simple mud or for sun-dried mud walls] *Camino de la perfección,* in Madre de Dios and Steggink, eds. (1967). Cf. Bilinkoff (1989) for the social and political context in which the first Carmelite foundations unfolded.

57. [That while he was prelate he would not consent to the foundation of a convent that professes to be so perfect by spoilt, chocolate-guzzling criollas. That we (the criollas) would bring three or four servants each to serve us] ("Fundación 70–71, AHCSJ).

58. For more on these racial commonplaces, see Alberro (1990). Cf. the opinion that chocolate, apart from an indigenous food, was an aphrodisiac and the references made in many Inquisition trials to its being used as an ingredient in love potions prepared by women. The history of the "gendering" of chocolate in the pre-Conquest to colonial period is very intriguing. For the México, chocolate was a drink for warriors preparing to do battle, while in the colony its consumers had become predominantly women and the substance consequently "feminized" (see Alberro 1992).

59. Peña (1728, 280; *vida* of María Josefa de Gracia).

60. Letona (1622, unpaginated).

61. [There is a legitimate custom in the Indies that everyone eats eggs and milk products during Lent and on other fast days. Thus the prohibition written into the rule will not apply to this kingdom or to any other where there is a similar custom. This is most definitely the case as the rule declares nuns should keep the customs of the region (they come from)] (Letona 1622, unpaginated).

62. Letona (1622, bk. 2).

63. The biographical format of the *vida* may also be considered in this light. Maravall (1990, 211) writes on the use of biography in the period by the ruling powers to sway and educate the masses.

CHAPTER 3

1. [End of quotation from the Venerable Mother, to whose thoughtful and effective words in the narration of this event we do not need to add, for appending or putting in anything would detract from the expressions and the liveliness with which she recounts everything] (Valdés 1765, 58).

2. The number of works dealing with the writing of biography and autobiography by women in this period is enormous. For an excellent overview of the writing of autobiography by Spanish nuns, see Herpoel (1987), Donahue (1989), Matter (1992), and Jacobsen Schutte (1992). For the autobiographical writings of Mexican nuns, see Myers, ed. (1993), Ferreccio Podestá, ed. (1984), Eich (1996), and Lavrin (1993). On the Hispanic historical and literary context, see Goetz (1994) and Spadaccini and Talens, eds. (1988). González Echevarría (1980) provides a good introduction to the generic and rhetorical complexities of New World autobiography. For an introduction to the intellectual and devotional universe of the convent in which these writings were produced, see Zarri (1990, 21–50). For an analysis of how autobiography written by women has changed and developed as a subject for academic research and study, see Stanton's article in Stanton, ed. (1984).

3. For a similar methodological stance, see Ross (1993, 12–13).

4. Cf. Claude Martin's reworking of the writings of his mother, Marie de l'Incarnation, into a hagiography of her for insight into how a woman's unofficial text was transformed by a man into a narrative worthy of publication and the different imperatives that dictated composition in each case. Martin is principally concerned in making his mother's words both doctrinally impeccable, by removing mystical terms, and rhetorically more decorous, by updating her antiquated Canadian/colonial French. Zemon Davis (1995, 129–132).

5. A selection of passages from sor Sebastiana's letters is to be found in Appendix 1.

6. See Haliczer (1996) for an account of how confession was transformed after Trent. Haliczer is principally interested in one aspect of religious acculturation through confession—the regulation of sexuality—but his argument provides insight into the more general tensions and difficulties surrounding the exercise of power and authority in the relation that is my concern here. For a broader account of the struggles with guilt and the penitential regimes of people who had professed religious vows, see Delumeau (1983, 339–363).

7. For an assessment of the *vida espiritual* as a literary genre, see McKnight (1997).

8. The most obvious exception to this generalization in New Spain is, of course, sor Juana Inés de la Cruz, whose publishing history (significantly most of the published work was secular in character) has much more of an affinity with the writing career of court poets than with that of the average writing nun.

9. Significantly, early historians of America also used this trope of suffering in writ-

ing to secure the authority of their accounts. See Pagden (1993, 67) on Las Casas and Oviedo edging themselves, as close as they dared, "to a secularized, scientific analogue of that state [martyrdom]." See also Phelan (1970, 59) on how the authority of experience and that of Divine illumination is combined in Jerónimo de Mendieta's writing: "Empirical experience was not Mendieta's only self-justification. He claimed that the Holy Ghost had revealed to him certain insights into the character of the Indians. Mendieta, consequently, spoke [. . .] both as a man of experience and as a mystic."

10. See Alberro (1988).

11. For a discussion of how criticism has evaluated the "autonomy" of Hispanic women's writing in relation to these constraints, see Ross (1993, 156), Arenal and Schlau (1989, 15–16), and Franco (1989, 15).

12. The manuscripts are held by the Biblioteca Nacional, Mexico City, and are numbered in the original (L31 f180).

13. [How I wish I were a saint!] (L10 f74).

14. Cesare Ripa's accompanying text in his *Iconologia* (1603, 216–217) makes the association of female spirituality and semblance absolutely clear: "la tesa china, con il velo che gli cuopre la fronte, la Corona & l'offitiuolo, dinotano che l'hippocrito mostra d'essere lontano dalle cose mondane & rivolto alla contemplatione dell'opere divine."

15. Bilinkoff (1989) examines the relation between Teresa de Jesús' religious reforms and the social structure of the city and convents in which it took place. Her argument that instability in the social structure was conducive to reform is particularly resonant in the very heterogeneous social context of eighteenth-century Mexico City.

16. Perhaps best known is Bernardo de Balbuena's, *La grandeza mexicana* (1603).

17. See Maravall (1990). For a philosophical perspective, see Deleuze (1993). Franco's (1989) discussion of the transgression of public space by American *ilusas* and *alumbradas* is very relevant in this context.

18. See Vallarta (1990) for an account of the production of didactic literature by a male confessor from the writing of women in his spiritual care in New Spain.

19. For an interesting contrast, see Ross' (1993, in particular chap. entitled "The Discourse of Paternity") account of Sigüenza y Góngora's approach to women's writings as sources for his own.

20. Valdés (1765, bk. 1, chap. 5, 34).

21. Gerson's treatise in *Oeuvres Complètes* (1974, 160–164) was written in response to another nun's spiritual experiences—Bridget of Sweden's visions. Gerson emphasizes the circumspection with which novices in things spiritual, especially women and young people, should be treated. Moreover, he warns against taking women's prolix narrations to their confessors too seriously. Note Valdés' (1765, bk. 2, Intro. 131) echo of Gerson's terminology, opposing frivolity and emptiness (*deleitación . . . vacía*) to solidity and truth ("virtudes sólidas, sin fingimiento ni simulación"). The Gerson reads: "Approbare enim falsas et illusorias aut frivolas visiones pro veris et solidis revelationibus, quid indignis,

quid alienius ab hoc sacro Concilio?" (Gerson 1974, vol. 9:179). On the tightening and rationalizing of procedures to ascertain the authenticity of visions experienced by women, see Christian (1981).

22. Valdés (1765, bk. 1, chap. 13, 99).

23. See Martin (1975). For sor Sebastiana's devotion for Loyola, see especially Valdés (1765, bk. 1, chap. 18) and for her reading of Alcántara (bk. 2, chaps. 1 and 17).

24. For a review of Sta. Teresa's relation to theology and theologians, see Steggink (1982).

25. Quoted in Bataillon (1966, 702).

26. Valdés (1765, bk. 2, chaps. 21–24 and 26, respectively).

27. Valdés (1765, bk. 2, chap. 25, 348–349).

28. Vives, *De tradendis disciplinis* (1531). The work was reprinted several times in the seventeenth century. There is an English translation by Watson (1913).

29. See Conley (1990, in particular chap. 4: "Rhetoric and Renaissance Humanism").

30. Valdés (1765, bk. 1, 1).

31. [The sixty arguments which I offer are nothing other than the letters she wrote to her confessors. Because each one is proof of her humility. I cannot give a truer testimony than them. To read them is to admire her abjection, in fact, it is one and the same act, for to read them is to be filled with wonder] (Valdés 1765, bk. 2, chap. 22, 307).

32. Valdés (1765, bk. 2, chap. 13, 241).

33. Valdés (1765, bk. 1, chap. 10, 58).

34. Valdés and sor Sebastiana's agreement on this subject is an indication that we should perhaps revise the usual critical reading of confessors as authoritarian dictators of writing and nuns as writers of apparently orthodox but really secretly subversive texts. Clearly, the relationship between nun and confessor, and between the writings of both, was often collaborative and more in the nature of partnership than competition. On nuns' writings as subversive palimpsests, see Ross (1993, 156–157).

35. [I do not know if what happened to Mother Sebastiana was miraculous or prodigious. I only narrate it as it appears in the documents I have in my power] (Valdés 1765, bk. 2, chap. 29, 385). Cf. Valdés' (bk. 2, Intro. 129) censure of the two types of confessor, one accepting of mysticism and the other skeptical, and his advocation of a "reasonable" middle path to be taken by confessors.

36. Cf. Birge Vitz (1991) on how the move to a more Humanist hagiography is tied to the reception of works. For an examination of how rhetoric complicates devotion, see Arrasse (1981). See especially how the cult of the image turns into the reverence accorded to the cultivated image in this period.

37. [Because she did not want to be a painted saint, of those that are formed by the soft strokes of the brush and the delicacy of colors, but a sculpted one, made by blows from the iron and the adze, wounds from the chisel, scratches from the scalpel, pains

from the scorper, until finally, shattering herself into pieces and fracturing herself completely, she would be a saint made through suffering] (Valdés 1765, bk. 1, chap. 16, 115). Cf. Perry (1991).

38. Valdés (1765, bk. 1, chap. 9, 60).

39. Peter Brown shows how even Ancient Christian friendships between devout women and priests were the subject of scurrilous speculation, citing the example of Origen's self-castration, an act intended to staunch such rumors. Brown (1989, 153–167) links this both to the concrete economic power widows wielded in the early Church and to the more abstract fear in which femininity, because more "open," condensed the deep preoccupation of male Christians with their own relations to the world. See also Haliczer (1995).

40. The text of Fray Luis' sermon is reprinted in Imirizaldu, ed. (1977); all references are to this edition. Granada (1504–1588) was possibly the most widely read of the mystical authors of this period. He also generated substantial controversy. His assertion that knowledge of God could only be reached on the paths of contemplation and not the roads of practical religion was considered to have encouraged heretical beliefs such as those held by the Alumbrados in Extremadura in the 1570's. His works were some of the first to be placed on the Index. Granada was deceived by the piety of María de la Cruz, the prioress of the Dominican convent in Lisbon, who had emerged as a holy woman in the early 1580's. By 1582, after the annexation of Portugal by Spain, María was presenting herself as mystical supporter of the Portuguese pretender, dom Antonio. She was eventually sentenced to perpetual exile in Brazil, having been found guilty of a variety of crimes including feigned sanctity and seditious statements about the Spanish monarchy. For information on the availability of Fray Luis' works in the New World, despite the ban placed on them, see Leonard (1949) and Hampe-Martínez (1993). Many of the nuns mentioned in the convent chronicles and *vidas* examined make references to Granada.

41. L27 f150.

42. L3 f25.

43. [With so much anger against my Venerable Father as if he were responsible for all my pains, though unaware of all that was happening to me. [. . .] and so I was ashamed, and also of the fact that my things seemed wicked to Your Grace, and if I were to go back to you I would get no consolation and you would say only what was necessary, the rest being dangerous. And suddenly I would feel such disgust for the Father of my soul that I would want to insult him with bad words. I was like a gentile] (L26 f146).

44. Cf. Arenal (1985).

45. Valdés (1765, bk. 1, chap. 15, 108). There was already a history of Indian institutions of this kind being eroded by the power of the Spanish authorities, and so the reaction of the *cacique* nuns is interpreted by Valdés as a natural resistance to a heterogeneity that will make their institution lose its particularity, and thereby its power.

46. *Limpieza de sangre* had already become a term loaded with cultural and class values in the Peninsula, and in the New World context its multivalent significations were even more evident. See Bernand and Gruzinski (1993).

47. See Valdés (1765, bk. 1, chap.17) for his condemnation of the patron's conditions. The Brigidine convent was founded by Basque nuns and financed by Basque patrons— clearly there was a strong sense of group identity and solidarity in the convent. Sor Sebastiana does not appear to have had the necessary connections.

48. Le Goff emphasizes the particularly "feminine" characteristics of this mediation, citing the Virgin and St. Lutagard as especially effective mediators for souls in purgatory. The role of the Beguines of Helfta in encouraging this idea of the "efficacy" of female intervention in matters connected to purgatory is well established, and perhaps the greatest exponent of the peculiarly feminine contribution to be made in freeing souls from "the third place" is Catherine of Genoa's (1447–1510) treatise on the subject (le Goff 1981, 482–483). On the power such mediation could bring to the Beguines, see Jo Ann McNamara (1991, 214): "by developing their powers to assist the dead, women of limited means and worldly prospects put themselves firmly among society's benefactors and outside the realm of the abject and needy poor."

49. Valdés (1765, bk. 1, Intro. 2, and chap. 1, 7).

50. Valdés (1765, bk. 2, chap.2, 141–142).

51. Valdés (1765, bk. 2, chap. 2, 142).

52. L15 f85; see also L6 f54.

53. L25 f136. In this description, some of the animals are monkeys, which in the New World were to be found both in the jungle and in the market place.

54. See Carrión (1994, 137) for an account of how Sta. Teresa's descriptions of hell serve to defamiliarize the domestic spaces usually considered so safe for women, thus opening up the entire issue of the degree of autonomy permitted women in writing if their rhetoric can be seen to have such violent effects on such sacrosanct symbols.

55. L28 f155; L39 f242.

56. L23 f129.

57. [I found myself in a terrifying place. It is impossible to describe it, but to make myself understood I will say it was like the saddest, most remote quarter of a city. It was very big and there were very few houses; to see them pained the soul with sadness. What looked like long-legged men walked about speaking an incomprehensible language. I saw a very high thing that looked like a tower; I do not know how to describe it. At the top there something like a stage, and there were people dancing and jumping] (L24 f134).

58. See McKnight (1997) for a description of how the Bolivian Madre Castillo's writings vary in their concordance with social, religious, and political orthodoxy according to their changing generic form.

59. [In this tragicomedy, there is nothing but appearance and the staging of virtue, as

well as the rottenness and disgusting lust of this woman. She has more self-love than a *beata*] (Quoted in Méndez 1989, 14).

60. [They are pleasures connected in the end to Mexican courtliness, spells, and toys with which Lady Mexico, though a lady and an adult, likes to be amused] (Valdés 1765, bk. 1, chap. 3, 18).

CHAPTER 4

1. [The Discalced (Carmelites) consider ourselves utterly obedient and meek toward our prelates, and we would not allow bad doctrines to influence this, whosoever held them] (Archivo General de la Nación, Mexico City, Ramo Inquisición 581, exp. 1, f30r; hereafter, AGN. Inq. Letter Mariana de la Encarnación, undated).

2. "Daba a entender se tenía por las religiosas algunos errores y herejías" (AGN Inq. 581, exp. 1. Title). It would have been hard for the Inquisition to refuse a request for an investigation from an archbishop, but, certainly in America, by no means impossible. In his chapter on the Inquisition's relation to the regular clergy, Richard Greenleaf (1969, 152–157) makes clear that, on the initiative of Inquisitor Archbishop Montúfar, the regular clergy lost power in the colony. Greenleaf insists, however, that this did not mean that the Inquisition was simply the tool of the episcopacy. In theory it was an independent religious institution, able to act impartially in cases involving both branches of the priesthood.

3. Teresa de Jesús (1982).

4. The convent of San Plácido in Madrid was tried in the eighteenth century. For an account of a French example, see Certeau (1980).

5. See Pagden (1995) on the extensive discussions about the difficulties of administering far-flung colonies undertaken by contemporary theoreticians of empire. The Mexican Carmelites' uncomfortable relation with ecclesiastic authority was to continue in the eighteenth century. The convent of Sta. Teresa la Nueva, which was founded by nuns from San José, came into conflict with José Lanciego y Eguilaz, a Benedictine archbishop appointed in 1713. Lanciego y Eguilaz resolved his disagreement with the nuns in a drastic manner by deposing the prioress, imprisoning her in San José, and eventually (in a manner reminiscent of how Ana de Jesús was sent to found convents in the Netherlands by the Spanish ecclesiastical authorities) dispatching her to Cuba as a founding mother for the island's first Carmelite convent. See Ramos Medina (1993).

6. "Visita de Descalzas," in *Obras Completas*, Madre de Dios and Steggink, eds. (1967, 647). It would not be unreasonable to suppose that the archbishops of Mexico City would have been familiar with this text of Sta. Teresa's.

7. Madre de Dios and Steggink, eds. (1967, 656).

8. [Because she preferred to found a monastery to a convent, as she was aware of the

importance of it, something which was to be confirmed later] (García de la Concha, ed., 1982, 155). In fact, an entire chapter of the book is given over to the first male Carmelite foundation (chap. 13): "En que trata cómo se comenzó la primera casa de la regla primitiva y por quién, de los Descalzos Carmelitas, año de 1568."

9. García de la Concha, ed. (1982, 199).

10. Sta. Teresa's account of these political intrigues can be traced in her correspondence, though references are, unsurprisingly, guarded (in Madre de Dios and Steggink, eds., 1967).

11. For an introduction to the controversy, see Torres (1995, 9–42).

12. See Steggink (1965). For an account of the theological factors that influenced Sta. Teresa's relation with various prelates and how they transformed the gender hierarchy of such relations, see Steggink (1982).

13. In the last quarter of the sixteenth century, division and animosity between *gachupines* and criollos within the Franciscan Order, for example, were endemic and coincided with the petitions for the renewal of *encomiendas* being requested by disgruntled lay criollos. The problems within the Franciscan Order gave rise to debates on the nature of the Indians and on the effects of the climate of the Americas, as well as punctilious legal arguments about the rights of these various groups in the colony. The introduction of the *alternativa* in 1624, a system whereby a criollo, a *gachupín,* and a *gachupín* who had professed in the Indies were elected alternately to the leading offices of each Franciscan province, only partially resolved the problem (see Brading 1991). The significance of the conflict between the secular and the regular clergy extended beyond these internal ecclesiastical differences, however, and some historians have traced the birth of a politicized idea of "nation," or at least of a criollo political identity to it. See Cuevas' characterization of the exclusion of Mexicans from high ecclesiastical office by the Crown as the final humiliation that drove the criollos to fight for independence (Cuevas 1921–1926). See also Lafaye (1974). For an interpretation that places the regular/secular conflict within a solidly European tradition of ecclesiastical dispute, see Wright (1982, 121–146). Wright points out, "Conflict between regulars and bishops [. . .] repeated, from the early seventeenth century, yet another aspect of the overseas export of problems internal to the Catholic church of the Counter-Reformation" (136).

14. See Pagden (1984, 51–93).

15. It could be argued that *pureza de sangre* in the New World is completely caught up in an aristocratic problematic where there is truly only ever one pure blood: that of the noble. The problem then becomes how to define the noble in the vertiginous social universe of the Indies. On the concept of honor in the period, see Maravall (1979).

16. Cf. Alberro (1988, Intro.).

17. Alberro (1988, 86). See Bernand and Gruzinski (1993, 307) on the impossibility of policing New World beliefs: "Un extraordinaire entrelacs de croyances que les autorités de la Nouvelle-Espagne ne se préoccupent guère d'extirper, à la fois parce qu'elles savent

l'entreprise irréalisable et parce que ce tourbillon d'images, d'espoirs et de rites ne se métamorphose ni en un mouvement hérétique ni en une protestation sociale." An attempt to define a New World psychology, using Inquisition cases as "ethno texts," can be found in Escandell Bonet (1980), "Una lectura psico-social de los papeles del Sto. Oficio." For an analysis of Inquisition trials involving heretical women that interprets the phemenon as a direct cultural imposition of Spanish norms, see Méndez (1989). The cases she discusses are all late eighteenth century.

18. One would expect the archbishop to be particularly touched by this, in effect, memento mori. Cf. Delumeau (1983, 363): "Ainsi, même pour les saints, la mort est parfois difficile et, à l'époque que nous étudions, la peur de l'au-delà fut d'abord et surtout le tragique privilège d'une élite chrétienne."

19. AGN Inq. 581, exp. 1, f5v: letter Mariana de la Encarnación, undated. This divine injunction is, of course, the ultimate proof of Truth. Mariana de la Encarnación is probably referring to the last chapter of *Libro de las fundaciones,* where Sta. Teresa writes about how a divine sign told her to change the obedience given by the convent in Avila from the archbishop to the male Carmelites.

20. ". . . y también por haber entendido que es acto libre el de elejir confesor, especialmente en este trance" [and because I have heard it said that choosing a confessor is a free act, especially in this circumstance] (AGN Inq. 581, exp. 1, f5r: letter Mariana de la Encarnación, undated).

21. AGN Inq. 581, exp. 1, f5r: letter Mariana de la Encarnación, undated.

22. AGN Inq. 581, exp. 1: letter to the king, 29 August 1657, unfoliated.

23. AGN Inq. 581, exp. 1: letter to the king, 29 August 1657, unfoliated.

24. AGN Inq. 581, exp. 1, f198v: letter Luis Becerra, 27 January 1661.

25. AGN Inq. 581, exp. 1, f199r: letter Luis Becerra, 27 January 1661.

26. AGN Inq. 581, exp. 1, f199r: letter Luis Becerra, 27 January 1661.

27. Cf. Haliczer (1996, Intro.).

28. Andrea de San Francisco defends her actions in going to the Inquisition by saying she was convinced to do so not only by other nuns in San José but by her own confessors. She claims she pleaded with Jacinto de la Serna to wait until the archbishop carried out a formal visitation to the convent (AGN Inq. 581, exp. 1, f118r: Andrea de San Francisco, 11 February 1661). The declaration she gives on 7 February 1661 is reproduced in Appendix 2.

29. AGN Inq. 581, exp. 1, f81v: Andrea de San Francisco, 4 February 1661.

30. AGN Inq. 581, exp. 1, f82r: Andrea de San Francisco, 4 February 1661.

31. AGN Inq. 581, exp. 1, f87v: Andrea de San Francisco, 7 February 1661. The echoes of a paradise lost are maintained by the description of the ideal concordance between the original couple of founding mothers, the destruction of whose friendship brings disaster to the cloister (AGN Inq. 581, exp. 1, f87v–88r: Andrea de San Francisco, 7 February 1661). According to sor Andrea, how far San José finds itself from Paradise increases under the

government of these *gachupinas* and is evident from the unhappiness in the cloister. Not only does one nun, Clara del Sacramento, want to hang herself, but most of the novices leave, terrorized by Margarita de San Bernardo (AGN Inq. 581, exp. 1, f102r–102v: Andrea de San Francisco, 9 February 1661).

32. It also, of course, reminds us of the original divisions between *gachupinas* and criollas that were so evident at the time of San José's foundation and that were discussed in Chapter 2. It seems as if this divisiveness was built into the very heart of New Spanish convents.

33. AGN Inq. 581, exp. 1, f92r: Andrea de San Francisco, 7 February 1661.

34. AGN Inq. 581, exp. 1, f92r–92v: Andrea de San Francisco, 7 February 1661.

35. AGN Inq. 581, exp. 1, f91v: Andrea de San Francisco, 7 February 1661.

36. AGN Inq. 581, exp. 1, f116v: Andrea de San Francisco, 11 February 1661.

37. AGN Inq. 581, exp. 1, f117r–117v: Andrea de San Francisco, 11 February 1661.

38. AGN Inq. 581, exp. 1, f114r: Andrea de San Francisco, 10 February 1661.

39. AGN Inq. 581, exp. 1, f114v–115v: Andrea de San Francisco, 10 February 1661.

40. AGN Inq. 581, exp. 1, f115v: Andrea de San Francisco, 10 February 1661.

41. AGN Inq. 581, exp. 1, f115v: Andrea de San Francisco, 10 February 1661.

42. See Ginzburg (1992) on the Inquisitor as Anthropologist. See also Kelley (1987).

43. AGN Inq. 581, exp. 1, f178v: Hijas de la Orden communal letter, 21 February 1661.

44. AGN Inq. 581, exp. 1, f175r: Hijas de la Orden communal letter, 21 February 1661. The gravity of this story's implications in terms of sorcery and superstition in an Inquisition context should not be underestimated.

45. AGN Inq. 581, exp. 1, f175r: Hijas de la Orden communal letter, 21 February 1661.

46. *Sus parlerias* [her chatter] *su buena labia* [her big mouth] *su demasía en hablar* [her excessive talk] (AGN Inq. 581, exp. 1, f175r–175v, and Hijas de la Orden communal letter, 21 February 1661). Cf. also Juana de San Elías' description of sor Andrea's seductive speech: "engañando con un modo tan parlero y halagueño que parece no hay mal en ella" [deceiving with a talkative and flattering manner that there seems to be no evil in her] (AGN Inq. 581, exp. 1, f184v: letter Juana de San Elías, undated). Also Catalina de la Cruz, "habla todo el día" [she speaks all day long], "es tan abundante en sus palabras que ahoga a quien la oye" [she is so excessive with her words that she drowns anyone who listens to her], and the incredibly damning, "decir palabras muy feas no de carmelitas descalzas sino de mujeres perdidas de ese mundo" [saying ugly words, not those of a Discalced Carmelite but of a lost woman of the world] (AGN Inq. 581, exp. 1, f160r–161v: letter Catalina de la Cruz, 18 February 1661).

47. AGN Inq. 581, exp. 1, f175v–176r: Hijas de la Orden communal letter, 21 February 1661, f177r. The letter describes how sor Andrea manages to deceive the archbishop. He takes her word as truth, according to the letter, and as a result neglects his duties to the convent, never visiting them to find out what is really going on. The accusation is clearly

one of "seduction"; again a serious charge in these circumstances. The accusation of being a self-conscious *reformadora* is repeated in Ana de San Bartolomé's undated letter, annexed to the communal one (AGN Inq. 581, exp. 1, f180r, as well as in Juana de Sta. Teresa's, f186v). Ana de San Bartolomé's letter is reproduced in Appendix 2 along with a letter from María de San Juan.

48. AGN Inq. 581, exp. 1, f17: Hijas de la Orden communal letter, 21 February 1661.

49. [With stratagems and tricks (. . .) some weak nuns who were less disciplined in religious observance] (AGN Inq. 581, exp. 1, f152r: Ana de San Bartolomé, 17 February 1661).

50. Cf. Juana de San Elías' remark that Andrea de San Francisco called nuns who disagreed with her *judías* for an equally inflammatory comment, given the context (AGN Inq. 581, exp. 1, f184r: letter Juana de San Elías, undated).

51. [. . . these will be the ones to put the last candle into her hands on her deathbed] (AGN Inq. 581, exp. 1, f176r: Hijas de la Orden communal letter, 21 February 1661).

52. AGN Inq. 581, exp. 1, f176v: Hijas de la Orden communal letter, 21 February 1661.

53. AGN Inq. 581, exp. 1, f190r: letter María de San Cirilio, undated. The ambiguity "indian"/"born in the Indies" is impossible to resolve, but the latter interpretation suggests a far wider application of the stereotype that fits in with Alberro's findings and ties in with the *gachupín* claim that all criollos were Indians beneath the skin (Alberro 1992).

54. AGN Inq. 581, exp. 1, f160r: letter Catalina de la Cruz, 18 February 1661.

55. AGN Inq. 581, exp. 1, f151r: Ana de San Bartolomé, 17 February 1661.

56. AGN Inq. 581, exp. 1, f183r: letter María de San Juan, undated.

57. AGN Inq. 581, exp. 1, f181v–182r: letter María de San Juan, undated.

58. AGN Inq. 581, exp. 1, f120v: Andrea de San Francisco, 11 February 1661.

59. AGN Inq. 581, exp. 1, f120v–121r: Andrea de San Francisco, 11 February 1661.

60. AGN Inq. 581, exp. 1, f121r: Andrea de San Francisco, 11 February 1661.

61. [This doctrine is heretical] (AGN Inq. 581, exp. 1, f122r: Andrea de San Francisco, 11 February 1661).

62. AGN Inq. 581, exp. 1, f122v: Andrea de San Francisco, 11 February 1661.

63. AGN Inq. 581, exp. 1, f124r: Andrea de San Francisco, 11 February 1661.

64. [Only what she has already said about asking for Carmelite confessors] (AGN Inq. 581, exp. 1, f124r: Andrea de San Francisco, 11 February 1661).

65. AGN Inq. 581, exp. 1, f169r: Clara del Santísimo Sacramento, 19 February 1661. The great majority of the accusations leveled by the nuns remain at this allusive, often metaphorical level. They retell anecdotes that may be interpreted as having a doctrinal dimension, but they never make this dimension apparent themselves. Thus, María de los Angeles, when answering the direct question of whether heterodox doctrines are held in the convent, recounts how during a meal and extraordinary mortification she hears Catalina de Cristo say that she was "losing her soul" because she was not fulfilling the Carmelite

rule. She also says she has heard Margarita de San Bernardo say that no nun in the convent was in a fit state for salvation because they were not fully Carmelites (AGN Inq. 581, exp. 1, f145r: María de los Angeles, undated).

66. AGN Inq. 581, exp. 1, f169v–170r: Clara del Santísimo Sacramento, 19 February 1661.

67. AGN Inq. 581, exp. 1, f156r: María del Niño Jesús, 17 February 1661.

68. AGN Inq. 581, exp. 1, f126r: Andrea de San Francisco, 11 February 1661.

69. AGN Inq. 581, exp. 1, f126r: Andrea de San Francisco, 11 February 1661.

70. AGN Inq. 581, exp. 1, f135r: Teresa de Jesús, 15 February 1661. In her testimony, María de los Angeles uses exactly the same metaphor, this time in reported speech. Clearly, the Hijas de la Orden themselves employed it (f143r: María de los Angeles, undated).

71. AGN Inq. 581, exp. 1, f136r: Teresa de Jesús, 15 February 1661.

72. AGN Inq. 581, exp. 1, f135v: Teresa de Jesús, 15 February 1661.

73. AGN Inq. 581, exp. 1, f134v–135r: Teresa de Jesús, 15 February 1661.

CHAPTER 5

1. [Since the birth of the new Eve in 1500, divine providence has shown her omnipotence by allowing more of the world to be discovered, principally the Indies, which had not been done for 5500 years . . . in the hope that the source of the divine spirit should be incorporated into the world through this general mothering] (Reprinted in Geneva, 1970). The quotation is from this reprinted edition, pp. 50–51. On Postel's stature as a thinker about "woman," see Maclean (1980, 22–26) and Screech (1953). On his conception of the New World, see Febvre's comments (1982, 107–122). A version of this chapter first appeared in *Gender and History* (1997).

2. [Having mentioned good Petronila (the Indian), there is no reason not to mention other humble little women, who today in the court of the Supreme King of Kings will be very great] (Sigüenza y Góngora 1683, Preface).

3. The literature on the history of the indigenous peoples under colonial rule is vast. A good overview, including a bibliographical essay, is provided by Gibson (1984). For seminal accounts of indigenous acculturation in New Spain, see Lockhart (1992), Clendinnen (1987), and Gruzinski (1988).

4. The testimonies of two priests, Manuel Pérez and Alejandro Romano, one for and one against the foundation, are reproduced in Appendix 3.

5. Nancy M. Farris provides details of the relationship of the indigenous population to the church hierarchy. She describes how an Indian community set up its own cult to the Virgin, an activity connected to the Indian revolt in Chiapas in 1712. Earlier, in 1610 in another border region, the Yucatán, two Maya Indian men proclaimed themselves

pope and bishop and ordained a number of other Indians. It was also usual for Indians to officiate at "dry" masses (when the Host was not consecrated) whenever an officially ordained priest was not available. Farris also cites the example of the apostate Maya in the Tipu region who taunted visiting friars with claims that his people had their own priests to celebrate mass using tortillas and pozole. Farris (1984, 318) identifies the definitively negative shift in official Spanish policy toward the establishment of an indigenous Catholic priesthood as taking place between the foundation of the Franciscan school/seminary at Tlatelolco in 1536 and the first Mexican Provincial Council in 1555, after which all such ideas were abandoned. See also Gruzinski (1991) on how the options taken by wealthy Indians making their wills in the eighteenth century, especially the foundation of *capellanías,* can be interpreted as strategies designed to ensure the ordination of male members of their families.

6. Cf. Ricard (1992); see especially the chapters on the foundation of the seminary for Indian boys in Tlatelolco. Cf. also Gonzalbo Aizpuru (1990).

7. See Cuevas (1921–1926, 4:189) and Muriel (1963).

8. This article is based on material consulted in the Archivo General de la Nación, sección Historia, abbreviated hereafter as AGN Hist. (AGN Hist. vol. 109, exp. 2, f39v–40r).

9. Cf. Pedro Valo de Villavicencio's assertion that his Jesuit colleagues testifying against the foundation have proved their case both in theological and legal terms, as well as from personal experience (AGN Hist. vol. 109, exp. 2, unfoliated).

10. José L. Sánchez Llora's figures for the printing of hagiographic works in Spanish revealingly set the peak years as the decades 1600–1610, 1610–1619, and 1620–1629, with a production of 79, 97, and 124 works, respectively. The figures for the last half of the seventeenth century average about 40 works per decade, considerably higher than the average production per decade for the whole preceding century, which is 13. Sánchez Llora's (1988, 375) figures are based on the library catalog of the Spanish humanist Nicolás Antonio and are intended to give an idea of editorial activity rather than exact numbers of publication. It was in this period of high production that the greatest number of hagiographies of women were published. For the "feminization" of hagiography as narrative, see Vauchez (1981, 41).

11. For the formalization of hagiography as a genre, see Weinstein and Bell (1982) and Caro Baroja (1978).

12. Of course, the New World's novelty and the unknown consequences of its climate, food, and so forth, became a subject of debate in connection with the huge Creole and mestizo populations that had grown by 1700 (see Alberro 1992).

13. Maclean (1980, 57). The varieties of social organization of the peoples who made up the México empire should not be underestimated. It is, however, justifiable to make a generalization in this case (see Clendinnen 1995). As for Spanish imposition of what they

considered "natural" family structures, it is interesting to recall how many of the Indians were forced to live in nuclear and patriarchal "units" in the hospitals set up by the early missionaries, most notably Vasco de Quiroga's in Santa Fe.

14. Vitoria, *De potestate ecclesiastica altera,* in Lawrance and Pagden, eds. (1995, 130).

15. Brown (1989, 271).

16. Maclean (1980, 81).

17. The classic study of the fortunes of Natural Slavery and other aspects of scholastic thought concerning the Americas is Anthony Pagden's, *The Fall of Natural Man* (1982).

18. Manuel Pérez mentions the papal bull in his testimony, though he mistakes the pope, in order to impress how the utterly barbaric nature of the indigenous peoples had caused many to doubt their rationality, obliging the Church to issue a binding statement (AGN Hist. vol. 109, exp. 2, unfoliated).

19. *Politics* 2.1254a28–b2 and 3.1254b2–16. (1995, 6–7). It is interesting in this context to note that the discussion that prompts such comments from Aristotle is on the "Natural patterns of rule as a justification of slavery." For an account of the recurrent appeal to pairs of opposites of various sorts, both in general cosmological doctrines and in accounts of particular natural phenomena in ancient thought, see Lloyd (1966).

20. Cf. the canonist Diego de Covarrubias' (1512–1577) statement that "all women are natural slaves in relation to their husbands" (quoted in Pagden 1982, 46).

21. Alejandro Romano (AGN Hist. vol. 109, exp. 2, f37v–38r) and Pedro Valo de Villavicencio (AGN Hist. vol. 109, exp. 2, f53r–53v).

22. *Novísima de Indias* (1571–1572, 27, bk. 6).

23. Cf. Brown (1989, 271).

24. AGN Hist. vol. 109, exp. 2, unfoliated.

25. AGN Hist. vol. 109, exp. 2, unfoliated.

26. AGN Hist. vol. 109, exp. 2, unfoliated. For an explanation of the classical genealogy of this kind of argumentation from opposites, see Lloyd (1966, especially chap. 2, "The Analysis of Different Modes of Opposition").

27. AGN Hist. vol. 109, exp. 2, unfoliated.

28. On the late medieval precedents for this legislation on the suitability of different kinds of grain, see Rubin (1991). Cf. Francisco de Vitoria's (1586, f38v) explanation that barley was an unsuitable cereal for making the Host, as it was not the food of men but of beasts.

29. Rubin (1991, 147) describes how the frequency of communion was also a source of concern for medieval theologians and how it changed from being an annual sacrament (instituted by the Fourth Lateran Council of 1215) to one permitted three times a year (Christmas, Easter, and Pentecost) as long as it was accompanied by proper confession. Discussions in this period about the appropriateness of sexual intercourse before receiving the Eucharist and the consensus that menstruating women should abstain from communion underline how the materiality of the sacrament had always been a source of

ambivalence. That it continued to be so during the Counter-Reformation and that such ambivalence required that the sacrament's practice be regulated carefully is also apparent from the controversy surrounding the Jansenists, who wrote opposing what they characterized as the Jesuit custom of administering the sacrament in a too frequent and indiscriminate manner. Delumeau (1977, 107–108) mentions Arnauld's *De la fréquente communion* (1642) in the context of the Jansenists' perceived "rigor" but makes clear that this was also a discussion central to thinkers like Charles Borromeo, whose orthodoxy was never in question. See Zarri (1990, 87–163) on frequent communion and women. Zarri provides a closely argued account of the Italian ecclesiastical hierarchy's interpretation of this practice by spiritually inclined women in the early and mid sixteenth century as constituting a threat to the (male) priesthood. Caroline Walker Bynum (1987, 56) pursues a similar argument.

30. AGN Hist. vol. 109, exp. 2, unfoliated.

31. AGN Hist. vol. 109, exp. 2, f29r–30r.

32. AGN Hist. vol. 109, exp. 2, f37r.

33. AGN Hist. vol. 109, exp. 2, f29v.

34. AGN Hist. vol. 109, exp. 2, f30r. Cf. Delumeau, ed. (1992).

35. "Videmus, vel in ipsa nostra Hispania homines in pagis quibusdam natos, si apud suos perseverent, ineptos haberi, ac ridiculos: eosdem traductos in scholas, aut curiam, aut celebres urbes mirae soltertiae, in genio praestare, nemeni cedere" (Acosta 1596, 150).

36. AGN Hist. vol. 109, exp. 2, unfoliated.

37. For an interpretation of the rediscovery of idolatry in the Spanish viceroyalties, see Bernand and Gruzinski (1992, 1993).

38. On the antipathy of José de Acosta (Jesuit historiographer and founder of the order's first *reducción* in Peru in 1578) toward the idea of making Indians more Spanish on the grounds that it would be "the downfall of everything," see Pagden (1982, 164). See also Girolamo Imbruglia (1983, 26) for the selective preservation of facets of indigenous culture in the Jesuit *reducciones*.

39. For a general account of narrative transformations in the New World, see Greenblatt (1992).

40. AGN Hist. vol. 109, exp. 2, unfoliated.

41. AGN Hist. vol. 109, exp. 2, unfoliated.

42. AGN Hist. vol. 109, exp. 2, unfoliated.

43. Diego de Covarrubias (1679, f684v, f685r, and f673r) often makes this analogy, both in order to prove Spanish authority over the Indians and in order to support arguments for universal monarchy.

44. Vigil (1986, 135).

45. Caro Baroja (1978, 490).

46. Pilar Gonzalbo Aizpuru (1987) argues that Indian women learned the lessons of assimilation and acculturation much more quickly than their male counterparts. She links

the fact that Indian women taught Christianity in convents were put into groups that ignored indigenous customs of social segregation and hierarchy to the rapid decomposition of the indigenous elite. A similar argument that women were special vectors for the transmission of cultural values is put forward by Solange Alberro (1988, 204) in relation to Inquisition cases concerning Jews. Alberro claims the *judaisante* family—and particularly the women in it—are a perfect metaphor of the process of assimilation and integration under way in the colony, and that in fact the very fabric of colonial Jewish religious practice was transformed as a result of the domestic and feminine sphere becoming its privileged space.

47. AGN Hist. vol. 109, exp. 2, unfoliated.

48. AGN Hist. vol. 109, exp. 2, unfoliated.

49. Bernand and Gruzinski (1992, 142). The authors also point out the importance the extirpators made of the distinction between traditions they considered to have been inherited mechanically and those they perceived to be the result of transformations wrought by personal initiative. Bernand and Gruzinski's formulation is clearly indebted to the work of Pierre Bourdieu and his notions of the quotidian and what he expresses as the habitus. See Bourdieu (1990).

50. AGN Hist. vol. 109, exp. 2, unfoliated.

51. See Ginzburg's (1992, 161) comments on the rejection of the "referential fallacy" by historians and his own optimism that "dialogic" sources may still hold information about "something which we must call, *faute de mieux,* (eternal reality)."

52. See the consequent resonance of Ginzburg's (1992, 159) description of the "anthropological attitude": "The essence of what we call anthropological attitude—that is, the permanent confrontation between different cultures—rests on a dialogic disposition."

53. AGN Hist. vol. 109, exp. 2, unfoliated.

54. AGN Hist. vol. 109, exp. 2, unfoliated.

55. Corcuera de Mancera (1992).

56. AGN Hist. vol. 109, exp. 2, unfoliated.

57. Vitoria, *De Indis,* in Lawrance and Pagden, eds. (1995, 235).

Afterword

1. Cervantes (1995, 459, Allen, ed.).

Appendix 2

1. Spaniards who have come to the Indies. From the Portuguese *cachopo,* meaning small boy.

2. This title denotes that Téllez had a university degree.

Appendix 3

1. The numbering of folios follows the original, which is extremely erratic.

2. The meanings of the Spanish *doncella* ["virgin" and "unmarried woman"] are, of course, considered to be synonymous by the writer.

3. A gruel made out of maize flour and water.

Bibliography of Works Cited

Manuscript Sources

Ana de San Bartolomé. 1650. "Vida de la madre Bernarda de San Juan." AHCSJ.

"Apuntes de algunas virtudes que señalaron varias religiosas de este convento antiguo de Nuestro Padre y Señor San José y Carmelitas Descalzas." Undated. Archivo Histórico del Convento de San José de Carmelitas Descalzas; hereafter AHCSJ.

Avendaño, Nicolás de. Undated. "Crónica de la fundación del convento de San José de Carmelitas Descalzas de México." AHCSJ.

"Carta." 1640. AHCSJ.

"Convento de Nuestra Señora de las Nieves: Crónica." Undated. [The chronicle consists of one volume, divided into five sections, and covers the period 1739–1783. It is possible to identify the various authors of the sections as follows:

A: María Catalina de la Concepción (copies the original Spanish chronicle dealing with the foundation of the mother house in Vitoria [Basque country] and includes a *vida* of St. Bridget);

B: Benita Francisca de San José;

C: Isabel Antonio de San Miguel (principal author, writing 100 pages of the 230-page document);

D: Inés Joaquina del señor San José (taking dictation from C);

E: possibly María Antonio de San Pedro (telling of C's death).]

"De algunas cosas que he visto en este convento y de la vida de la Madre Bernarda de San Juan." Undated. AHCSJ.

Historia. Vol. 109, exp. 2. 1723. ff. 8–56. "Diligencias ejecutadas en virtud de la real cédula de su majestad sobre la licencia pedida por el excelentísimo señor marqués de Balero, virrey y gobernador y capitán general que fué de este reino, para la fundación de un convento para religiosas de San Francisco en esta ciudad." Archivo General de la Nación, Mexico City.

Inés de la Cruz. Undated. "Fundación." AHCSJ.

Inquisición. Vol. 581, exp. 1. 1661. "Autos hechos en el convento de San José de religiosas Carmelitas Descalzas de esta ciudad sobre una carta escrita a la superiora de dicho convento por el señor arzobispo don Mateo de Buqueiro en que daba a entender se tenía por las religiosas algunos errores y heregías." Archivo General de la Nación, Mexico City.

Isabel de la Visitación. Undated. "Relato de una relación de lo que le sucedió." AHCSJ.

Margarita de San Bernardo. 1630. "Apuntes sobre la vida de la hermana Beatríz de Santiago." AHCSJ.

María de Santa Inés. 1650. "Vida de Bernarda de San Juan." AHCSJ.

María del Niño Jesús. 1640. "Escritos." AHCSJ.

Mariana de la Encarnación. Undated. "Fundación." AHCSJ.

Méndez, J. B. Undated. "Historia de la fundación." AHCSJ.

Petronila de San Ildefonso. 1640. "Vida de Bernarda de San Juan." AHCSJ.

"Relatos extraordinarios de la religiosa fundadora Inés de la Cruz." 1640. AHCSJ.

Rosa Figueroa, A. de la. 1755. "Crónica suscinta del convento de Sta. Clara de México en dos cuadernos. Primer cuaderno: disquisiciones cronológicas por Fr. [. . .] Segundo cuaderno; descripción del voraz incendio acaecido en la iglesia y convento de Sta. Clara de Mexico." Instituto Nacional de Historia y Antropología.

"Sta. Catalina de Sena: Crónica." Undated. [The main text is the "Libro de memorias" belonging to Beatríz de las Vírgenes (1620–1663), who was prioress of the convent six times. On two occasions, the *vidas* of nuns recounted in Beatríz de las Vírgenes' book are supplemented by the information contained in Alonso Franco y Ortega's (1645) *Historia de la provincia de Santiago en México: Orden de predicadores en la Nueva España.*]

Santísima Trinidad, S. de la. Undated. "Cartas." Biblioteca Nacional, Mexico City.

"Vida de algunas religiosas primitivas del convento de San José." Undated. AHCSJ.

"Vida de la Madre Juana de San Esteban." 1650. AHCSJ.

"Vida de la Madre María de la Natividad." Undated. AHCSJ.

"Vocación, vida y visiones de la Madre Ana. Se señalan los milagros de la fundadora Inés de la Cruz." Undated. AHCSJ.

PRINTED WORKS

For ease of reference, no distinction has been made between primary and secondary sources.

Acosta, J. de. 1596. *De procuranda indorum salute.*

———. 1984. 2 vols. Edited by Luciano Pereña. Madrid: CSIC. [Modern edition of Latin text with Spanish translation.]

Alberro, S. 1988. *Inquisition et société au Mexique, 1571–1700.* Mexico City: CEMCA.

————. 1992. *Del gachupín al criollo o de cómo los Españoles en México dejaron de serlo.* Mexico City: Colegio de México.

Andrade, A. de. 1642. *Tratado de la Virgen.*

Arasse, D. 1981. "Entre dévotion et culture: Fonctions de l'image religieuse au XV siècle." In *Faire croire: Modalités de la diffusion et de la réception des messages religieux du XII au XV siècles.* 130–146. Rome: Ecole Française de Rome.

Arenal, E. 1985. "Sor Juana Inés de la Cruz: Reclaiming the Mother Tongue." *Letras Femeninas* 11 (1–2): 63–75.

Arenal, E., and. S. Schlau. 1989. *Untold Sisters: Hispanic Nuns in Their Own Works.* Albuquerque: University of New Mexico Press.

Aristotle. 1995. *Politics.* Translated by Trevor J. Saunders. Oxford: Clarendon.

Augustine, St. 1978. "Confessions." In *Complete Works.* Edited by R. M. Hutchins. Translated by E. Bouverie Pusey. London: Encyclopaedia Britannica.

Balbuena, B. de. 1604. *La grandeza mexicana.* Mexico City.

Bataillon, M. 1966. *Erasmo y España: Estudios sobre la história espiritual del siglo XVI.* Mexico City: Fondo de Cultura Económica.

Bennassar, B. 1982. *Un siècle d'or espagnol.* Paris: Robert Lafont.

Bernand, C., and S. Gruzinski. 1992. *De la idolatría: Una arqueología de las ciencias religiosas.* Mexico City: Fondo de Cultura Económica.

————. 1993. *Histoire du Nouveau Monde: Les métissages, 1550–1640.* Paris: Fayard.

Bethell, L., ed. 1984. *The Cambridge History of Latin America.* 11 vols. Cambridge: Cambridge University Press.

Bilinkoff, J. 1989. *The Avila of St. Teresa: Religious Reform in a Sixteenth-Century Convent.* Ithaca: Cornell University Press.

Birge Vitz, E. 1991. "From the Oral to the Written in Medieval and Renaissance Saints' Lives." In *Images of Sainthood in Medieval Europe.* Edited by R. Blumenfeld-Kozinski and T. Szell. 97–114. Ithaca: Cornell University Press.

Blumenfeld-Kozinski, R., and T. Szell, eds. 1991. *Images of Sainthood in Medieval Europe.* Ithaca: Cornell University Press.

Bourdieu, P. 1990. *In Other Words: Essays towards a Reflexive Sociology.* Cambridge: Polity Press.

Brading, D. A. 1991. *The First America: The Spanish Monarchy, Creole Patriots, and the Liberal State, 1492–1867.* Cambridge: Cambridge University Press.

Brown, P. 1989. *The Body and Society: Men, Women, and Sexual Renunciation in Early Christianity.* London: Faber and Faber.

Canny, N., and A. Pagden, eds. 1987. *Colonial Identity in the Atlantic World, 1500–1800.* Princeton: Princeton University Press.

Capua, R. of. 1517. *Vita e dialogo.* Venice.

Caro Baroja, J. 1978. *Las formas complejas de la vida religiosa: Religión, sociedad y carácter en la España de los siglos XVI y XVII.* Madrid: Akal.

Carrión, M. M. 1994. *Arquitectura y cuerpo en la figura autorial de Teresa de Jesús.* Madrid: Antropos.

Castillo Graxeda, J. del. 1692. *Compendio de la vida y virtudes de la venerable Catarina de San Juan.* Puebla: Diego Fernández de León.

Certeau, M. de. 1977. *L'Ecriture de l'histoire.* Paris: Gallimard.

————. 1980. *La possession de Loudun.* Paris: Gallimard.

Cervantes, M. de. 1995. *Don Quijote de la Mancha.* Edited by J. J. Allen. Madrid: Cátedra.

Chang Rodríguez, R. 1982. *Violencia y subversión en la prosa hispanoamericana, siglos XVI y XVII.* Madrid: Turanzas.

Chicharro, D., ed. 1990. *Vida.* By Teresa de Jesús. Madrid: Cátedra.

Christian, W. A., Jr. 1981. *Apparitions in Late Medieval and Renaissance Spain.* Princeton: Princeton University Press.

Clendinnen, I. 1987. *Ambivalent Conquests: Maya and Spaniard in the Yucatán, 1517–1570.* Cambridge: Cambridge University Press.

————. 1995. *Aztecs: An Interpretation.* Cambridge: Cambridge University Press.

Conley, T. M. 1990. *Rhetoric in the European Tradition.* Chicago: University of Chicago Press.

Corcuera de Mancera, S. 1992. *El fraile, el indio y el pulque: Evangelización y embriaguez en la Nueva España.* Mexico City: Fondo de Cultura Económica.

Covarrubias, D. de. 1679. "De servitute captivorum in bello." In *Opera omnia.* Geneva.

Cruz, A. J., and. M. E. Perry. 1992. *Culture and Control in Counter-Reformation Spain.* Minneapolis: University of Minnesota Press.

Cuevas, M. 1921–1926. *Historia de la iglesia en México.* 4 vols. Mexico City: Patricio Sanz.

Davis, N. Z. 1995. *Women on the Margins: Three Seventeenth-Century Lives.* Cambridge: Harvard University Press.

Deleuze, G. 1993. *The Fold: Leibniz and the Baroque.* Translated by T. Conley. London: Athlone.

Delumeau, J. 1977. *Catholicism between Luther and Voltaire: A New View of the Counter-Reformation.* London: Burns and Oates.

————. 1983. *Le péché et la peur: La culpabilisation en Occident XIII–XVIII siècles.* Paris: Fayard.

————, ed. 1992. *La religion de ma mère: Le rôle des femmes dans la transmission de la foi.* Paris: Cerf.

Donahue, D. 1989. "Writing Lives: Nuns and Confessors as Auto/biographers in Early Modern Spain." *Journal of Hispanic Philology* 13:230–239.

Eich, J. L. 1996. "The Mystic Tradition and Mexico: Sor María Anna Agueda de San Ignacio." *Letras Femeninas* 22:19–32.

Escandell Bonet, B. 1980. "Una lectura psico-social de los papeles del Sto. Oficio:

Inquisición y sociedad Peruanas en el siglo XVI." In *La Inquisición Española: Nueva visión, nuevos horizontes.* Edited by J. Pérez Villanueva. 437–467. Madrid: Siglo XXI.

Faire croire: Modalités de la diffusion et de la réception des messages religieux du XII au XV siècles. 1981. Rome: Ecole Française de Rome.

Farris, N. M. 1984. *Maya Society under Colonial Rule: The Collective Enterprise of Survival.* Princeton: Princeton University Press.

Febre, L. 1982. *The Problem of Unbelief.* Translated by B. Gottlieb. Cambridge: Harvard University Press.

Ferreccio Podestá, M., ed. 1984. *Relación autobiográfica de Ursula Suárez (1666–1749).* Santiago: Biblioteca Nacional.

Flores Valdés, R. G. 1707. *Sermón en la honras fúnebres que hizo el religiosísimo convento de San Felipe de Jesús de madres Capuchinas de México a la venerable madre sor Teresa María de Guzmán, abadesa que fue y fundadora de dicho convento.* Mexico City: Francisco Ribera Calderón.

Franco, J. 1989. *Plotting Women: Gender and Representation in Mexico.* London: Verso.

Franco y Ortega, A. 1645. *Historia de la provincia de Santiago en México: Orden de predicadores en la Nueva España.* Mexico City.

García de la Concha, V., ed. 1982. *Libro de las fundaciones.* By Teresa de Jesús. Madrid: Espasa Calpe.

Gerson, J. 1974. *Oeuvres complètes.* Paris: Desclée.

Gibson, C. 1984. "Indian Society under Spanish Rule." In *The Cambridge History of Latin America.* Edited by L. Bethell. 11 vols. 2:361–400. Cambridge: Cambridge University Press.

Ginzburg, C. 1992. *Clues, Myths, and the Historical Method.* Baltimore: Johns Hopkins University Press.

Goetz, R. 1994. *Spanish Golden Age Autobiography in Its Context.* New York: Peter Lang.

Gonzalbo Aizpuru, P. 1987. "Tradición y ruptura en la educación femenina del siglo XVI." In *Presencia y transparencia: La mujer en la historia de México.* Edited by C. Ramos et al. 32–50. Mexico City: Colegio de México.

———. 1990. *Historia de la educación en la época colonial: El mundo indígena.* Mexico City: Colegio de México.

González Echevarría, R. 1980. "The Life and Adventures of Cipión: Cervantes and the Picaresque." *Diacritics* 10:15–26.

Granada, L. de. 1977. "De las caídas públicas, 1588." In *Monjas y beatas embaucadoras.* Edited by J. Imirizaldu. 200–270. Madrid: Editora Nacional.

Greenblatt, S. 1992. *Marvellous Possessions: The Wonder of the New World.* Oxford: Oxford University Press.

Greenleaf, R. 1969. *The Mexican Inquisition of the Sixteenth Century.* Albuquerque: University of New Mexico Press.

Gruzinski, S. 1988. *La colonisation de l'imaginaire: Occidentalisation et sociétés indigènes dans le Mexique espagnol, XV à XVIII siècles.* Paris: Archives Contemporaines.

———. 1991. "Familias, santos y capellanías: Bienes espirituales y estrategias familiares en la sociedad indígena, siglos XVII y XVIII." In *Familia y poder en Nueva España: Memoria del tercer simposio de Historia de las Mentalidades.* 173–193. Mexico City: INAH.

Haliczer, S. 1996. *Sexuality in the Confessional: A Sacrament Profaned.* Oxford: Oxford University Press.

Hampe-Martínez, T. 1993. "The Diffusion of Books in Colonial Peru: A Study of Private Libraries in the Sixteenth and Seventeenth Centuries." *Hispanic American Historical Review* 73 (2): 211–233.

Herpoel, S. 1987. *Autobiografías por mandato: Una escritura femenina en la España del Siglo de Oro.* Doctoral dissertation. St. Ignatius University, Antwerp.

Hufton, O. 1995. *The Prospect before Her: A History of Women in Western Europe, Vol. 1, 1500–1800.* London: HarperCollins.

Ife, B. W. 1985. *Reading Fiction in Golden Age Spain: A Platonist Critique and Some Picaresque Replies.* Cambridge: Cambridge University Press.

Imbruglia, G. 1983. *L'Invenzione del Paraguay: Studio sull'idea di communità tra seicento e settecento.* Naples: Bibliopolis.

Imirizaldu, J., ed. 1977. *Monjas y beatas embaucadoras.* Madrid: Editora Nacional.

Jacobsen Schutte, A. 1992. "Inquisition and Female Autobiography: The Case of Cecilia Ferrazzi." In *The Crannied Wall: Women, Religion, and the Arts in Early Modern Europe.* Edited by C. A. Monson. 105–118. Ann Arbor: University of Michigan Press.

Juana Inés de la Cruz, sor. 1989. *Obras completas.* Mexico City: Porrua.

Kelley, D. 1987. "Civil Science in the Renaissance: The Problem of Interpretation." In *The Languages of Political Theory in Early Modern Europe.* Edited by A. Pagden. 57–78. Cambridge: Cambridge University Press.

Lafaye, J. 1974. *Quetzalcóatl et Guadalupe: La formation de la conscience nationale au Mexique, 1531–1813.* Paris: Gallimard.

Lavrin, A. 1965. "Ecclesiastical Reform of Nunneries in New Spain in the Eighteenth Century." *The Americas* 22 (2): 182–203.

———. 1991. "Unlike Sor Juana? The Model Nun in the Religious Literature of Colonial Mexico." In *Feminist Perspectives on Sor Juana Inés de la Cruz.* Edited by S. Merrim. 61–86. Detroit: Wayne State University Press.

———. 1993. "La vida femenina como experiencia religiosa: Biografía y hagiografía en Hispanoamérica." *Colonial Latin American Review* 2 (1–2): 1–26.

le Goff, J. 1981. *La naissance du purgatoire.* Paris: Gallimard.

Leonard, I. A. 1949. *Books of the Brave: Being an Account of Books and of Men in the Spanish Conquest of the Sixteenth Century.* California: University of California Press.

Letona, B. de. 1622. *La perfecta religiosa: Vida de Gerónima de la Asunción*. Mexico City.

Lloyd, G. E. R. 1966. *Polarity and Analogy: Two Types of Argumentation in Early Greek Thought*. Cambridge: Cambridge University Press.

Lockhart, J. 1992. *The Nahuas after the Conquest: A Social and Cultural History of the Indians of Central Mexico, Sixteenth through Eighteenth Century*. Stanford: Stanford University Press.

Loreto López, R. 1991. "La fundación del convento de la Concepción: Identidad y familias en la sociedad Poblana, 1593–1643." In *Familias Novo Hispanas, siglos XVI al XIX*. Edited by P. Gonzalbo Aizpuru. 163–177. Mexico City: Colegio de México.

Maclean, I. 1980. *The Renaissance Notion of Woman: A Study in the Fortunes of Scholasticism and Medical Science in European Intellectual Life*. Cambridge: Cambridge University Press.

Madre de Dios, E. de la, and O. Steggink, eds. 1967. *Obras completas de Teresa de Jesús*. Madrid: Biblioteca de Autores Cristianos.

Maravall, J. A. 1979. *Poder, honor y elites en el siglo XVII*. Mexico City: Siglo XXI.

———. 1990. *La cultura del barroco: Análisis de una estructura histórica*. Barcelona: Ariel.

Martín, M. A. 1975. *Los recogidos: Nueva visión de la mística Española, 1500–1700*. Madrid: Fundación Universitaria.

Matter, E. A. 1992. "The Personal and the Paradigm: The Book of María Domitila Galluzzi." In *The Crannied Wall: Women, Religion, and the Arts in Early Modern Europe*. Edited by C. A. Monson. 87–103. Ann Arbor: University of Michigan Press.

McKnight, K. J. 1997. *The Mystic of Tunja: The Writings of Madre Castillo, 1671–1742*. Amherst: University of Massachusetts Press.

McNamara, J. A. 1991. "The Need to Give: Suffering and Female Sanctity in the Middle Ages." In *Images of Sainthood in Medieval Europe*. Edited by R. Blumenfeld-Kozinski and T. Szell. 199–221. Ithaca: Cornell University Press.

Méndez, M. A. 1989. "Ilusas o alumbradas: ¿Discurso místico o erótico?" *CMHLB Caravelle* 52:5–15.

Monguió, L. 1983. "Compañía para Sor Juana: Mujeres cultas en el Virreinato del Perú." *University of Dayton Review* 16 (2): 45–92.

Monson, C. A., ed. 1992. *The Crannied Wall: Women, Religion, and the Arts in Early Modern Europe*. Ann Arbor: University of Michigan Press.

Muriel, J. 1963. *Las indias caciques de Corpus Cristi*. Mexico City: UNAM.

Myers, K. A. 1993. *Word from New Spain: The Spiritual Autobiography of Madre María de San José (1656–1719)*. Liverpool: Liverpool University Press.

Novísima de Indias. 1571–1572.

Pagden, A. 1982. *The Fall of Natural Man: The American Indian and the Origins of Comparative Ethnology*. Cambridge: Cambridge University Press.

———. 1987. "Identity Formation in Spanish America." In *Colonial Identity in the Atlantic World, 1500–1880.* Edited by N. Canny and A. Pagden. 51–93. Princeton: Princeton University Press.

———. 1991. "Ius et Factum: Text and Experience in the Writings of Bartolomé de las Casas." *Representations* 33 (Winter): 147–162.

———. 1993. *European Encounters with the New World: From Renaissance to Romanticism.* New Haven: Yale University Press.

———. 1995. *Lords of All the World: Ideologies of Empire in Spain, Britain, and France, c.1500–c.1800.* New Haven: Yale University Press.

Pardo, F. 1676. *Vida y virtudes heróicas de la madre María de Jesús, religiosa profesa en el convento de la Limpia Concepción de la Virgen María, Nuestra Señora, de la ciudad de los Angeles.* Mexico City: Viuda de Bernardo Calderón.

Peña, J. I. de la. 1728. *Trono Mexicano en el convento de religiosas pobres Capuchinas, su construcción y adorno en la insigne ciudad de México.* Madrid.

Perry, M. E. 1991. "Subversion and Seduction: Perceptions of the Body in Writings of Religious Women in Counter-Reformation Spain." In *Religion, Body, and Gender in Early Modern Spain.* Edited by A. Saint-Saëns. 67–78. San Francisco: Mellon Research University Press.

Phelan, J. L. 1970. *The Millennial Kingdom of the Franciscans in the New World.* Berkeley: University of California Press.

Postel, G. de. 1553. *Les très merveilleuses victoires des femmes du nouveau monde.* Reprinted 1970. Geneva: Slatkine.

Poutrin, I. 1987. "Souvenirs d'enfance: L'apprentisage de la sainteté dans l'Espagne moderne." *Mélanges de la Casa de Velazquez* 23 : 331–354.

Ier Congreso internacional del monacato femenino en España, Portugal y América, 1492–1992. 1993. León: Universidad de León.

Purkiss, D. 1992. "Producing the Voice, Consuming the Body." In *Women, Writing, History, 1640–1740.* Edited by I. Grundy and. S. Wiseman. 140–158. London: Batsford.

Ramos Medina, M. 1990. *Imagen de santidad en un mundo profano.* Mexico City: UIA.

———. 1993. "Monjas sumisas pero justas." In *Ier Congreso internacional del monacato femenino en España, Portugal y América, 1492–1992.* 155–162. León: Universidad de León.

Regla y ordenaciones (Concepcionistas). 1635. Mexico City.

Relación histórica de la fundación de este convento de nuestra señora del Pilar, Compañía de María, llamado vulgarmente La Enseñanza, y compendio de la vida y virtudes de nuestra muy reverenda madre María Ignacia Azlor y Echeverz. 1793. Mexico City: Felipe Zúñiga y Ontiveros.

Ricard, R. 1992. *La conquista espiritual de México: Ensayo sobre el apostolado y los métodos misioneros de las ordenes Mendicantes en la Nueva España de 1523–1524 a 1572.* Mexico City: Fondo de Cultura Económica.

Ripa, C. 1603. *Iconologia.* Rome.

Ross, K. 1993. *The Baroque Narrative of Carlos de Sigüenza y Góngora: A New World Paradise.* Cambridge: Cambridge University Press.

Rubin, M. 1991. *Corpus Cristi: The Eucharist in Late Medieval Culture.* Cambridge: Cambridge University Press.

Ruggiero, G. 1993. *Binding Passions: Tales of Magic, Marriage, and Power at the End of the Renaissance.* Oxford: Oxford University Press.

Sahagún, B. de. 1988. *Historia general de las cosas de Nueva España.* Intro. and Notes by A. López Austin and J. García Quintana. 2 vols. Madrid: Alianza Editorial.

Saint-Saëns, A., ed. 1991. *Religion, Body, and Gender in Early Modern Spain.* San Francisco: Mellon Research University Press.

Salmerón, P. 1675. *Vida de la venerable madre Isabel de la Encarnación, Carmelita Descalza, natural de la ciudad de los Angeles.* Mexico City: Francisco Rodríguez Lupercio.

Sampson Vera Tudela, E. 1996. "Voyages in the New World Cloister." *History and Anthropology* 9 (2–3): 191–206.

———. 1997. "Fashioning a *Cacique* Nun." *Gender and History* 9 (2): 171–200.

Sánchez Llora, J. L. 1988. *Mujeres, conventos y formas de la religiosidad Barroca.* Madrid: Fundación Universitaria.

Screech, M. A. 1953. "The Illusion of Postel's Feminism: A Note on the Interpretation of His *Très merveilleuses victoires des femmes du Nouveau Monde.*" *Journal of the Warburg and Courtauld Institutes* 16 : 162–170.

Sigüenza y Góngora, C. de. 1683. *Parayso occidental plantado y cultivado por la liberal y benéfica mano de los muy católicos y poderosos reyes de España nuestros señores en su magnífico real convento de Jesús María.* Mexico City: Juan Luis de Ribera.

Spadaccini, N., and J. Talens, eds. 1988. *Autobiography in Early Modern Spain.* Minneapolis: Prisma.

Stanton, D., ed. 1984. *The Female Autograph: Theory and Practice of Autobiography, from the Tenth to the Twentieth Century.* Chicago: Chicago University Press.

Steggink, O. 1965. *La reforma del Carmelo Español: La visita del general Rubeo y su encuentro con Sta. Teresa.* Rome: Institutum Carmelitanum.

———. 1982. "Teresa de Jesús: Mujer y mística ante la teología y los teólogos." *Carmelus* 1 : 111–129.

Surz, R. E. 1995. *Writing Women in Late Medieval and Early Modern Spain: The Mothers of Saint Teresa.* Philadelphia: University of Pennsylvania Press.

Taylor, W. B., and F. G. Pease, eds. 1993. *Violence, Resistance, and Survival in the Americas: Native Americans and the Legacy of Conquest.* Washington, D.C.: Smithsonian Institution.

Teresa de Jesús, Sta. 1967. *Obras completas.* Edited by E. de la Madre de Dios and O. Steggink. Madrid: Biblioteca de Autores Cristianos.

———. 1982. *Libro de las fundaciones.* Edited by V. García de la Concha. Madrid: Espasa Calpe.

———. 1990. *Vida.* Edited by D. Chicharro. Madrid: Cátedra.

Torres, C. 1995. *Ana de Jesús, cartas 1590–1621: Religiosidad y vida cotidiana en la clausura femenina del Siglo de Oro.* Salamanca: Ediciones Universidad de Salamanca.

Valdés, J. E. 1765. *Vida admirable y penitente de la venerable madre sor Sebastiana Josefa de la Santísima Trinidad.* Mexico City: Biblioteca Mexicana.

Vallarta, L. 1990. "Los espacios del encierro: Voces sin sonido: José Eugenio Ponce de León y su modelo de mujer religiosa." *Relaciones* 45:33–61.

Vauchez, A. 1981. *La sainteté en occident aux dernièrs siècles du Moyen Age: D'après les procès de canonisation et les documents hagiographiques.* Rome: Ecole Française de Rome.

Vida de la venerable virgen sor Ana María de San José, abadesa del convento real de Descalzas y provincia de Santiago de Salamanca. 1641. Mexico City: Francisco de Robledo.

Vigil, M. 1986. *La vida de las mujeres en los siglos XVI y XVII.* Madrid: Siglo XXI.

Vitoria, F. de. 1586. *Summa sacramentorum ecclesiae.*

———. 1995. *Political Writings.* Edited by J. Lawrance and A. Pagden. Cambridge: Cambridge University Press.

Vives, J. L. 1531. *De tradendis disciplinis.* Antwerp.

Walker Bynum, C. 1987. *Holy Feast and Holy Fast: The Religious Significance of Food to Medieval Women.* Berkeley: University of California Press.

Watson, F. 1913. *Vives on Education.* Cambridge: Cambridge University Press.

Weber, A. 1990. *Teresa of Avila and the Rhetoric of Femininity.* Princeton: Princeton University Press.

Weinstein, D., and R. M. Bell. 1982. *Saints and Society: The Two Worlds of Western Christendom, 1100–1700.* Chicago: Chicago University Press.

Wright, A. D. 1982. *The Counter-Reformation: Catholic Europe and the Non-Christian World.* London: Weidenfeld and Nicolson.

Zarri, G. 1990. *Le sante vive: Profezie di corte e devozione femminile tra '400 e '500.* Turin: Rosenberg and Sellier.

Index

Alcántara, Pedro de, 43
Aristotle, 83–84

Carmelites
  character of, 139, 143–144
  and communion, 65–66
  confessional practices of, 56, 66
  establishment of in New Spain, 15
  and government of convent, 144
  history of in New Spain, 16–17
  and internal conflict, 58–59
  male and female branch of, 57–59
  and manipulation of history, 65
Catherine of Siena, Saint, 46–47
city
  and barbaric Indian past, 84–85, 158–159
  role of convents in, 6, 14, 40
  visions of, 51–52
clergy
  and government of convent, 131, 139
  secular and regular, 55
climate
  and excessive femininity, 53
  pernicious effects of, xiv, 32
  religious vocation and, 29
colonial culture. See New Spanish culture
colonial practices
  orthodoxy of, x–xi
  and quotidian, 33
confessional relationship
  and acculturation, 37
  instability of, 46–47
  and psychological turmoil, 48–49
  sexual roles in, 47
confessor
  choice of, 61
  emotional dependence on, 36, 48, 55
  as interpreter, 43
convent community
  aggression in, 139–140
  dissimulation, 68
  disunion, 26, 64, 127–129, 133–134, 144, 146–147
  ethnic variety of, 29, 31, 33
  and family, 26, 28–29
  and gossip, 138, 144–145
  hagiographic representation of, 25
  and humility, 115–116
  and obedience, 127–128
  and particular friendships, 28
  snobbishness in, 132
  and surveillance, 144
  and Teresian abolition of titles, 27
  and torment, 116–117
  and worldliness, 117
convents
  ceremonies of foundation of, 18
  conflict in, 74, 116–117
  ecclesiastic visit of, 129
  and election rigging, 130
  and female asceticism, 82
  government of, 70–72, 131
  hierarchy in, 138, 145–146
  images and relics in, 50–51
  for Indian women, 78–80

and political influence, xv
punishment in, 131
relaxation of, ix, 130, 138–139
convent writings
adaptation of Teresian model, 21
as historical sources, xi–xii
sense of community in, 10
See also women's writing
Counter Reformation
hagiography in, 80
influence of in New Spain, 40
and manifestations of spirituality, 22
role of confessor in, 47
criollas, xiv
and apologetic New World project,
49–51
characteristics of, 31–32
and political power, 59
symbolic worth of, 41
Cruz, sor Juana Inés de la, xii

dialogic accounts, 94–95

empire
cultural and religious hegemony, 41
history of, 98
and narration, 99
role of city in establishment of, 6,
52
See also colonial practices
ethnography, xiv, 4
exemplary
ambiguity, 49
and purgatory, 3
representation of America, 49
extirpaciones, 89, 92–93

feminine spirituality
and bewitchment, 54
New World manifestations of, 53
See also New Spanish culture; women;
women's writing

food
chocolate, 32–34
politics of, xiv

gachupinas, xiv
characteristics of, 30
and conflict in convent, 128, 133
and courtliness, 132
and cunning, 131
and honor, 64–65
privileges enjoyed in New Spain, 30–31
and sexual innuendo, 132
Gerson, Jean, 42
Granada, Luis de, 47–48

hagiography
antihagiography, 66–70
artifice, 69
audience, 45
canon of authoritative texts, 42–43
Counter Reformation use of, 42, 44, 80
didactic purpose of, 9, 12, 44
eschatology, 4, 7, 12
heroine in, 64
and human nature, 80
juridical character of, 8
and modernity, 34
and naturalism, 64, 68–69
novelistic discourse, 21
reformer in, 68
and regulation of writing, 41
representation of social conformity, 22
and silence, 67
social context, 70
and St. Augustine, 22
and superstition, 43
transcendental narration, 4, 7
travel narrative, xii

Ignatius of Loyola, Saint, 43
Indias, xiii–xiv
acculturation, 152

alcoholism, 95, 152
and Christian thought, 86–87
and classical thought, 84–85
communion, 85–86
and convent community, 158–159
and extremes, 85
and Franciscan Order, 89
and government of convent, 161
inconstancy of, 159
intellectual capacity of, 92
and Jesuit Order, 89
and marriage, 159
and misogynist thought, 87–88
as nuns, 78–80
pagan history, 92
perseverance of, 152
rationality of, 83
and understanding, 153, 160–161
virtues, 154
weakness, 69, 162
Inquisition
confessor in, 60, 63
in convent, 147
and dissimulated sanctity, 53
docta ignorantia, 70–73
and doctrine, 66
fear of, 38
forensic rhetoric, 66
and heresy, 60
jurisdiction of, 60
and obedience, 63

martyrdom
hagiography, 22
and journey to New World, 5
and Sta. Teresa in New World, 34
writing and, 38

Natural Law, 81–83
New Spanish culture
exemplarity, 78
gender, 80–81, 91–92

identity, x
optimism, 76
orthodoxy, 50–51
saints, cult of, in, 39
women's spirituality, 61–62
nuns
education of, 130–131
and persona of reformer, 137
and religious hierarchy, 62
and usurping of male privileges, 5

picaresque, 20–21
pureza de sangre
New World context, 50, 59, 93–94
and Sta. Teresa, 29–30
purgatory. *See* exemplary

reform
representation of, 25

Teresa of Avila, Saint
adaptation and transformation of literary forms, 21
birthplace, significance of, 31
and convent government, 67
and divine ordination of Mexican convents, 16
and feminine tradition, xi
and heroic virtue, 22
influence of works on writing nuns, 19
intimate and personal style, 19
and literary and spiritual tradition, 15
and practicalities of foundation, 15, 18
relation to prelates, 57
and secular clergy, 65
and simplicity in writing, 23
and unity of convent community, 27
testimony
confessional letters, 44
debates on Indies, 78
Inquisition, 70
literary genre, 2

personal experience, 90–91, 96–97,
  154, 159, 160
transmission of culture, xi
  and Inquisition, 59–60
  and women, 93–94
travel narrative, xii
  personal experience, 7–11
  pilgrimage, 7
  and purgatory, 3

vida. See hagiography

women
  Early Modern notions of, 82–83
  theological understanding of, 78
women's writing
  access to, xii
  and anxieties, 109
  articulacy in, 24, 110

audience, 37
and confessor, 36, 115
and discomfort, 54
and *docta ignorantia*, 23, 70–73
and emotion, 38–39, 114–115
and exemplarity, xii
and feminine tradition, 15, 35
and intimate and personal style, 19
and naturalism, 10, 75
and obedience, 110
orthodoxy of narrative, 37
and personal experience, 73
and personal need, 61
and reticence, 24
and simplicity, 45
allusion to Sta. Teresa, 20
and submission to God, 45
and visions, 111–114